Literature

Critical Issues and Themes

Twentieth-Century Literature

Critical Issues and Themes

Philip Thody

First published 1996 by
MACMILLAN PRESS LTD
Houndmills, Basingstoke, Hampshire RG21 2XS
and London
Companies and representatives
throughout the world

ISBN 0–333–61533–6 hardcover   *820.9D*
ISBN 0–333–61534–4 paperback

A catalogue record for this book is available
from the British Library.

10   9   8   7   6   5   4   3   2   1
05   04   03   02   01   00   99   98   97   96

Printed in Malaysia

Contents

Acknowledgements

Not a word of this book could have been written without the help given to me with the mysteries of the Word Processor, first by Patricia de Castries in Stanford, then by Janet Kish, Annette Torode, Lesley Pearce and Bill Williams in Leeds, and especially by Sarah Meadows, of Oxford and London.

Preface

Twentieth-Century Literature: Critical Issues and Themes makes no claim to be anything but a personal view. Its ideal reader is someone who shares my own interest in history, politics, philosophy and religion, and who is occasionally tempted, as I am, to see literature as a kind of collective autobiography written by those who are most sensitive to what is happening in their society. I am writing for the person who wants to know what books are about, who wishes to test her or his reactions against those of somebody else, and who is interested in what makes the literature of the twentieth century different from that of earlier periods. Since all views and preferences are subjective, the information as well as the ideas and opinions in this book should be supplemented by consulting the section entitled Suggestions for Further Reading.

While I agree with T. S. Eliot's remark in *The Function of Criticism* that

> The critic, one would suppose, if he is to justify his existence, should endeavour to discipline his personal prejudices and cranks – to which we are all subject – and compose his differences with as many of his fellows as possible in the pursuit of true judgement[1]

I see this as an ideal which one can try to follow rather than an attitude which can be consistently adopted. It is inevitable that the fact that I am an agnostic in matters of religion, a conservative in my political views, and a sceptical empiricist in philosophy should influence my judgements. It is honest to warn the reader about this from the outset.

In 1748, in his *Enquiry concerning Human Understanding*, David Hume gave a piece of advice to his readers which I am often tempted to reproduce, albeit in slightly milder form, when discussing literary theory. 'If we take in our hand', Hume wrote,

> any volume; of divinity, or school metaphysics, for instance: let us ask, Does it contain any abstract reasoning concerning quantity or number? No. Does it contain any experimental reasoning concerning matters of fact or existence? No. Commit it then

to the flames. For it can contain nothing but sophistry and illusion.

The equivalent of this in literary criticism is to say:

> Take down any volume of literary theory and ask yourself: does
> it illustrate its argument by reference to authors such as Jane
> Austen, Charles Dickens, Ernest Hemingway, Tolstoy, Thomas
> Mann or Proust? No. Does it contain an analysis of works such
> as Goethe's *Faust*, *The Divine Comedy* or *Don Quijote*? No. Does
> it explain why the plays of Racine are still performed while
> those of his contemporary Pradon are not, or why Shelley's
> *Ozymandias* is a better poem than Emma Lazarus's *The New
> Colossus*? No. Then put it back on the shelves. For it can con-
> tain nothing but sophistry and delusion.

The work of Roland Barthes, like that of the thinkers whom he
has influenced, nevertheless offers so intriguing a challenge to so
many of the presuppositions on which the appreciation and discussion of literature have been based in the past that some account has to be given of what he said. My reasons for thinking
that Barthes is wrong, though in a very interesting way, provide
one of the arguments running through this book.

Philip Thody
Stanford–Leeds
1993–4

A Guide to Contents

Chapter 1 begins with a discussion of the way writers in the twentieth century have treated the problem of religious faith. I then move on, in the same chapter, to discuss the importance of the theatre, the tendency of writers in the twentieth century to live in exile, and their fondness for experimentation. Chapters 2 and 3 talk about attitudes towards childhood, and Chapters 4, 5 and 6 about the problems of realism. Chapter 7 provides a transition to the discussion of ethics by looking at the treatment by twentieth-century writers of the problem of cowardice. Chapter 8 studies some of the moral dilemmas raised by novelists and playwrights in the twentieth century, Chapter 9 carries on this discussion through a study of novels about the future, and Chapter 10 looks more particularly at the plays of Shaw, Steiner and Sartre.

Chapter 11 tries to analyse what influence writers such as Bertrand Russell, Solzhenitsyn, Brecht and Dürrenmatt had on the behaviour of governments during the Cold War, and Chapter 12 examines the theme of madness in Pirandello, Evelyn Waugh, Peter Weiss and Jean Genet. The closing chapter examines the work of García Márquez, Kafka, Salman Rushdie and Toni Morrison in the context of the movement known as magical realism.

Endnote markers in the text in standard type denote references. Those in bold indicate notes which offer further information.

1

Themes, Variations and Constants

I

The nature of disbelief: comparisons and contrasts between Camus, Salman Rushdie, Kingsley Amis and David Hare; and Martin du Gard, Bertrand Russell, and Somerset Maugham. Huxley and Sartre on pregnancy and biology. A glance at humanism in Anthony Burgess and Auden; a parallel with Matthew Arnold; a mention of 'Catch 22'.

1900 is not an important literary date. The publication in 1880 of Dostoievski's *The Brothers Karamazov* was a much more important event in the early development of a specifically twentieth-century literature, as was also the first performance in 1879 of Ibsen's *A Doll's House*. Although no woman playwright has so far equalled the achievements of Simone de Beauvoir, Germaine Greer or Kate Millet in using the long essay to set out the case for what Simone de Beauvoir's 1949 essay called *Le Deuxième Sexe* (*The Second Sex*), Ibsen's play is at one and the same time a forerunner of the revival of the theatre which is so marked a feature of twentieth-century literature, and the first major attempt since the *Lysistrata* of Aristophanes, in 411 BC, to use literature to call into question the authority of men over women. When, in 1988, Angela Holdsworth prepared a major documentary for the BBC subtitled 'The Story of Women in the Twentieth Century', it was a fitting tribute to Ibsen that the main title should be *Out of the Doll's House*. There is, in this respect, some irony in the fact that apart from Joan Littlewood, whose 1963 musical *Oh What A Lovely War!* made so many of the attitudes of the English poets of the 1914–18 war popular with a wider public, no other woman has made her mark in the twentieth-century theatre as an author or a director. When Eileen Atkins and Claire Higgins spoke in a programme on BBC radio 4 on 13 October 1994, about the roles which were, for an actress, 'our Hamlet and our Lear', they found

1

themselves talking about Tennessee Williams's Blanche Dubois in *A Streetcar named Desire* (1947) and Princess in *Sweet Bird of Youth* (1956), both of them characters created by a man. In the theatre, if not in the novel and the essay, women have so far been allowed to excel only on the level of interpretation.

Dostoievski's importance as a political writer is evident in Alexander Solzhenitsyn's remark, in November 1993, that he was the only writer of the nineteenth century to have foreseen the twentieth-century phenomenon of totalitarianism. The originality of his novels is not, however, limited to the way *The Possessed* predicted both the ruthlessness and the ultimate failure of the Bolshevik revolution of 1917. In spite of the fact that Dostoievski was himself a convinced believer in the truth of Christianity, especially as embodied in the doctrines of the Russian Orthodox Church, the arguments whereby the rebellious Ivan Karamazov rejects any idea of a providential deity provide a kind of leitmotif for another of the central strains in twentieth-century literature, the reasons put forward by novelists and playwrights for not believing in God.

Thus one of the main themes in Camus's 1947 chronicle, *La Peste* (*The Plague*), is the argument that no God who was all-powerful and all-good could permit the physical suffering of the innocent. Initially, when the plague breaks out and begins to devastate the town of Oran, the priest Paneloux preaches a sermon in which he explains to his parishioners that God has sent the disease to punish them for their wickedness. But when Judge Othon's seven-year-old son Philippe dies of the plague, in 'a grotesque parody of the cruxifixion', Paneloux has no answer to Dr Rieux's objection that 'he, at least, was innocent'. The sight of the child's suffering makes Paneloux so aware of how mistaken he was in his first sermon that he preaches a second one, in a totally different style, in which he effectively gives up any attempt to defend the traditional Christian concept of God. Instead of talking about a loving and providential deity who knoweth the fall of the sparrow (Matthew, 10:29), he presents his congregation with a God whose ways are totally inexplicable in terms of human concepts of right and wrong. If men and women then worship Him, and Paneloux still calls upon them to do so, it will be because the incomprehensible nature of His actions is a proof of a divine nature which transcends and even contradicts our own idea of what is right and wrong.

The argument is neither a new nor a complicated one. Nor is it only in the twentieth century that agnostics have pointed out that if God is all good, He would want to save the child; that if He is all powerful, He would be able to do so; and drawn the conclusion that since the child dies, God must either be indifferent to the sufferings of children, or be unable to do anything about them, or must simply not exist. Although Voltaire's 1759 short story *Candide* set out with the relatively limited aim of refuting the optimism of Leibnitz and the early Pope, its permanent interest stems from the fact that it too ends up by calling into question any idea that the world could have been created by a benevolent deity. Tennyson's *In Memoriam* may end with an affirmation of faith. What stick in the mind are stanzas LIV and LV in which Tennyson already foresees, in 1850, the disappearance from the universe of any kind of purpose or providence which is so marked a feature of the intellectual revolution announced nine years later by the publication of Darwin's *The Origin of Species*. It is nevertheless in the twentieth century that the problem of disbelief comes to be expressed more and more frequently in terms similar to the ones which Salman Rushdie uses in *The Satanic Verses* when he comments on how the location of her cancer proved to Mirza Saeed's infertile wife Mishal that

only a vicious deity would place death in the breast of a woman whose only dream was to suckle new life.[1]

Whether you look at authors who write with obviously philosophical ideas in mind, like Rushdie or Camus, or at authors whose main intent is to comment on social issues, or even simply to entertain their readers, the reasons expressed by twentieth-century writers for not believing in a personal God tend to recur in the same form. In David Hare's 1990 play about the problems of the Church of England, for example, *Racing Demon*, Lionel Espy's mistress, Frances Parnell, cries out

There isn't any justice, God knows. You're not a moral God. Your style is more: 'What a sweet baby! Give it cancer!'. Just glimpse happiness, board the wrong aircraft, and pfft! The whole thing's a joke.

If there were better justice then I'd believe in you. I like the idea of justice better than God. Because God is arbitrary.[2]

If there is a God, suggests Penelope Lively in the words she puts into the mouth of her heroine, Claudia Hampton, in her 1987 novel *Moon Tiger*, He is certainly not the being envisaged by any of the traditional religions. Claudia is dying of cancer, and thinking of spending her last days writing a history of the world. When her daughter, Lisa, tells her that she personally is not too sure about God's existence, Claudia replies that she has no doubts at all. Who else, she asks, could 'bugger things up so effectively?'[3]

As might be expected, Kingsley Amis expresses his reluctant agnosticism in less obviously impassioned tones. As befits one of the galaxy of humorous writers who, like P. G. Wodehouse, David Lodge, and Tom Sharpe, have shown to what perfection the tradition of Sterne, Dickens and Fielding can be brought in twentieth-century English literature, he adopts a slightly bluff, common-sense approach. What he cannot understand, as he explains in the 1970 postscript to his earlier essay 'On Christ's nature', is why

> if God wanted human beings to have religion, he did not simply give it to them, instead of arranging the world in one way and then sending somebody along to explain that really the whole set-up was different.[4]

A distinction should nevertheless be made, on theological grounds, between the central example which Ivan Karamazov gives for not believing in God and the arguments developed by Camus in *The Plague*. When, in Chapter iv of Book V of Part II of *The Brothers Karamazov*, the one entitled 'Rebellion', Ivan explains to his saintly brother Alyosha why he 'most respectfully' returns God his entrance ticket, he concentrates on a story about the cruelty shown by a Russian general to the children of one of his serfs. Because the child, a little boy of eight, had 'thrown a stone in play and injured the paw of the general's favourite hound', the general assembles his whole household, including the boy's mother, comes out in full hunting gear, and has the boy pursued and torn to pieces by his hounds. Like the accounts of the children in Marghanita Laski's 1949 novel *Little Boy Lost*, on whose naked bodies the Nazi guards throw acid to make them go more quickly into the gas chamber, the scene is unforgettable in its horror. But it does not, on theological grounds, constitute an argument against the existence of God.

God, in Christian theology, gave all men the great gift of free will. Only thus, it is argued, could they freely choose salvation, and come to know and worship Him with full awareness of what they were doing. But free will implies the ability to choose between good and evil, and if Russian landowners and Nazi guards choose evil rather than good, this does not prove that there is no God. It merely illustrates the consequences of having a God who, in His creation of man, chose to make him free. The advantage, in the presentation of the agnostic's case against the existence of God, of Camus's choice of the plague is that it is a disease for which man cannot be held responsible. Unlike lung cancer or AIDS, it is not the result of people having chosen to behave in a particular way. If anyone is responsible, it is therefore God; unless one chooses to accept the Darwinian hypothesis, and see the world as the product of an evolutionary process which has no place for purpose or providence.

Although he did not specifically mention Darwin – French writers are, as a general rule, less interested than their English counterparts in the natural sciences – this was Camus's position, as it is that of E. M. Forster, Orwell and Bertrand Russell. It is difficult to see how, except by the total rejection of the whole basis for modern biology, it can be faulted on philosophical grounds, any more than the view of human history as having purpose and direction can be defended against the mention of Auschwitz or the Gulag. It is of course true, as Christian apologists have pointed out, that there is some irony in the frequency with which twentieth-century agnostics base their rejection of God on the idea of the undeserved physical suffering of the innocent. Since, they observe, there has been no period in human history during which human beings have caused so much undeserved physical and mental suffering to one another as they have in the twentieth century, it shows a peculiar blindness to their own faults for men to start laying the blame on God.

In the twentieth century, playwrights and novelists have tended to base their reply to this argument on the words which Bernard Shaw put into the mouth of Saint Joan in his 1923 play: 'By what judgement can I judge by but mine own?' In spite of the scriptural authority for the argument presented by Paneloux in his second sermon in *The Plague* – Job 13:15; 42:2–6; Corinthians I, 1:19–23 – it is difficult for human beings living in a secular society to accept that the principles of rational argument and scientific enquiry should stop the moment one comes into contact with religious belief. Men

may have caused immeasurable suffering to their fellows. But as
George Orwell commented in his 1946 essay 'How the Poor Die',

> People talk about the horrors of war, but what weapon has
> man invented that even approaches in cruelty some of the
> commoner diseases?[5]

There is also the humanist argument, again put forward by Camus,
Forster and Orwell, that one of the unique qualities of human
beings is to demand a justice for which there is no evidence in
the natural universe, and even to try to create it.

Arguments about religion have been part of the stock in trade
of Western literature from classical times onwards, with Lucretius
putting forward, in *De Natura Rerum*, in the last century before
Christ, many of the agnostic arguments which resurfaced in the Renaissance, and Euripides, in fifth-century Athens, using the theatre
to cast doubt upon the wisdom of the Gods. One of the features
which most obviously distinguishes twentieth-century literature
from that of its immediate predecessors has been a kind of return to this aspect of the classical tradition and a move away
from the kind of arguments put forward in the eighteenth or in
the nineteenth century. For Gibbon or Hume, Christianity was
unacceptable for a mixture of intellectual and social reasons, and
Voltaire had other objections to it apart from those based on the
physical suffering of the innocent. There was, for Gibbon and
Hume, no way in which Christianity could be shown to be true,
and both writers agreed with Voltaire in stressing the disastrous
effect on society produced by the intolerance to which Christianity gave rise. In the nineteenth century, it was a set of primarily
intellectual arguments which led men and women away from the
Christian faith. The techniques used in what became known as
the Higher Criticism, a term describing the application to the texts
both of the Old and the New Testament of the same principles of
textual analysis which had been used for writers such as Homer
or Thucydides, showed that few of the books presented as canonical
by the Church could possibly have been written in their officially
received form by the authors to whom the Church attributed them.
At the same time, there was no way in which the description of
creation in Genesis could be reconciled with the evidence on which
Darwin based his theory of evolution.

In this respect, the account given in 1913 by the French novelist Roger Martin du Gard of how his hero, Jean Barois, stops believing in Christianity makes one of several outstanding works which punctuate that *annus mirabilis* – others were Thomas Mann's *Death in Venice*, Shaw's *Pygmalion*, Apollinaire's *Alcools* and Unamuno's *Del sentimento trágico de la vida* – into a very nineteenth-century piece of writing. For there is no mention in *Jean Barois* of the essentially moral objections which other, more characteristically twentieth-century authors such as Camus, direct against Christianity. It is the combination of Darwin and nineteenth-century scientific determinism, coupled with the impact of the Higher Criticism, which leads Martin du Gard's hero first of all to lose his faith, and then to devote his life to the very nineteenth-century activity of propagating the gospel of rationalism in a highly militant and aggressive form.

The plot of the novel also has a distinctly nineteenth-century air to it. Just after he has given a well-attended lecture entitled 'The Future of Disbelief' – not a topic likely to attract a large audience in the 1990s – Barois is involved in a road accident in which he thinks he is about to die. What worries him most intensely is that he suddenly finds himself, at the moment of the accident, reverting to the habits inculcated in him by the religious training he received in his childhood, frantically crossing himself and reciting the 'Hail Mary'. Thoroughly ashamed of what he sees as a totally atavistic type of behaviour, and determined that a similar accident will not provide his clerical opponents with the argument that even the most fervent agnostic turns to God at the moment of death, he draws up a last will and testament in which he denounces, in advance, any convérsion to Christanity into which he may be led by illness or old age. When, in response to the terror of death which he is depicted as inheriting from his father, he undergoes just such a conversion in the last years of his life, his pious daughter, with the connivance of the priest who has attended his last moments, ensures that Barois's death will be used for the correct purposes of religious edification. He burns the detailed and lengthy document in which Barois reaffirms his agnosticism, and in which he had written:

> I deserve to die, as I have lived, combatant and defiant, without capitulating, without whoring after idle hopes, without fearing my return to the primal matter that nourishes the slow process of evolution.

I do not believe in an immortal, independently existing soul.

I do not believe that mind and matter are mutually exclusive entities. The 'soul' is a complex of psychic phenomena, and the body a complex of organic phenomena ... I have never found thought existing apart from matter and a living body; and I am aware of one universal substance only, living substance ... Life had no beginning, and it will go on producing life for ever. But I know that my personality is but an agglomeration of matter, whose disintegration will end it absolutely.[6]

Although he won the Nobel Prize for Literature in 1937, and did not die until 1958 – the year in which Camus wrote a long and very enthusiastic Introduction to the *Pléiade* edition of his collected works – Martin du Gard is an author whose themes and preoccupations illustrate how delicate a task it can be to make a clear distinction between those writers who simply belong chronologically to the twentieth century and those who strike the modern reader as offering some unmistakable witness to its essential temper. It is not only by its rhetoric that Jean Barois's will is unmistakably the work of a man of the nineteenth century. Its insistence on a wholly materialistic universe is a reminder of the importance of a number of ideas which a twentieth-century writer would simply not bother to express. At the same time, and in a way which Martin du Gard may not have foreseen, the doctrines which Jean Barois is so keen to deny offer an instructive guide as to what the nineteenth-century Catholic was expected to believe.

The philosopher Bertrand Russell, who became the fifth English writer to receive the Nobel Prize for Literature when the award was bestowed on him in 1950, also voiced objections to Christianity which have a distinctly nineteenth-century air to them. The lecture he gave in March 1927 to the South London Branch of the National Secular Society, an organisation of the kind that Jean Barois would have greatly appreciated, scarcely deals with what C. S. Lewis calls, in one of his most interesting pamphlets, *The Problem of Pain*, and which William Nicholson's 1993 play, *Shadowlands*, shows Lewis as having to confront in a less intellectual context when his wife Joy dies of cancer. Instead, Russell deals in the characteristically pellucid style which was one of the factors which most justified the decision of the Swedish committee to give him the prize, with each of the traditional arguments for God, and effectively demolishes them. The 'first cause' argument, the argument from design and the moral argument are all very quickly disposed of, with a particularly telling case against the last one. As though in direct reply to the words which Dostoievski puts into the mouth of the rebellious Ivan Karamazov – 'If God does not exist, then everything is permitted' – Russell points out the logical fallacy involved in claiming that it is only through a belief in God that human beings can distinguish between right and wrong:

> The point which I am concerned with is that, if you are quite sure that there is a difference between right and wrong, you are then in this situation: is this difference due to God's fiat or is it not? If it is due to God's fiat, then for God Himself there is no difference between right and wrong, and it is no longer a significant statement to say that God is good. If you are going to say, as theologians do, that God is good, you must then say that right and wrong have some meaning which is independent of God's fiat, because God's fiats are good and not bad independently of the mere fact that He made them. If you are going to say that, you will then have to say that it is not only through God that right and wrong came into being, but that they are in essence logically anterior to God.[7]

Arguments of this kind, however, even for readers with the same admiration for them as I have, seem to belong to a period which came to an end before the First World War. This is partly because theologians themselves no longer argue as they used to in Russell's day. As Saki's Clovis remarked, as early as 1901, 'It is very difficult to be an unbeliever nowadays. The theologians have left one with so little in which not to believe', and the publication in 1963 of John Robinson's *Honest to God* showed how prescient he had been. The curiously dated air of both Russell's and Martin du Gard's arguments also stems from a characteristically twentieth-century similarity between believers such as Graham Greene, Evelyn Waugh, François Mauriac and Georges Bernanos, and unbelievers like Camus or Orwell. Each group has approached religion from such a different point of view from their nineteenth-century predecessors that they scarcely seem to be talking about the same phenomenon as the defenders and opponents of Christianity in the past. The doctrines rejected by Jean Barois do not figure widely in the novels written by twenti-eth-century believers. Nor do the agnostics give much sign of thinking that they are worth rejecting.

There is also the fact that the liberation from religious belief which the real Russell and the fictional Jean Barois celebrated with such enthusiasm has not brought about the improvement in human behaviour which they, as typical men of the nineteenth century, had so confidently expected. From this point of view, Somerset Maugham's description of Philip Callow's loss of religious faith at the end of Chapter XVIII of the semi-autobiographical novel which he published in 1915, *Of Human Bondage*, has almost as old-fashioned a ring as Russell's *Why I am Not A Christian* or Jean Barois's Last Will and Testament. Philip was, writes Maugham,

> freed from degrading fears and free from prejudice. He could go his way without the intolerable dread of hell-fire. Suddenly he realised that he had lost also that burden of responsibility which made every action of his life a matter of urgent conse-quence. He was responsible only to himself for the things he did. Freedom! He was his own master at last. From old habit, unconsciously he thanked God that he no longer believed in Him.[8]

It is also a passage which has dated for other reasons. Few young people nowadays have the same painful recollections of the religious exercises which, Philip recalls, had for so many years been forced upon him, and which led him to think with such acute distaste of the

> collects and epistles which he had been made to learn by heart, and the long services in the Cathedral through which he had sat when every limb itched with the desire for movement.[9]

One may regret this change for other reasons. English has rarely been better written than by the group of largely anonymous theologians who drew up the 1662 Prayer Book. Yet although the end of this kind of church-going has brought about an improvement in human happiness which is almost on the same level as the availability of cheap and reliable contraception, there are other ways in which virtual disappearance of religious belief has been a mixed blessing. Maugham's own liberation from belief did not inspire him with any belief in the ability of human beings either to act morally or to achieve happiness. His characters are all, as the title of one of his collections of short stories puts it, *Creatures of Circumstance*, unable to overcome the accidents of existence which lead them to their doom. Only occasionally, as in the short story 'The Facts of Life', is there a lightening of the darkness.

Since the twentieth century has been peculiarly rich in authors whose experimental approach to literature occasionally makes them rather difficult to read, Martin du Gard, Russell and Maugham are also interesting for another contrast which they provide. All three belonged to the characteristically nineteenth-century tradition which the author Anatole France – who did not in fact die until 1921 – summed up when he said that 'la clarté est la politesse de l'homme de lettres' (clarity is the politeness of the man of letters). From a purely literary point of view, the fact that Martin du Gard is so clear and compulsive a read is a factor which is almost as important as his belief in scientific determinism in placing him by the side of Kipling, Galsworthy or Somerset Maugham in the not unflattering category of those who bring into the twentieth century a set of attitudes and beliefs which were already fully developed in the nineteenth.

This is not to say that all characteristically twentieth-century writers go in for experimentation, or that they have forgotten the intellectual revolution produced by Darwin, or that they are unaware of how radically the progress of the biological sciences has changed man's concept of himself. It is much more that the revelation of man's fundamental similarity to all other forms of biological life has become so familiar that it can regain the power to shock only by being used in an unexpected form, as when Aldous Huxley uses a mixture of scientific precision and comic satire in two of the descriptions of Marjorie Carling's pregnancy in his 1928 novel *Point Counter Point*:

Marjorie felt sick and tired. Six months from now her baby would be born. Something that had been a single cell, a cluster of cells, a little sac of tissue, a kind of worm, a potential fish with gills, stirred in her womb and would one day become a man – a grown man, thinking, remembering, imagining. And what had been a blob of jelly within her body would invent a god and worship; what had been a kind of fish would create and, having created, would become the battle-ground of disputing good and evil; what had blindly lived in her as a parasitic worm would look at the stars, would listen to music, would read poetry.

A cell had multiplied itself and become a worm, the worm had become a fish, the fish was turning into the foetus of a mammal. Marjorie felt sick and tired. Fifteen years hence a boy would be confirmed. Enormous in his robes, like a full-rigged ship, the Bishop would say: 'Do ye here in the presence of God, and of this congregation, renew the solemn promise and vow that was made in your name at your Baptism?' And the ex-fish would answer with passionate conviction: 'I do'.[10]

It is a passage which one sometimes suspects might have inspired Jean-Paul Sartre in the account which he gives of how Mathieu Delarue, in the first volume of *Les Chemins de la liberté* (*The Paths to Freedom*), *L'Age de raison* (normally translated as *The Age of Reason* but better rendered as *The Years of Discretion*) thinks about the foetus growing in the womb of his mistress, Marcelle Dubuffet, and which he is trying to arrange to have aborted as soon as possible:

There was a tiny, human creature, conscious, furtive, deceitful and pathetic, with a white skin, wide ears, and tiny fleshmarks, and all manner of distinctive signs such as are stamped on passports, a little man who would never run about on the streets with one foot on the pavement and the other in the gutter; eyes, green, like Marcelle's or dark like Mathieu's, which would never see the vitreous skies of winter, nor the sea, nor any human face.[11]

It is a surprisingly moving passage to find in an author who never showed any enthusiasm for fatherhood, and whose life-long companion, Simone de Beauvoir, was one of those who led the right to legalise abortion in France in the 1970s. In that respect, it is a reminder of the way in which many authors write books that are much better from a literary point of view than some of their social or philosophical theories, or their life-style, would allow.

One of the best ways for readers to approach Sartre's existentialism, especially if they are unfamiliar with the style of thinking fashionable in the Europe of the 1920s and 1930s, is to think of it as the translation of the Darwinian hypothesis into the more general terms traditionally used in philosophical discourse. When Sartre talks about the absurd, as he does at some length in his 1938 novel, *La Nausée* (*Nausea*), he presents the term as being virtually synonymous with 'accidental' or 'contingent'. What he means by this is that all forms of biological life, whether animal, vegetable or human, could well be totally different from what they are, or could equally well not exist at all. There is no such thing as the kind of inner necessity which governs the world of logic or mathematics, and even less of the providence which traditionally presided over the Christian view of creation. For Darwin, the process of evolution is also without purpose or providence, in that a different series of random genetic variations from the one which actually produced the world as it is at the moment could well have given rise to a set of totally different life forms.

Sartre himself, however, had little time for either the physical or the biological sciences, and makes no mention of Darwin at any point in his work. Like Huxley, he used literature to express philosophical ideas, but always gave the impression of writing for an audience which was not interested in the links between science and literature which seem so natural in English-speaking countries. His vision of the world is nevertheless remarkably similar in many ways to that of Huxley, and the definition which he gave in 1964 of human beings as 'des animaux sinistrés' (animals struck with disaster)[12] implies the same absence of belief in the personal, providential God of traditional Christianity which, in the twentieth century, has characterised all the conscious or unconscious disciples of Darwin. Where he went further than Camus was in regarding protests against the acts of injustice supposedly perpetrated by an absent god as a complete waste of time, and metaphysical speculation of this type as an excuse not to make more of an effort to eliminate the social injustice created by men. The one mention of Christ in his published work presents him as a political agitator executed by the Romans. In so far as God, for him, is so thoroughly dead as not even to be worth a mention, let alone a protest, Sartre may well come to be seen as a forerunner of what intellectual life will be like in the twenty-first century.

The remark which Anthony Burgess, a lapsed Catholic, made to explain his loss of faith offers a further illustration of the difference between the reasons which authors tended to give for their disbelief in the nineteenth century and those which are more characteristic of our own time. The position which he came to adopt was, Burgess said, 'one that could be called Manichean'. That meant, he added, that he believed it was 'the wrong God who is temporarily ruling the world, and that the true God has gone under'. In a phrase which recalled Camus's belief that it is the peculiar duty of man to try to bring order and justice into a world which God gives every appearance of having deserted, Burgess pointed out that his pessimism did not prevent him from believing that the world 'has much solace to offer: love, food, music, the immense variety of race and language, literature and the pleasure of artistic creation'. Burgess's attitude, like that of English writers such as Orwell or E. M. Forster, was essentially a humanist one, and in that respect again not entirely new. Already, in 1856, Matthew Arnold was writing in *Dover Beach* that only loyalty in love between human beings could offer solace in a world which had no ultimate meaning, and there are similarities as well as differences between his attitude and the one which Auden expressed in *Lullaby*, in 1936, when he wrote:

> Lay your sleeping head, my love,
> Human on my faithless arm;
> Time and fevers burn away
> Individual beauty from
> Thoughtful children, and the grave
> Proves the child ephemeral:
> But in my arms till break of day
> Let the living creature lie,
> Mortal, guilty, but to me
> The entirely beautiful.

The Auden of *Lullaby*, like the Arnold of *Dover Beach*, accepts that the world has no purpose, and history no meaning. It is also an attitude expressed by one of the best and most accessible of Dylan Thomas's poems, 'Do not go gentle into that good night', especially in the way the concluding stanza

> 'And you, my father, there on that sad height,
> Curse, bless, me with your fierce tears, I pray,
> Do not go gentle into that good night,
> Rage, rage against the dying of the night',

catches the despair behind the humanist ethos expressed in Auden's *Lullaby*. Indeed, Auden's pessimism goes further than that of Arnold, in that he recognises the transience not only of human life but of love itself. There is nothing in *Lullaby* of the wish for fidelity which comes near to giving *Dover Beach* something of the emotional resonance of the vows which form so central a part of the Christian sacrament of marriage. But the two poems are similar in that both express a kind of defiant as well as a depairing humanism, with private human relationships as the only possible source of meaning in an absurd universe: 'Ah, love,' writes Arnold, in a poem which moves Mrs Bowles to tears when Montag reads it out to her in Ray Bradbury's 1954 novel, *Fahrenheit 451*,

> Let us be true
> To one another! For the world which seems
> To lie before us like a land of dreams,
> So various, so beautiful, so new,
> Hath really neither joy, nor love, nor light,
> Nor certitude, nor peace, nor help for pain;
> And we are here as on a darkling plain
> Swept with confused alarms of struggle and of flight
> Where ignorant armies clash by night.

It is a phrase which recurs in a book of so indisputably twentieth-century a temper that its title has passed into the language, Joseph Heller's 1961 novel, *Catch 22*. The rules governing the bombing unit to which the central character Yossarian is attached in the Second World War state very clearly that a man can be grounded only if he is insane. But when it is only a matter of time before the plane in which one is flying is shot down, and the number of missions after which a man is automatically grounded is constantly being increased, first from 25 to 40, then from 40 to 50, to 60 and finally to 80, the request to be grounded is an irrefutable proof of sanity; and consequently the best of all reasons why, in the view of the authorities, one should continue to fly. The immediate absurdity of the individual situation of each aviator is mirrored by what Heller, writing of the staple diet of war films projected for the entertainment of the troops, describes as 'ignorant armies which clash by night'.[13] Like human life in general, war and politics are manifestations of a fundamental absurdity which characterises all experience except perhaps the personal relationships which E. M. Forster prized above all else.

II

Some new themes in the twentieth-century literature inspired by Christianity; exemplified in François Mauriac, Graham Greene, Evelyn Waugh and others; the persistence of more conventional attitudes in Claudel; also an example of another revival, that of the theatre; a contrast with the apparent decline of an interest in poetry; some quotations and some reservations about the alleged decline; a reminder of Christopher Fry; possible reasons for the revival of the theatre.

Not all twentieth-century writers are agnostics or disbelievers. George Orwell's remark that 'prose literature, as we know it, is the product of the Protestant centuries, of the autonomous individual',[14] may well be an accurate observation as far as literary history is concerned. The number of twentieth-century authors who write novels on specifically Catholic themes, and from an identifiably Catholic viewpoint, is nevertheless surprisingly high.

François Mauriac and Georges Bernanos in France, like Graham Greene and Evelyn Waugh in England, showed in the middle years of the century how the novel could be used to explore ethical problems which were characteristic of the twentieth century, but in no way peculiar to practising Catholics. In more recent times, David Lodge and Muriel Spark have dealt with Catholic themes in a more comic mode, and done so in a way which neither the supporters nor the opponents of Christianity in the nineteenth century would have thought possible. The position adopted by such authors has rarely been a strictly orthodox one, and has been characterised by an indifference which I have already noted to the very precise doctrines which Jean Barois is so anxious to reject. They have dealt far more with sinners than with saints, and with sinners whose behaviour often seems highly irrational to observers who share the secular standards of contemporary society. It is also sometimes difficult to remember, when reading Mauriac, Greene or Evelyn Waugh, that the central ethical teaching of Christianity is in the Sermon on the Mount.

The type of Catholicism which these authors explore is also a reminder of how difficult it is to say which authors are, and which are not, characteristic of twentieth-century literature, and of how inseparable such a distinction is from one's own value judgements. One of the most famous of all French Catholic writers, Paul Claudel, did not die until 1950, and his plays enjoyed an extraordinary popularity in both London and Paris in the 1940s and 1950s. The impression which his world view gives is nevertheless that of a mind firmly fixed in the nineteenth century, if not some time before. He is said for example, to have replied to André Gide's plea in favour of the virtue of tolerance which is so characteristic of twentieth-century liberalism with a pun whose intended meaning was very clear to the average native speaker of French: 'La tolérance? Mais nous avons des maisons pour cela, me semble-t-il'. Since brothels in France, until they were made illegal in 1946, were known as 'des maisons de tolérance', it was as though Alan Bennett intended the Headmaster in his 1968 play *Forty Years On* to be taken absolutely seriously when he made him declaim: 'When a culture is reduced to looking for its humour in the public lavatory, the writing is on the wall.'

There is nevertheless one way in which Claudel belongs very much to the twentieth century: his success as a playwright fits in with a development that transcends ideological boundaries as completely as it ignores geographical ones. Whatever one may think of their political or religious opinions, or even of the moral implications of what they present as happening on stage, it is very difficult to imagine the plays of Albee, Anouilh, Beckett, Brecht, Hare, Ionesco, David Mamet, Arthur Miller, Eugene O'Neill, Pirandello, Pinter, Shaw, Sartre, Tom Stoppard and Alan Bennett himself falling into the same oblivion which now characterises the work of playwrights who, like Dion Bouicicault, William Douglas Jerrold, Thomas William Robertson, Georges de Porto Riche, Eugène Scribe and Victorien Sardou, were as well known in their day as the Howard Brenton of *The Romans in Britain* or the Tony Kushner of *Angels in America* are in the 1990s.

The excellence of the playwrights of the twentieth century also offers, at first sight, another contrast with the nineteenth century: the apparent eclipse of poetry as a dominant literary genre by fiction and by the theatre. In the nineteenth century, in the United States as well as in England and France, poets such as Longfellow and Whitman, Wordsworth, Tennyson and Browning, Lamartine and Victor Hugo, were national figures whose books sold almost as many copies as the work of the great novelists of the age. This is less obviously the case to-day, where few American poets are as well known as novelists such as Hemingway, Faulkner or Toni Morrison, and no French poet can rival the popularity with the reading public of a Camus or a Michel Tournier, let alone of Françoise Sagan or Marguerite Duras. This is partly the result of a tendency which I discuss in more detail later on: what seems at times to be an almost perverse cult of difficulty which characterises certain twentieth-century writers. In this respect, there is no way in which T. S. Eliot or Saint-John Perse could be as widely read as Tennyson or Hugo. The meaning does not leap swiftly enough off the page. Even if the nineteenth-century habit of reading poetry aloud at social or family gatherings were to be revived, neither *The Four Quartets* nor *Anabase* would be very suitable items in a young man's repertoire. But poetry is a more important literary genre than might at first sight appear, and there is a considerable if sometimes surprising appetite for it.

Thus in the 1993 film *Four Weddings and a Funeral*, John Hannah, playing the part of David, recites W. H. Auden's *Funeral Blues*, at the funeral of his friend, Charles.[15] For the first few weeks after the beginning of the film's triumphant run in the United States, it was impossible, from New York to San Francisco, to buy a copy of Auden's poems. Four stanzas which had originally been written in 1936, in collaboration with Christopher Isherwood, for a not oversuccessful verse drama, *The Ascent of F6*, set to music by Benjamin Britten, and subsequently offered to the cabaret singer, Heidi Anderson, had suddenly reminded people of the capacity, which poetry alone possesses, to give permanent and moving expression to an emotion and a mood.

There are other examples of comparable reminders, albeit of a somewhat different type. In 1942, in one of his war broadcasts, Winston Churchill quoted a poem by Arthur Hugh Clough (1819–61), 'Say not the Struggle naught availeth'. Quite spontaneously, people learned it off by heart. It perfectly matched the national mood. In what could not have been a more different context, the detective Lemmy Caution in Jean-Luc Godard's 1965 film, *Alphaville*, carried around with him a copy of Paul Eluard's 1926 collection, *Capitale de la douleur*. The volume was immediately reissued in paperback, a reminder of the role which some of Eluard's later poems, like those of Aragon, another former surrealist who had joined the Communist party, had played in the resistance movement. I talk later of the impact which the English poets of the First World War – Edward Blunden, Wilfred Owen, Siegfried Sassoon, Robert Graves – had on the mood of their fellow-countrymen. The revulsion against war which was so marked a feature of the 1920s and 1930s found perfect expression in their verse, which still profoundly influences young people to-day.

In a cooler emotional temperature, some of the success of the poetry of Philip Larkin stems from the way he embodies a way of looking at experience which reflects something of the national mood in the England of the second half of the twentieth century.[16] Neither is it only in poetry that a characteristically twentieth-century refusal of romanticism finds convincing literary expression. In 1942, Jean Anouilh gained great success on the Parisian stage with his version of the Antigone legend, and it has remained one of his most frequently performed plays. It is not his best, which is probably the 1956 *Pauvre Bitos*, but it did present an intriguingly different version of the character of Creon. Instead of being, as he is in Sophocles, a tyrant duly punished for the *hubris* he shows in defying the laws of gods and men, he becomes a conscientious but weary administrator, almost a character from a novel by C. P. Snow or a policeman in Graham Greene, the embodiment of the attitude which A. E. Housman evoked in his poem about the soldiers in the British Expeditionary Force sent to defend Belgium in 1914:

These, in the days when heaven was falling,
The hour when earth's foundations fled,
Followed their mercenary calling
And took their wages and are dead.

Their shoulders held the sky suspended;
They stood, and earth's foundations stay;
What God abandoned, these defended.
And saved the sum of things for pay.

Like other literary periods, the twentieth century has also been visited with false dawns. In post-war England, T. S. Eliot's *The Cocktail Party*, in 1950, following on from the pre-war success of *Murder in the Cathedral* and *The Family Reunion*, together with the triumphs of Christopher Fry in *A Phoenix Too Frequent* in 1946 and *The Lady's Not for Burning*, in 1949, seemed to foreshadow a

rebirth of the poetic drama. Lines in *The Lady's Not For Burning*
such as Thomas Mendip's

> I've been unidentifiably floundering in
> Flanders for the past seven years,
> Prizing open ribs to let men go
> On the indefinite leave which needs no pass

struck an immediate chord with an audience which, in 1949,
contained a fair number of men who had been doing exactly that,
while the comment that

> The spheres churned on,
> Hoping to charm our ears
> With sufficient organ-music, sadly sent out
> On the wrong wave of sound

expressed one of the themes in the then popular philosophy of
existentialism with an appropriately English lightness of touch.
Alison Eliot's evocation of the last days of her father –

> And on he went
> Still deeper into the calculating twilight
> Under the twinkling of five-pointed figures
> Till Truth became for him the sum of sums
> And Death the long division

– may nowadays seem unbearably precious. In what were still
austerity years, they raised as immediate and as appreciative a
wave of laughter as the lines in the long speech in *A Phoenix Too
Frequent* in which Dynamene mourns her dead husband:

> I am lonely,
> Virilius. Where is the punctual eye
> And where the cautious voice which made
> Balance sheets sound like Homer and Homer sound
> Like balance sheets? The precision of limbs, the amiable
> Laugh, the exact festivity? Gone from the world.
> You were the peroration of nature, Virilius.
> You explained everything to me, even the extremely
> Complicated gods. You wrote them down,

In seventy columns. Dear, curling calligraphy!

Appropriately enough, in a culture which had just survived one of the greatest crises ever to threaten its existence, both plays end with the triumph of life. Dynamene, who has sworn to starve herself to death in her husband's tomb, ends up by handing over his body to the young soldier whose fascination with her has led him to neglect his duty to watch over the six corpses of men hanged for dissent and left on public display. One of them has been stolen, and the cold Virilius takes his place. The story, as Chrisopher Fry informs his audience in a note, 'was got from Jeremy Taylor who had it from Petronius'. In *The Lady's Not For Burning*, set in '1400 more or less exactly' Thomas Mendip saves Alison Eliot from being hung as a witch; and marries her.

There is no particular need to regret that this apparent revival of the verse drama was so short lived, or that it should have been overtaken in the 1950s and 1960s by the almost aggressively unpoetic drama of John Osborne, Arnold Wesker and Harold Pinter. The success of a playwright is perhaps more closely linked than that of the novelist or poet to a series of social and political changes which go beyond literature itself. The disappearance of verse drama has not led to a narrower range of theatrical experience. Although audiences have remained predominantly middle class, as they were in the nineteenth-century theatre for almost all genres except melodrama, this class has grown very much larger and is a great deal more varied and open-minded in its attitudes than the nineteenth-century bourgeoisie. This is partly because the spread of higher education has created a far more appreciative and intelligent audience than the playwrights of the nineteenth century could ever have hoped to enjoy. When almost every major town in the United Kingdom and the United States has a university attached to it, the success of a play such as Tom Stoppard's 1972 *Jumpers* is assured. Everyone recognises his George Moore as the lecturer who tried to teach them ethics and caught himself up in a tangle as he did so.

It is true that, in more recent days, the immediate success of David Mamet's 1992 play, *Oleanna*, owes less to its setting in a university than to its criticism of the excesses to which the women's movement has allegedly given rise in the United States. The relationship between Carol and John is nevertheless understandable only in a society in which mass higher education has become the norm, but in which Tennyson's vision in *The Princess* of 'sweet girl-graduates in their golden hair' has not been achieved in quite the way he had in mind. The way in which Carol, the student, so completely ruins the life of her teacher, John, by the ruthlessness with which she exploits the power which the popularity of feminism has given her, moved some members of the audience, not all of them men, to burst out in applause when he finally lost his temper and struck her. The war between the sexes, already brilliantly exploited in an academic setting in Edward Albee's 1962 drama *Who's Afraid of Virginia Woolf?*,[17] gave an additional meaning in *Oleanna* to the line in Sonnet 94, 'Lilies that fester smell far worse than weeds'.

The success of the theatre in the twentieth century is also linked to other, more deep-rooted social factors. The disasters of the 1914–18 war, followed by the Depression of the 1930s and the Second World War, totally destroyed the confidence in its own values which had made the middle class of the nineteenth century so hostile to plays which, like those of Ibsen, called these values into question. Nowadays, in contrast, it is almost as though the twentieth-century playwright has chosen to adopt something of the same technique as Cousin Amos when preaching in the Church of the Quivering Brethren in Stella Gibbons's *Cold Comfort Farm*. For as Amos looked scornfully round at his congregation, drew a deep breath, and announced at the top of his voice: *'Ye're all Damned!'* the result was, as Stella Gibbons observed, that

> an expression of lively interest and satisfaction passed over the faces of the Brethren, and here was a general rearranging of arms and legs, as though they wanted to sit as comfortably as possible, while listening to the bad news.[18]

The relationship between a Beckett, a Brecht, a Dürrenmatt, a Pinter or a Sartre and their audience is often very similar. Indeed, the Austrian playwright Peter Handke originally made his name by a play entitled *Offending the Audience*, originally performed in 1966, in which four characters come on stage and insult the audience for the very fact of being middle class.

III

The arrival of authors from outside the European mainstream; a ca-
veat about their intellectual novelty; an interest in experimentation
and the habit of exile; one not peculiar to the twentieth century. Huxley
and others with a taste for grand guignol.

Lord Melbourne once remarked that he wished he knew as much
about anything as Tom Macaulay did about everything, and there
are few nineteenth-century writers who can rival Macaulay in
the self-confidence with which he expressed some of the most
politically incorrect views to be found in any major British historian.
But when Macaulay said, in 1835, that while he was 'quite ready
to take the Oriental learning at the valuation of the Orientalists
themselves', and added that he had 'never found one among them
who could deny that a single shelf of a good European library
was worth the whole native literature of India and Arabia'[19] there
was a strong temptation, for some time afterwards, to extend his
argument to other cultures. Indeed, it was only in the late nineteenth century that the balance began to change, with Russian
novelists such as Dostoievski, Tolstoy and Turgeniev inspiring a
new approach to fiction in France and England, and two Scandinavian dramatists, Ibsen and Strindberg, helping to revive the
theatre in Western Europe and beyond.
  The impact of Russian and Scandinavian writers on a literary
tradition which had previously drawn its models principally
from Greece and Rome points to another central development in
twentieth-century literature: its internationalisation. With Goldsmith,
Sheridan and Swift, Southern Ireland had always contributed to
the development of what, in this respect, is rather curiously known
as English literature. In the late nineteenth and early twentieth
century, with Shaw, Wilde, Synge and O'Casey, the debt which
the English-speaking theatre owes to the country which has perhaps
suffered most from having England as its nearest neighbour grew
even greater. In the rest of the century, the development of literature throughout the world has shown how thoroughly the
dominance of Europe has given way to a more representative
manifestation of world-wide literary activity. Go into any book-
shop in Western Europe, North America or Australasia, and look
at the shelves. In addition to the work of the Russian, Scandinavian
and Irish writers whose work made such an impact on Western

Europe at the turn of the century, you will find South Americans such as Gabriel García Márquez or Vergas Llosa, Indian-born writers like Salman Rushdie, as well as the works of Toni Morrison, who won the Nobel Prize for Literature in 1993, or those of the West Indian novelist Narayan and the Kenyan playwright Soye Wolinka. Literature has long ceased to be what it was until the closing years of the nineteenth century, an activity mainly practised by Caucasian males – and occasionally by white-skinned women – living in Western Europe or North America.

'Up to a point, Lord Copper', as Mr Salter was in the habit of replying in *Scoop*, Evelyn Waugh's 1936 'novel about journalists', every time his chief said something obviously wrong but which his wealth, power and autocratic temperament prevented a mere foreign editor from querying. Since the questions which authors ask their readers and themselves still tend to be discussed in a framework which has its intellectual origins in Western Europe, the internationalisation of literature remains a more relative phenomenon than might at first sight appear. No substitute has yet been found for the heady mixture first created when the Greek insistence on asking questions was brought into contact with the Jewish passion for justice. No system of thinking which links the monotheistic insights of Islam with the spirituality of the Buddhist tradition has yet provided a powerful rival to the models which Marx and Freud provided when they grafted their secular religions on to the powerful growth which their Jewish ancestors created when they invented Christianity. The triumphs of the Japanese in applying Western technology have not been matched by a comparable inventiveness in pure science or speculative philosophy. In a political context, only a relatively small number of countries have succeeded in following the model established in Western Europe and North America. And just as no powerful alternative pattern has arisen outside Western Europe and North America in the way men organise their society and try to make sense of their experience through religion, philosophy and politics, so there has been no major take-over bid to challenge the literary forms first established in the Europe of the Renaissance and the Industrial Revolution.

The arrival on the scene of writers from outside the dominant mainstream of Western Europe and North America is nevertheless linked to two other phenomena which have been more marked in our time than at any previous period: a taste for experimentation, and the tendency of writers to become exiles. The two features are not necessarily related, and not all the experiments are entirely new. The technique of differed narrative in Italo Calvino's 1979 *Se une notte d'inverno un viaggatore* (*If on a winter's night a traveller*), like the interweaving of its ten different plots, is not all that disconcerting to the admirer of *Tristram Shandy*. The first use of the interior monologue, or stream of consciousness, was by a Frenchman, Emile Dujardin, in a novel called *Les Lauriers sont coupés*, published in 1888, and acknowledged by Joyce himself as one of his sources for his use of the same technique in *Ulysses*, in 1922. Nor is experimentation necessarily linked to exile. Dujardin spent the whole of his life in France, as did the most aggressively experimental of late twentieth-century French novelists, Georges Pérec. In England, the interior monologue was exploited by Virginia Woolf in *Mrs Dalloway* in 1925 and *The Waves* in 1931. Like other members of the Bloomsbury group, she rarely went abroad. In the United States, William Faulkner used the stream of consciousness technique in *The Sound and the Fury* in 1929, and in *As I lay dying* in 1930. He left the Deep South and his imaginary Yoknapatawpha County only rarely, most notably to receive the Nobel Prize for Literature in 1950.

There nevertheless is a tendency for twentieth-century writers to live abroad, as well as for their host country to profit greatly from their presence. Samuel Beckett and Eugène Ionesco lived more or less the whole of their adult lives in France, albeit for different reasons, and brought an entirely new note to the French stage. It was also the countries which remained most immune to the great twentieth-century disaster of totalitarianism which benefited most from the exiles who chose them as a place of residence. Arthur Koestler, whose use of fiction to put forward an explanation for the readiness of those accused in the Moscow state trials of the 1930s to confess to crimes they had never committed produced in 1940 one of the best political novels ever written, *Darkness at Noon*,[20] explained why. 'I chose as my home country', he wrote in the second volume of his autobiography, *The Invisible Writing*,

> a country where arrows are used only on dart-boards, suspicious of all causes, contemptuous of systems, bored by ideologies, sceptical about Utopias, rejecting all blueprints, enamoured of its leisurely muddle, incurious about the future, devoted to its past.[21]

Aldous Huxley rarely lived in England after he had left for the United States in 1937, proclaiming as he did so that 'Europe is no place for a pacifist', and the fact that he spent the last thirty years of his life in California led to an unexpected parallel with the work of Steinbeck. The 'newspaper fellow' mentioned in *The Grapes of Wrath* as deriving no pleasure from his possession of millions of acres because his mother had made him so terrified of dying is clearly modelled on the same legend which provided Huxley with the Jo Stoyte of his 1946 novel, *After Many a Summer*. In Huxley, the novel ends with Jo Stoyte, whose maternal grandmother had taught him how terrible a thing it is to fall into the hands of a living God, preparing to follow the example of the Fifth Earl of Gonister, who had succeeded, way back in the eighteenth century, in postponing mortality by consuming a diet of 'raw, triturated Viscera of freshly opened carp'. The fact that the Fifth Earl has, when they find him, fulfilled the biological destiny of man, 'a foetal ape who has not had time to grow up', does not cause Jo Stoyte too much apprehension. Anything, after all, is better than death, though one wonders what William Randolph Hearst, who is said to have provided one of the models for Jo Stoyte, as he is alleged to have done both for Orson Welles's *Citizen Kane* and for Steinbeck's 'newspaper fellow', would have thought about it all.[22]

Twentieth-century writers are as ruthless in their search for good copy as any of their predecessors, and are not averse to altering the facts to get a good story. Nor do they shy away from the nineteenth-century genre known as *grand guignol*. In Muriel Spark's 1959 novel, *Memento Mori*, Dame Lettie Colston is battered to death by her own walking stick. The description in the chapter entitled 'Good Friday Fare' in Book One of Günter Grass's *The Tin Drum* (1959) of the eels crawling out of the 'fresh and genuine horse's head' which has just been dredged from the Baltic is not for sensitive stomachs. In Howard Brenton's *The Romans in Britain*, produced at the National Theatre in London in 1980, a Roman soldier tries to bugger one of the native Britons, only to comment: 'Arseful of piles. Like fucking a fistful of marbles.' While in Edward Bond's *Saved* (1965), a baby is stoned to death on stage by a group of hooligans.

IV

An accompanying shift of the traditional balance with the growth of American influence on French literature; the relative coolness of the English to continental ideas. Roland Barthes and the problem of realism; a precursor to some of his ideas in L. C. Knights; Barthes's theories discussed in the context of Salman Rushdie and Gabriel García Márquez; a comparison with F. R. Leavis; Orwell on Kipling.

Jean-Paul Sartre's remark, in 1938, that he considered the American novelist John Dos Passos as 'the greatest writer of our time'[23] was one of a number of comments by leading French writers which illustrated another significant shift in the literary relationship between Europe and the rest of the world. Traditionally, it had been the Americans who imitated French or European models, and American authors like Henry James who came to Europe to perfect their art or find a more appreciative audience. Then, after André Malraux had described William Faulkner's novel *Sanctuary*, in his 1933 preface, as 'the intrusion of Greek tragedy into the detective story', the balance began to shift, at least temporarily. Camus made no secret of the debt which he owed Hemingway in finding the right style in which to describe the experience of Meursault in *L'Etranger* (*The Outsider*), in 1942, pointing out that what he described as Hemingway's 'behaviourist technique' was perfect for describing a man who was apparently totally unaware of what was going on. Sartre himself borrowed the same techniques which Dos Passos had used in the three volumes of his *USA Trilogy*: *42nd Parallel* (1930), *1919* (1931), *The Big Money* (1936) to recreate the atmosphere of the 1938 Munich crisis in *The Reprieve*, the second volume of *The Paths to Freedom*, in 1945, while Simone de Beauvoir's novel about responsibility, *Le Sang des Autres* (*The Blood of Others*), also published in 1945, owed an obvious debt to the use of different time frames in Faulkner's *The Sound and the Fury*.

It was the first time that European writers had used transatlantic models to express a set of very European ideas, and the lender derived as many benefits as the borrower. It is unlikely that Faulkner would have been awarded the Nobel Prize as early as he was had not so many leading European writers spoken with such enthusiasm of his work. French existentialism was more easily absorbed into the mainstream of American literary and philosophical thinking by being presented in familiar models, and the fruitful nature of the exchange marked the beginning of the period in which America became far more receptive to new ways of literary and philosophical thinking than the United Kingdom. There, continental theories tended to be looked upon with a certain suspicion, and it was not only the now forgotten C. E. M. Joad, who dismissed Sartre's *Existentialism is a Humanism* with the remark that 'if M. Sartre has conceived the unutterable, he should not try to express it',[24] who expressed reservations. A. J. Ayer was equally sceptical when he defined *Being and Nothingness* as 'very largely an exercise in the misuse of the verb "to be"'.[25]

Resistance to foreign intellectualism is, of course, part of the British tradition, and Max Beerbohm was merely expressing a commonly held attitude when he commented of the philosophy of Bergson how very depressed he felt at his inability to keep up with these advanced thinkers as they vanished into oblivion. If David Lodge had offered his readers an English academic explaining the ideas of Roland Barthes with the same energy and enthusiasm which Maurice Zapp showed in the lecture he delivers in *Small World*, he would have lost a good deal of the credibility which he rightly enjoys as the best of all the many chroniclers of academic life in the twentieth century. But Maurice Zapp is an American. He smokes cigars, makes love in unorthodox ways, is disturbed when he looks out of the aeroplane window and sees that the machine in which he is about to take off has propellers, and is open to the excitement of literary theory; and especially to those theories stemming from the ideas of Roland Barthes.

At first sight, it might seem strange to present Roland Barthes (1913–1980) as one of the key figures in the development of literature in the second half of the twentieth century. He wrote neither novels, plays nor poetry, and made a point of insisting that he was not a literary critic. Criticism, for him, involved formulating judgements, and this he regarded as a typical example of the intellectual intolerance and pretentiousness which, in his view, characterised bourgeois society. What he did was more important than this, at least in the eyes of his admirers, since he put forward a theory of literature which brought together the ideas developed in a number of new disciplines and used them to suggest that one of the central traditions on which European literature had been based in the past, that of realism, stemmed from a fundamental misunderstanding of what literature was as well as of what it could do.

This tradition was expressed in its clearest form by Balzac in his 1842 *Avant Propos* to the series of novels to which he gave the overall title of *La Comédie humaine*, a term deliberately chosen to suggest a parallel to Dante's *Divina Commedia*. French society, wrote Balzac, was the historian; he personally was merely the secretary, transcribing a pre-existent reality. The same presupposition lay behind Zola's decision to devote the 20 volumes of the Rougon-Macquart series to providing his readers with the inner history of the Second Empire, and is implicit in almost any other novelist of the nineteenth or early twentieth century: here is external reality, and there is the novelist; the job of the latter is to provide an accurate transcription of the former. Hugh Walpole expressed the idea in its clearest and most uncompromising form when he said that 'the test of a character in any novel is that it should have existed before the book that reveals it to us begins, and that it should continue after the book is closed' and his claim has the value of highlighting the reasons for which many readers have believed almost as firmly in the existence of Becky Sharpe, Mr Pickwick or Huckleberry Finn as in that of their next-door neighbour; and often derived a great deal more pleasure from it. Neither Dos Passos nor Steinbeck nor Martin du Gard nor Sartre himself would, in this respect, have seen their task as fundamentally different from that of Thackeray, Dickens or Mark Twain, any more than would the Christopher Isherwood who began his *Berlin Diary* of 1930 with the phrase: 'I am a camera with its shutter open, quite passive, recording, not thinking'. There are the facts – the misadventures of Sally Bowles, the sexual antics, financial problems and mysterious behaviour of Arthur Norris – and here is the writer, telling you the truth about something which he presents with the same certainty of its external, objective existence as I have of the table on which I am writing this book. Just as we can all see that the table is oblong, we can all agree that Becky is a wicked little schemer whose conduct is nevertheless forgivable because of the obstacles she has to overcome, Mr Pickwick a delightful old gentleman with a surprisingly resilient belief in the justice of his own cause, Huck Finn the archetypal American of the Mississipi valley in the early nineteenth century, Sally Bowles a pretentious pain in the neck, and Mr Norris an unprincipled villain whose charm would have made us just as incapable as William Bradshaw was of expelling him completely from our lives.

The extent to which this depiction of an external and independent reality was seen as one of the proper functions of literature can be seen in the habit of many readers, as well as some critics, of discussing whether Dickens had described the 'real' David Copperfield or Flaubert the 'real' Emma Bovary. In French literature, it has so dominated the discussion of Alain Fournier's *Le Grand Meaulnes* as to have almost overshadowed the literary value of the book. The idea that imaginative literature was about something which had actually happened also recurred in arguments as to whether the author had personally experienced the emotions which he described, and whether his poem or novel therefore passed the test of being a sincere account of what he had done or felt. While both these attitudes are now equally unfashionable, the initial version of what the French were to turn into a theory of literature which they thought of as invalidating all previous concepts was first put forward by a critic writing in English.

Thus in 1933, when Roland Barthes was just 20, the Shakespearian scholar L. C. Knights gave a lecture at King's College, London, entitled 'How many children had Lady Macbeth?' When subsequently published in book form by The Minority Press, Cambridge, the lecture was described in *The Listener* as '*The Communist Manifesto* of the new critical movement', and its attack on what was then the dominant and widespread belief that characters in fiction or the theatre had an existence of their own which was independent of the words on the printed page gave it an impact comparable to that of Marx's pamphlet. It was pointless, argued Knights, to look at the apparent contradiction between Lady Macbeth's claim in Act I, scene iii to have 'given suck, and know how tender 'tis to love the babe that milks me', and Macduff's despairing remark, in Act IV, that it will be impossible for him to avenge himself on Macbeth for the murder of his 'dam and all his pretty ones' because: 'He hath no children'. A poem works, argued Knights, using the word to describe any work of imaginative literature, by 'calling into play, directing and integrating certain interests'. The belief in the reality of characters in fiction or the theatre was an illusion created by the skill which the writer showed in exploiting the human capacity to imagine.

The rejection of the idea of an independent, guaranteeing reality lying behind works of art is fundamental to Barthes's theory of literature. This theory is not always easy to grasp, and he belongs

to a fairly extensive school of twentieth-century writers about literature whose style makes their books and essays much more
difficult to understand than the plays, novels or poems which they
are discussing. Indeed, in the case of Georges Bataille, Maurice
Blanchot, Malcolm Bowrie, Hélène Cixous, Jacques Derrida, Stephen
Heath, Luce Irigaray, Julia Kristeva, Jacques Lacan, J. Hillis Miller,
Toril Moi, Gayatri Chakravorty Spivak, Philippe Sollers and, indeed, in that of many others in addition to Barthes himself, it is
so hard to grasp what they mean that one adopts the paradoxi-
cal position of reading the play, novel or poem supposedly under analysis in order to understand what the critic is saying.

The best way of approaching Barthes's theory – though not
one which his admirers would endorse – is through his own essay on all-in wrestling, in which he contrasts a sport in which
there is no real contest or conflict with one in which, as in boxing or fencing, real blows are exchanged and real victories won.
What the all-in wrestlers are doing, observes Barthes, is merely
pretending to fight; and what the audience goes to see is not the
conflict itself but merely the external signs of the passion which
traditionally accompanies any kind of struggle. The shouts of anger,
the howls of agony, the threats of vengeance, the protestations of
innocence, are all make-believe, what Pooh-Ba in *The Mikado* describes as 'merely corroborative detail, intended to add a touch
of verisimilitude to an otherwise bald and unconvincing narrative'. Nothing is really happening, and what the audience sees in
a work of literature, as in an all-in wrestling match, is not a rep-
resentation of what is taking place in the real world. It is merely
a series of signs inviting it to react in a particular way to a set of
imaginary events.[26]

There is an important sense in which Barthes is right, and an
equally important one in which he is wrong. Dickens may have
used certain of his own father's characteristics to create Mr Micawber,
and the starting point for Emma's adulterous misfortunes may
have been the unfortunate Delphine Delamare. In neither case,
however, does the believability of the character stem from the
accuracy with which the author has copied a real person. If Emma
Bovary or Mr Micawber strike us as real, it is because of the skill
with which the author has manipulated the signs and conventions
of a particular literary code, just as our tendency to leap from
our seat at an all-in wrestling match is a tribute to the skill with
which Mick MacManus has exploited the conventions of the

particular branch of entertainment in which he so excels. When, in 1969, John Fowles presented the reader with two alternative endings to *The French Lieutenant's Woman*, one in which Charles Smithson married Ernestina Freeman and settled down to a respectable life in business, the other in which he disappointed all the expectations of the bourgeois reader in continuing to pursue the mysterious Sarah Woodruff, he was putting into practice a number of the implications of Barthes's rejection of traditional realism. John Fowles was naturally very conscious of this aspect of a novel which has many other themes to it, and wrote in Chapter XIII that 'The story I am telling is all imagination. The characters I create never existed outside my imagination.'

The existence of the alternative ending to *The French Lieutenant's Woman* also offers another justification for using Barthes's essay on all-in wrestling as a starting point for analysing his ideas. If you follow the wrestlers on their tour, you will see that they not only take it in turns to win or lose. They also omit or include certain features of their perfomance, as well as occasionally making certain additions, a fact which again indicates how absent any idea of a real conflict with real emotions is.

The development of Barthes's theories into the practice known as deconstructionism underlines the extent to which he is going further either than the arguments advanced by L. C. Knights or than the comment made by Coleridge in 1818, in *On Poesy and Art*, when he talked about that 'willing suspension of disbelief for the moment which constitutes poetic faith'. For the deconstructionists, and most notably for Jacques Derrida, language itself is so shifting and unreliable that no true statement can be made about anything, and the systematic application of his and Barthes's theories to novels, poetry and plays involves the virtually wholesale rejection of many of the reasons for which literature was admired, appreciated and studied in the past. Such an application requires, for example, the abandonment of any hope of our learning anything from literature about how human beings behave in their private or their public lives, how they organise their social or sexual experiences, how they feel about God, nature, money, children, politics or even literature itself.

I think that this view of literature is true only to a very limited extent. The books I discuss in this introduction to some of the themes in twentieth-century literature tell us something about twentieth-century experience which we would not have been able to find elsewhere. *Sons and Lovers* is so totally and obviously rooted in personal experience that any suggestion that all Lawrence is doing is manipulating a set of signs totally misses the point. What he is doing is to use literature to make sense of his own experience, just as Albert Camus did when he described his childhood in the novel *Le Premier Homme* (*The First Man*) which was in his briefcase in manuscript form when he was killed in a car accident on 4 January 1960, but which was not published until 1994. Over and above the biographical similarities between the two authors – both were from the working class, both nearly died of tuberculosis when very young men, both were pagan sun worshippers, both had great difficulty adjusting to the atmosphere of the intellectual milieu into which their talent gave them immediate access – there is the fact that both are describing what it was like for them to be brought up in a very specific society. One expects, as Pascal observed, to find an author, and one is delighted to discover a man.

There is also the very obvious fact that works of literature can contain specific items of information whose accuracy can be checked against other sources. In *Moon Tiger* for example, Penelope Lively makes Claudia Hampton give a number of details about Operation Barbarossa. It is, Claudia writes in her diary, speaking of her own projected History of the World, 'in these words that reality survives', and explains just what this reality is:

The snow, the twenty degrees below zero temperatures of the winter of 1941; the Russian prisoners herded into open-air pens and left till they died of cold or starvation; the furnace of Stalingrad; the thirty destroyed cities, the seven million slaughtered horses, the seventeen million cattle, the twenty million pigs. And beyond the words the images: the skeletal buildings pared by fire to chimney stacks and naked walls; the bodies chewed by frost; the screaming faces of wounded men. This is the record; this is what history comes down to in the end; this is the language of war.[27]

The presence of such a passage, which can be paralleled in the work of many other writers, notably Tolstoy, does not mean that *Moon Tiger* ceases to be a novel. However vulnerable it may be to a Barthesian critique by the role which it plays in creating the imaginary character of Claudia Hampton, the evocation of the

German invasion of Russia in 1941 also has what Barthes would call a 'signifié' or a referent:[28] it talks about a historical event which did take place.

Robert Browning also put the case against Barthes better than any of the twentieth-century critics who have doubted the value of structuralism and deconstructionism when he made Fra Lippo Lippi say:

> We're made so that we love
> First when we see them painted, things we have passed
> Perhaps a thousand times nor cared to see;
> And so they are better, painted – better to us,
> Which is the same thing. Art was given for that;
> God uses us to help each other so
> Lending our minds out.

Writers do not copy reality, and only the most naïve critics or theoreticians have ever pretended that they did. The stories they make up have the more interesting property of making us see what is already there, and which we might otherwise have missed. When, as also happens, they also offer us the reassurance that somebody else sees things as we do, or has had the same kind of experience that we have, they perform what is perhaps a more valuable service: they challenge us to wonder whether our vision of the world is the right one.

Barthes's ideas also play a central role in the peculiarly twentieth-century practice of trying to define the nature of literature. Since the word itself did not take on its current meaning in English until 1812, it is perhaps not surprising that attempts to define it should make their appearance so relatively recently, and that previous ages should have tended to argue more about the merits of particular ways of writing than about the nature of the activity in which poets, essayists, novelists and playwrights are all equally involved. Although Barthes's own concept of literature, as I shall argue, is far from value free, the issues he raises have an interesting philosophical edge to them, especially as far as what it is tempting to call the mimetic fallacy is concerned. Discussions of realism in the nineteenth century rarely got beyond the issue of what the author did or did not have the moral right to offer his readers. In taking the question further than what tended to become a rather boring argument about censorship and morality, and querying the very suppositions on which the writing of fiction, in particular, tended to be based, Barthes livened the matter up considerably.

There are, however, a number of reasons for treating Barthes's ideas with a certain scepticism. It has always been traditional, in English, to talk about works of the imagination, and to distinguish the novelist from the historian by referring to the former as an imaginative writer. This does not mean that what the novelist imagines is necessarily untrue in every sense of the word, and one of the most recent developments in literature, the movement known as 'magic realism', offers a useful opportunity to see how Barthes's ideas need to be modified if they are to offer a satisfactory answer to the genuine problem which he raises, that of how descriptions of events which never took place can still tell us something about ourselves and the world we live in. The reader of novels such as Salman Rushdie's *The Satanic Verses* or Gabriel García Márquez's *One Hundred Years of Solitude* is clearly not expected to see what happens in them as being realistic in the same sense that he might be required to see the plot and characters of E. M. Forster's *A Passage to India* or Conrad's *Nostromo* as realistic. The adventures of Gibreel Farishta and Saladin Chamcha, or the events which take place in and around the imaginary town of Macondo, could not have happened in the same way as the misfortunes of Dr Aziz or the exploits of Conrad's hero. Rushdie and Forster nevertheless resemble each other, in spite of their totally different aesthetic and political ideas, in that they say something about England and India which goes beyond the manipulation of arbitrary signs around an empty content. So, too, do García Márquez and Conrad in the insights which their novels offer into the political culture of South America.

A further reason for suspecting that Barthes has not quite got it right lies in the nature of the illusion which he is rejecting. However much it might be possible, by quoting statements by writers about what they thought or hoped they were doing, to show that Walpole and Arnold Bennett were not alone in thinking about characters in novels in the way they did, the idea that readers genuinely believed in the reality of fictional events is very much a straw man. Balzac himself cannot have failed to recognise the difference in kind between the events in *La Comédie humaine* and what actually happened in Restoration France, and whatever insights Christopher Isherwood's novels and short stories may offer into the atmosphere of Berlin in the 1930s, they do not live up to his claim that they are a photographic reproduction of the way real people lived before and immediately after the advent of the Third Reich. Barthes often gives the impression of making an imperfect distinction between the experienced consumer of imaginative literature, who knows perfectly well that there is a difference between *War and Peace* and the acount of the 1812 invasion of Russia offered in any history book, and the inhabitants of the village of Macondo in García Márquez's *One Hundred Years of Solitude* who

> became indignant over the living images that the prosperous merchant Bruno Crespi projected in the theatre with the lion-head ticket windows, for a character who had died and was buried in one film and for whose misfortune tears of affliction had been shed would reappear alive and transformed into an Arab in the next one.[29]

Although the starting point for Barthes's theories was in the officially value-free disciplines of Saussurian linguistics and semiology, these theories tend to be normative rather than descriptive. Like those of F. R. Leavis in England, they tell the reader what literature ought to be like rather than what it actually is, and it is very clear that Barthes thought Philippe Sollers a much better writer than Maupassant. Leavis's description in *The Great Tradition* of D. H. Lawrence as 'in the English language, the great genius of our time' is, naturally, a claim of a very different kind from Barthes's refusal to accept that literature can tell us anything at all about either the external world or about ourselves. What Leavis admired in Lawrence was not only his reverence for life and the authenticity of his moral responses, but his ability to tell the truth about human experience. The two critics nevertheless resemble each other in that they both ask the reader to see their idea of what is good literature as the only one which is intellectually respectable.

Thus there were, for Leavis, only five novelists who deserved to be included in what he called 'the great tradition': Jane Austen, George Eliot, Joseph Conrad, Henry James and D. H. Lawrence. He specifically excluded Fielding, observing that he was

> important not because he leads to Mr J. B. Priestley but because he leads to Jane Austen, to appreciate whose distinction

is to feel that life is not long enough to permit one's giving much time to Fielding, or any to Mr Priestley.[30]

Since Sterne, the Brontës, Thackeray, Trollope and Thomas Hardy didn't make it into *The Great Tradition* either, and even Dickens came to be included in the canon only as an afterthought, the tradition which Leavis admires is a fairly narrow one. The way in which he expressed his preferences also casts doubt on the view that the study of great literature makes people more tolerant. Few of Leavis's own books live up to the criterion which Holden Caulfield set out when he wrote of Hardy's *The Return of the Native* that 'what really knocks me out is a book that, when you've all done reading it, you wish the author was a terrific friend of yours and you could call him up on the phone whenever you felt like it'.[31]

It is perhaps significant, in this and other respects, that the attempt to define literature, which has taken a strictly intellectual form in France, should have assumed a semi-religious, neo-puritanical one in England.

There have, however, been some more open-minded and dissentient voices which have contributed to the debate about the nature of literature, and in 1942 George Orwell pointed out that Middleton Murry, an influential critic of the 1920s and 1930s, attributed to Thackeray the lines in which Kipling expressed the impossibility of reaching a satisfactory definition of literature:

There are nine-and-sixty ways, of constructing tribal lays
And Every-Single-One-Of-Them-Is-Right![32]

This was, Orwell observed, what might be called a Freudian error, in that Kipling was not then regarded as sufficiently fashionable to be quoted in a literary discussion among civilised intellectuals. Even nowadays, it would make a better impression on colleagues as well as on examiners if one were to express the same idea in more philosophical terms, and this is quite easy. All one needs to do is follow the example of William of Ockham (c. 1285–c. 1349) who taught that essences were not to be multiplied beyond necessity; in other words, that you should avoid complicated concepts and keep it simple. Thus one can point out, as would a philosopher in the nominalist tradition created by William of Ockham, that there are a large number of men listed in the telephone directory under the name of Robinson; but no quality common to them other than the possession of that name. Similarly, there are a very large number of books catalogued by librarians under the section marked 'Literature'. But it is as hard to find any quality which they all genuinely share as it is to discover the essence of Robinsonism in all the men who bear that name. The only danger in this argument is for examinees. The authorities at Oxford never allowed William to proceed beyond the status of under-graduate.

V

Rudyard Kipling as an author expressing a number of attitudes useful for defining the spirit of twentieth-century literature by its opposite. A view of his work supported by references to Evelyn Waugh, Conrad and Pierre Boule.

Kipling did not die until 1935, and writers as impeccably twentieth-century in their style, preoccupations and attitudes as T. S. Eliot, George Orwell and Kingsley Amis have written about him with considerable enthusiasm. There are nevertheless few readers, and even fewer literary critics, who would see him as a typically twen-tieth-century author. Like Roger Martin du Gard, though for very different reasons, he represents a prolongation into the twentieth century of a number of attitudes which are seen as belonging so completely to the nineteenth century that they can be used as an automatic contrast in order to define how people feel in the twen-tieth. This does not make these nineteenth-century attitudes wrong, and many of them can be found in as quintessentially a twenti-eth-century author as Joseph Conrad.

Thus, like Conrad, Kipling believed in the importance of cour-age, in the value of keeping one's word and seeing the job through to the end, of accepting responsibility for other people's mistakes as well as for one's own, and for not shirking one's duty to those less fortunately placed than oneself. It was the ethic of the officer class, which Conrad himself had absorbed during his years as a Master Mariner, and which was neatly expressed in the two rules which Guy Crouchback is given in *Men at Arms*, the first volume of Evelyn Waugh's trilogy *Unconditional Surrender*, when he joins the Halberdiers:

No Halberdier officer eats until he has seen the last meal
served.
No Halberdier officer sleeps until he has seen the last man
bedded down.

The irony of events which characterises Waugh's presentation
of the Second World War, subsequently described in 1946 in *Scott
King's Modern Europe* as 'a sweaty tug of war between teams of
indistinguishable oafs',[33] underlines how difficult it is to apply
these ideals to real situations. Part of the essentially twentieth-
century quality of Waugh's fiction lies in his understanding of
how inappropriate traditional moral values can become in the
new situations in which men find themselves. These values nevertheless inspire rules which both Kipling and Conrad would have
fully endorsed, and there is, in both writers, the same pessimism
about the ultimate justice of the universe which makes the observance of the moral values which men create for their own conduct
so essential.

There are, however, a number of reasons why any mention of
the values admired by Kipling and Conrad, and embodied in the
ethic of the Halberdiers, would be greeted with a certain scepticism by most twentieth-century literary critics as well as by many
of their younger readers. One of these is that these values pre-
suppose a set of power relationships in society which is seen as
totally inappropriate in a democratic and egalitarian age. The very
term 'officer class' has virtually disappeared from modern English, and there are few easier ways of raising a smile in literary
or intellectual circles in either England or America than to recite
the opening lines of Kipling's *The White Man's Burden*, a poem he
published in 1899 to celebrate the assumption by the United States
of responsibility for the Philippines:

Take up the White Man's burden,
   Send forth the best ye breed –
Go bind your sons to exile
   To serve your captors need;
To wait in heavy harness
   On fluttered folk and wild –
Your new-caught, sullen peoples,
   Half devil and half child.

The immediate explanation for the laughter is the mixture of culturalism and racialism which makes Kipling so unacceptable an author for the twentieth-century reader. Conrad's *Heart of Darkness* was published in the same year as *The White Man's Burden*, and ushered in a style of writing about imperialism which is at one and the same time totally different from Kipling's vision and highly typical of the twentieth century. One of the first things that Marlow sees when he arrives in what is obviously the Belgian Congo is six black men, clad in rags, their ribs showing through their skin, each with an iron collar on his neck connecting him to his fellow slaves by a chain whose 'bights swung between them, rhythmically clinking'. Kurtz's famous last words – 'The horror! The horror!' – apply just as obviously to what white men have done to the countries they have conquered as to the vast indifference of the universe which provides the metaphysical background to all Conrad's tales.

One of the most haunting images from *Heart of Darkness* is that of a French man-of-war anchored off the African coast. 'There wasn't even a shed there', comments Marlow,

> and she was shelling the bush. It appears that the French had one of their wars going on thereabouts. Her ensign drooped limp like a rag; the muzzles of the long six-inch guns stuck out all over the low hull; the greasy, slimy swell swung her up lazily and let her down, swaying her thin masts. In the empty immensity of earth, sky, and water, there she was, incomprehensible, firing into a continent.[34]

As Marlow is also made to put it

> The conquest of the earth, which mostly means the taking it away from those who have a different complexion or slightly flatter noses than ourselves, is not a pretty thing when you look at it too much,[35]

and his remark, like the image of the French battleship firing pointlessly into the jungle, is one which applies just as effectively to the American intervention in Vietnam between 1966 and 1973 as to the relationship between European imperialism and tropical Africa in the nineteenth century.

It is, however, by no means certain that Conrad would have

endorsed the very specific reading of *Heart of Darkness* which inspired Francis Coppola's adaptation of it in 1969 to the Vietnam war in the film *Apocalypse Now*. Conrad might well have wondered whether there was, in spite of all the horrors of the war, a political case for resisting the left-wing totalitarianism of the Viet Cong. In *Heart of Darkness*, the Europeans are in Africa solely to make money. What interests them is the price of ivory, not the exercise of power. The Vietnam war, in contrast, was fought for political motives. However misguided the Americans may have been in their application of the 'domino theory', they derived no financial benefit from their policy in Vietnam, and Conrad's rejection of capitalist imperialism did not inspire him with any enthusiasm for revolution. His two most obviously political novels, *The Secret Agent* (1907) and *Under Western Eyes* (1911) are in many ways highly conservative. Foreigners, and especially Russians, are given to murderous excesses, whose pointlessness underlines the advantages of the more restrained and ponderous approach to politics characteristic of the British Isles. After 1917, Conrad was occasionally annoyed by what he saw as the uncritical enthusiasm shown by English-speaking intellectuals towards the Bolshevik revolution. Long before Orwell had tried to warn against the dangers of totalitarian dictatorship, Conrad had anticipated the dangers of believing that all the values of bourgeois democracy had to be jettisoned to make way for the new values of the triumphant revolution.

There are other, complementary reasons to explain why twentieth-century writers and audiences are so automatic in their rejection of the moral values regarded as axiomatic in the nineteenth century. One of Kipling's best-known poems, *If*, praises self-reliance, courage and perseverance, resilience in face of difficulty or defeat, and modesty in success. These virtues, it is universally agreed, were so squandered in the trenches between 1914 and 1918, so useless in the Depression of the 1930s, so pointless in the face of the prospect of nuclear annihilation during the Cold War, and are nowadays so inappropriate to the revival of capitalism made possible by the disintegration of the Soviet Union as to be positively dangerous to anyone trying to put them into practice in the real world. In 1942, George Orwell was already out of step with the atmosphere of literary London when he said that however much you laughed at the tradition in which you were brought up, a moment always came when the sands of the desert were sodden red and What have I done for thee, England, my England? Nowadays, it is extremely unlikely that either of the quotations would even be recognised.[36]

Orwell's attitude was in this as in other respects very different from that of the London theatre audience of 1973 to Curly's reply to Mrs Dunning in *Knuckle*, the first play of David Hare's trilogy, *The History Plays*. For when she wondered why all the words in which her generation believed, 'words like honour and dignity' were now 'just a joke', Curly's response was that it was a very simple one. It was, he explained, 'because of some of the characters they've knocked around with' and his reply evoked an immediate murmur of agreement and potential applause throughout the theatre.[37] However inadequate Marxism may have turned out to be when used as a basis for trying to reorganise society, the scepticism which it helped to breed towards the values taken for granted in the nineteenth century remains one of the constants of twentieth-century literature.

The characters in twentieth-century literature who try to observe a Kiplingesque ethic may well be perfectly sincere in what they are trying to do. They nevertheless fail, and do so precisely because of the inadequacy of the ethic they are trying to apply. What matters in the first instance to Colonel Nicholson, the hero of Pierre Boule's 1954 *The Bridge on the River Kwai*, is the observance of the rules of warfare, and especially the article in the Geneva Convention which states that commissioned officers shall not be required to do manual work. Once he has begun to impose what he considers as the beginning of a necessary semblance of civilisation by making the Japanese yield on this immediate issue, and thus accept that some rules exist, he is led on by his concern for the welfare and morale of his men to ensure that they work properly. But his desire to show the Japanese how British soldiers can turn defeat into triumph by building the bridge more quickly and efficiently than their captors then leads him to a position where he is guilty of aiding and abetting the enemy.

It is only in the very successful film which was made out of the book, in 1957, that Nicholson is allowed to redeem himself. In the book, he is not given the chance of realising that he has, precisely by sticking to the rules and behaving with a sense of responsibility towards his men worthy of a Kipling hero and officer of the Indian Army, become a traitor to his own country and been led into aiding and abetting the enemy. There, the bridge which he has made his men build is not blown up by the small commando force sent to destroy it; and the train goes safely through. The quotation from Conrad which Boule puts at the beginning of the novel embodies one of the most frequently discussed questions in twentieth-century literature, that of the difficulty of deciding on the right action in an absurd world:

> No, it was not funny; it was rather pathetic; he was so representative of all the past victims of the great Joke. But it is by folly alone that the whole world moves, and so it is a respectable thing on the whole. And, besides, he was what one would call a good man.

VI

More on Kipling as an author defining the spirit of twentieth-century literature by its opposite. The examples of Norman Mailer, Nicholas Monsarrat, Irwin Shaw and others; similarities and contrasts between Kipling and the English poets of the First World War; a reference to Simone de Beauvoir.

Kipling does not idealise war. He knows, as Orwell wrote in 1942,

> that bullets hurt, that under fire everyone is terrified, that the ordinary soldier never knows what the war is about or what is happening except in his own corner of the battlefield, and that British troops, like other troops, frequently run away.[38]

There is nothing in his poetry comparable to a poem which Philip Larkin included in 1973 in *The Oxford Book of Twentieth Century English Verse*, Julian Grenfell's 'Into Battle', written in 1915 shortly before Grenfell himself was killed in action:

> The naked earth is warm with Spring,
> And with green grass and bursting trees
> Leans to the sun's gaze glorying,
> And quivers in the sunny breeze.
>
> And life is colour and warmth and light,

And a striving ever more for these;
And he is dead who will not fight;
And who dies fighting has increase.

Some of the poems in *The Barrack Room Ballads* (1892), as Orwell pointed out in his 1942 essay, are as realistic in tone as the work of the poets who, unlike Grenfell, concentrated on the horrors of the 1914–18 war. But Kipling does not countenance cowardice, and would have been horrified by the way that Joseph Heller does so in *Catch 22*. The poem in the second book of *Barrack Room Ballads*, 'That Day', which offers a very realistic account of how a regiment breaks and runs, takes the unfashionable attitude of attributing its cowardice to the failure of the officers to enforce proper discipline. The argument that war is a pointless activity conducted largely for their own self-aggrandisement by incompetent senior officers, and which is at the heart of Yossarian's decision to opt out in *Catch 22*, would have struck Kipling as rather naïve; and it does seem a little strange that an author who, like Heller, is Jewish, should present the Second World War as one which was not worth fighting. Kipling sees war as an inevitable part of the human condition, and even presents the 'savage wars of peace' which the White Man has to fight as part of his burden as a necessary part of the process whereby what he, Kipling, sees as a better way of organising society is imposed throughout the world. It is left to authors like Conrad and Pierre Boule to underline how simplistic and inadequate the Kiplingesque attitude is.

Nobody who has written about warfare, from Homer onwards, has any sympathy for the general staff, and Kipling is no exception. There is not much difference in attitude between his poem *Stellenbosch*, with the lines

The General got his decorations thick,
(The men that backed his lies could not complain)
The Staff had D.S.Os till we were sick
And the soldier – had to do the job again

and one of the most typical of the poems inspired by the First World War, Siegfried Sassoon's 'The General':

'Good morning; Good morning!', the General said,
When we met him last week on our way to the line.

Now the soldiers he smiled at are most of 'em dead,
And we're cursing his staff for incompetent swine.
'He's a cheery old card', said Harry to Jack
As they slogged up to Arras with rifle and pack.
. . . .
But he did for them both with his plan of attack.

But for Kipling, the enemy was the enemy, and his cry in 1914
was that the Hun is at the gates. For writers of a more twentieth-
century temper, the only enemy is war itself, perhaps accompanied
by the politicians seen as responsible for causing it and the civ-
ilians at home who are more bellicose than the men in the firing
line. Few writers in the history of literature can have had a more
permanent influence on the generations succeeding them than the
English poets of the First World War, and they are virtually unani-
mous in condemning not only the war in which they were involved but the very activity of war itself.

Tennyson was Poet Laureate for the last forty years of his long
life, and a new volume of his poems would sell 20,000 copies in
a week. In 1878, his poem *The Revenge. A Ballad of the Fleet* had
its hero, Sir Richard Grenville, urge his men into action with the
lines

Let us bang these dogs of Seville, the children of the Devil,
For I never turned my back upon Don or Devil yet

which would probably, less than a hundred years later, have laid
him open to prosecution under the Race Relations Act. There is a
marked contrast with Captain Ericson's attitude in Nicholas
Monsarrat's *The Cruel Sea*, one of the best and most successful
novels about the Second World War. As the crew of the German
submarine which *Compass Rose* has just sunk struggle towards
his ship through the icy, oil-covered waters of the North Atlantic,
Ericson's comment is that he expects them to 'look pretty much
like us'.

In spite of the fact that the enemy they were fighting was peculiarly unpleasant by any standards, the only feeling which Norman Mailer's soldiers have in his 1948 novel, *The Naked and the
Dead*, is the horror of an unpleasant job that has to be done in
appalling conditions, coupled with an intense suspicion of their
own society. The villain is Major-General Cummings, who spends

his time denouncing the failure of liberalism, and preparing himself, after the war, to take personal charge in an America which has more or less willingly adopted Fascism as the only way of dealing with its problems. Another major American novel about the Second World War, Irwin Shaw's *The Young Lions* (1949), gives as sympathetic a portrait of the young German, Christian, as it does of the American soldiers fighting against him. The only villains are the anti-semitic Southerners who torment Noah Ackerman, and the lazy and incompetent Captain Coughlan, whose boastings are equalled only by his cowardice.

There are other aspects of Kipling's work which, like Tennyson's *The Revenge. A Ballad of the Fleet*, provide a kind of negative identity test for trying to decide whether an author belongs to the twentieth century by a mere accident of birth, or whether he is emotionally, intellectually and politically in sympathy with its most characteristic attitudes. Although Kipling wrote the line which provided Somerset Maugham with the title for one of his best short stories about the supposed inability of Englishmen to understand female sexuality – 'For the colonel's lady and Judy O'Grady are sisters under the skin' – there is not a word in his work that would bring a blush to the most modest cheek. Whereas one of the great themes in twentieth-century literature is that of liberation, both in what an author can talk about and in the contribution which writers can make to the liberation of women and other previously oppressed groups, Kipling had an unshakable belief in the need for what Edmund Burke, the first genuinely conservative thinker in the intellectual history of Europe, called in his *Reflections on the Revolution in France*, in 1790, 'the principles of natural subordination'.

Not all Kipling's work was infected with the racialism which runs through *The White Man's Burden*, and he was not a man who believed that people of Anglo-Saxon origin were morally superior to everybody else. The best known of all his poems, *Gunga Din*, is a celebration of the superiority in courage, endurance and generosity of an Indian water-carrier over the British soldiers he is required to serve. But Kipling was undoubtedly a sexist, and another of his poems, *The Female of the Species*, not only gave Sapper, the creator of Bulldog Drummond the title for the novel in which his brave but anti-semitic hero triumphs over the wicked Irma, relict of the villainous Carl Petersen.[39] It also suggests that the greater ruthlessness traditionally attributed to women stems from

the fact that they are biologically programmed to produce and
protect the young, and will do anything to achieve this aim. It
would be difficult to imagine a point of view more different from
Simone de Beauvoir's observation that 'You are not born a woman.
You become one'. And whereas the quintessential role of the twentieth-century writer has become to disturb the presuppositions
on which the existing social order is based, Kipling thought that
the institutions already developed by men were perfectly adequate if all those who were called upon to do their duty were
faithful to their calling.

2

Visions of Childhood I: The Child Unhappy on its own Account

I

Twentieth-century attitudes towards children more reminiscent of the pre-romantic period than of the nineteenth century; Dylan Thomas and Philip Larkin; Sons and Lovers *and* Le Grand Meaulnes *as transitional texts; reflections on* The Catcher in the Rye.

A comparison between Sons and Lovers *and* Paddy Clarke Ha Ha Ha.

When W. C. Fields remarked that a man who hated children and dogs could not be wholly bad, he was expressing a truth which would have delighted the heart of the principal theoretician of seventeenth-century French classicism, Nicolas Boileau. Just as the sacred mysteries of the Christian religion were not, in Boileau's view, a suitable subject for profane literature, so the place of children was strictly offstage. Boileau's friend Racine proved him right in two ways: in his first great tragedy, *Andromaque* (1666), the audience is spared the sight of Astyanax, the son of the dead Hector whom Andromache must use all her wiles to protect from the murderous vengeance of the Greeks; in his last, and least performable play, *Athalie* (1691), the child Joas (the story is taken from 2 Kings 2, 11 and 2 Chronicles, 22–3) is an insufferable little prig whom it would be a pleasure to see pitched into the real world of childhood as depicted in William Golding's 1954 novel *Lord of the Flies*, Susan Hill's *The King of the Castle*, or even the William books. Compared to Racine's Joas, even Hubert Lane could step into the world of Kipling's *Stalky and Co.* (1899) with no questions asked and manage to survive.

If there are children in books written for an adult readership in the twentieth century, they are depicted with a lack of illusions which would have delighted the Mr Wopsle who took the opportunity of Christmas dinner at Mrs Jo's in Chapter 4 of *Great Expectations* to denounce them as 'naterally wicious'. Treatments of pre-pubescent sex are, fortunately, as rare as attempts to show that Rousseau was right when he began his book on education, *Emile*, in 1762, with the claim that 'everything is good as it leaves the hands of the Father of Things, everything degenerates in the hands of men'. Sex may appear to hold no mysteries for Adrian Mole, but his knowledge remains on an intellectual level. His actual behaviour reflects a rather touching teenage clumsiness. The whole plot of L. P. Hartley's 1953 novel *The Go-Between* depends upon the fact that the twelve-year-old Leo does not understand about sex. Nabokov's Lolita is not very interested in sex, but she is no angel either. The central theme in the book is not her sexuality, but Humboldt Humboldt's well-analysed obsessions. Where twentieth-century writers are much more realistic than their eighteenth- and nineteenth-century predecessors is in their readiness to accept that children have as great a capacity for evil as the adults around them. The vision of childhood which is characteristically twentieth century is the one which goes back beyond Rousseau and the Romantics to the more depressing implications of the La Fontaine fable, *Les Deux Pigeons*. After one of the pigeons has been attacked by a vulture and is lying wounded on the ground, a child takes his sling and casually finishes it off. 'Cet âge', comments La Fontaine, 'est sans pitié' (It is an age without pity). It is a comment which recurs, in an appropriately macabre form, in the anecdote which concludes *Moscow Stations*, Stephen Mulrine's 1994 dramatised version of Venedikt Yerofeev's novel. When a drunken passenger falls on to the track in a Moscow railway station, and has both legs cut off by a passing train, two children jump down on to the track and decorate the top part of the corpse by placing a cigarette in the corner of its mouth.[1]

It is true that there are few Wordsworthian clouds of glory hanging round the Maggie Tulliver of George Eliot's *The Mill on the Floss*. She disapproves of herself with the same intensity as does her virtuous and priggish brother Tom. But she is impulsive and absent-minded, not evil or selfish. The way the Reed children bully Jane Eyre is realistic by any standard. But they are merely following the example of their appalling mother, and this section of the novel is well within the tradition which dominated in the nineteenth century, whereby the sufferings of children are caused mainly by adults. Another characteristic of nineteenth-century literature, the poetic idealisation of childhood, took a long time to disappear. It was a dominant feature of the poetry of Dylan Thomas as late as the 1940s, with poems such as *Fern Hill*, and its opening stanza:

> Now as I was young and easy under the apple boughs
> About the lilting house and happy as the grass was green,
>   The night above the dingle starry,
>   Time let me hail and climb,
> Golden in the heydays of his eyes,
> And honoured among wagons I was prince of the apple
> towns,
> And once below a time I lordly had the trees and leaves
>   Trail with daisies and barley
>   Down the rivers of the windfall night.

It is not until Philip Larkin's ironically titled poem, 'I remember, I remember', in 1954, with its insistence on the boredom of childhood and its acknowledgement that 'Nothing, like something, happens anywhere,' that the myth of the splendour of childhood started to be seen in poetry for what it can often be.

William Golding's *Lord of the Flies* was turned down by 15 publishers before finally being accepted in 1954 by Faber and Faber, and it was clearly a gamble for a publishing house to expose its readers to books which queried the myths about childhood created by Rousseau and Wordsworth. Three of the novels which help to make 1913 into a crucial year for the development of twentieth-century literature – D. H. Lawrence's *Sons and Lovers*, Alain Fournier's *Le Grand Meaulnes* (a title best translated as *The Milk of Paradise*), and the first volume of Proust's *A la recherche du temps perdu* (*Remembrance of Things Past*) – each dealt, among other things, with the world of childhood. But while Proust and Lawrence are rightly seen as two of the founding fathers of modernism, the account which their novels, like that of Alain Fournier, give of the world of childhood still has strong reminiscences of the nineteenth century. None of the children in their books behaves badly either towards each other or to the adults around them, none is ever bored, and none suffers by being excluded by other children. Each of them, in particular, seems more like a young adult than a normal child in that he has a clearly formulated ideal which he is anxious to pursue, whether it is the ambition to become a writer in Proust, Paul Morel's desire to compensate his mother for her unhappiness in the first part of *Sons and Lovers*, or the longing to find the lost domain in *The Milk of Paradise*. The readiness with which both Proust and Alain Fournier subscribe to the idea which Baudelaire expressed in 1856 when he said that genius was 'childhood rediscovered at our bidding' ('l'enfance retrouvée à volonté') makes them more like the younger brothers of Wordsworth than the great-grandsons which they are on chronological grounds.

It is significant in this respect that the crucial experience described by Proust in *Combray*, the opening section of *Remembrance of Things Past*, should take the Narrator back not to his manhood or adolescence, but to his childhood. One day, when he is sometime in his early thirties, the Narrator is feeling tired and depressed, and happens to eat a *petite madeleine*, a small cake dipped in tea. When he is then filled with an unexpected and inexplicable ecstasy, he finds the secret of his bliss in the fact that the sensation is absolutely identical to the one which he used to have when he was a very little boy, and his aunt offered him a piece of the same cake every Sunday morning as he was about to go to church. Similar episodes take place later in the novel, especially in the final volume, *Time Regained*, and their recurrence inspires the Narrator with the ambition to discover their real meaning by writing a book in which they provide the starting point and principal theme. He sees the fact that chance physical sensation can bring the whole past flooding back into his memory as a providential accident which cannot be allowed to escape without being cast into the permanent framework of a work of art. But what matters most of all, in the first instance, is that the experience of the *petite madeleine* takes the Narrator back to what he sees as the magic world of childhood.

Matters are slightly different in *Le Grand Meaulnes*, in that the crucial period is adolescence. When Augustin Meaulnes explains to his friend François Sorel just why the magic domain which he had come across in his wanderings continues to exercise such a spell on him, what he stresses is the fact that he had, at that point in his very early youth, reached a state of total purity which he knew that he would never be able to find again. Whatever other features there are in both writers, and especially in Proust's treatment of voyeurism, homosexuality and sado-masochism, which enable us to say that they belong to the twentieth century by other factors than chronological accident, this insistence on the bliss and purity of childhood places them clearly in the tradition of nineteenth-century romanticism. It was a very rich and fertile tradition, which lasted a long time. Enough of it was still alive as late as 1945 to enable J. D. Salinger to make early childhood the one ideal still capable of making Holden Caulfield feel happy. What most touches his heart is the purity of his younger sister, Phoebe, and the way in which this awareness of her purity intensifies the repulsion which he feels for almost every manifestation of the adult world with which he comes into contact would not have seemed at all strange to Baudelaire.

In practically every other aspect, however, *The Catcher in the Rye* seems to have been written to destroy what it is tempting to see as another typically nineteenth-century myth, that of the well-balanced and fully integrated adolescent. The continued popularity of *The Catcher in the Rye* with teenagers in the schools and universities of England and America shows that Salinger's attack on this myth was aimed at a highly receptive audience. What delights these readers of his novel is, among other things, the spectacle of a hero whose mixture of incompetence and honesty frees them from the burden of being an ideal son or daughter themselves. If Holden is so disorganised that he leaves all the equipment belonging to the school's fencing team on the New York subway, is so bad at his studies that he is being constantly required to move schools, this is presented as being as much the fault of the adult world as of his own inability to cope. He has, the reader is given to understand, been so heartbroken by the death of his brother Allie that nobody will ever be able to grasp the intensity of his grief. But while the adult world can offer him no consolation, the memories of childhood can; even if they are only of how Jane Gallagher kept all her kings on the back row when she was playing checkers so as not to run the risk of losing them.

The element of hysteria which recurs on so many of its pages, linked with the uncertainty which Salinger has both about his own values and about his principal character, makes the traditional comparison with *Huckleberry Finn* hard to sustain. While the story of Huckleberry Finn is that of a boy who discovers a sense of responsibility, and ends up by saving the runaway slave, Jim, *The Catcher in the Rye* presents an adolescent who has very little sense of responsibility either for himself or for anybody else.

One of the great moments in the cinema of the 1990s comes when the young negro mythomaniac Paul, in the adaptation of John Guare's 1990 play, *Six Degrees of Separation*, draws the attention of his astonished upper-middle-class hosts, Ouisa and Frances Kitteredge, to the passages in the text which make Salinger's novel a manual for teenage murderers. Quoting chapter and verse, he points out that Holden describes his baseball hat as 'a people shooting hat', and he concludes his account of how reluctant he is to have fist fights with people by saying: 'I'd rather push a guy out of the window or chop his head off with an ax than sock him on the jaw'.[2] Paul also makes two other specific claims: that 'the nitwit Chapman, the one who shot John Lennon', said that he did it because he wanted to draw the attention of the world to *The Catcher in the Rye*, and that the 'reading of the book would be his defence'; and that young Hinckley, 'the whizz kid who shot Reagan and his press secretary, said that if you want any defence, all you have to do is read *Catcher in the Rye*'.[3] It is consequently not surprising that the rich New Yorkers and their South African guest, who are totally taken in by Paul's claim to be the son of Sydney Poitier, immediately resolve to read the book again.

It is improbable that these charges against Holden will ever seriously reduce the attraction he exercises on adolescents. They will continue to be impressed by the keenness of his nose for phonies, and by his intense awareness of being an outsider in a society whose values he does not accept. If *The Catcher in the Rye* strikes the reader as a characteristically twentieth-century text, in the sense that it is very difficult to imagine it as having been written at any other period, it is nevertheless for reasons which strike middle-aged readers as slightly odd. It is only too easy for such readers to imagine what a nightmare it would be to have Holden as their child, and to feel uneasy about a book which seems to justify a style of behaviour which is as self-defeating as it is ungrateful and irresponsible. Since, however, Holden Caulfield's parents seem to have treated him with too much generosity, it is also a book which links up with another aspect of Proust's treatment of childhood, the one which moves the blame for the child's unhappiness away from the adults around it and on to the child itself.

The convention of the child made unhappy by adults remained alive long enough for Lawrence to exploit it in his account of the unhappiness which Paul Morel feels at the brutal way in which his father treats his mother. This is still in the tradition established

by Dickens, albeit with the introduction of a more modern, potentially Freudian vein, as Lawrence shows how Paul's attachment to his mother is at the root of the problems he encounters
with Miriam and Clara. It is nevertheless instructive to compare
Sons and Lovers, perhaps the greatest of all novels about the English working class at the turn of the century, with the novel which
won the Booker Prize for fiction in 1993, Roddy Doyle's *Paddy
Clarke Ha Ha Ha*.[4] The contrast is partly a technical one. While
Doyle allows us no viewpoint other than that of the ten-year-old
Paddy, Lawrence is writing within the nineteenth-century convention of the omniscient narrator. The principal character, the
fairly obviously autobiographical Paul Morel, does not appear
until the stage has been clearly set by the account of the early
married life of the Morels. For readers who see Lawrence the
man as being, in a sense, more interesting than even the greatest
of his individual books, the portrait of Walter Morel holds a particular fascination. As a young man, Lawrence disliked his father,
and identified himself almost completely with his artistically-
minded, puritanical mother. In later life, and especially in *Lady
Chatterley's Lover*, it was the sensual values of his father which
were presented as better than those of the socially ambitious petty
bourgeoisie or the intellectualised middle class.

There was, it is true, an element of uncertainty here. Lawrence's
decision to present Arthur Mellors as a man who could speak
standard English when he chose to do so, and who had held
commissioned rank in the army, suggests a characteristically English
preoccupation with social class. Even as late as 1928, the hero of
a novel could not be as totally proletarian as everybody is in the
Dublin of 1967 evoked in *Paddy Clarke Ha Ha Ha*. *Sons and Lovers*,
from this point of view, is certainly a better novel than *Lady
Chatterley's Lover*. The relationship between Walter and Gertrude
Morel does more than ring true on psychological and sexual
grounds. It tells us something about the English working class
which remained true for decades after the publication of Lawrence's novel, and which was clearly part of a pattern established
in the early years of the industrial revolution. With few exceptions, carefully noted by Lawrence, the man's contribution to the
home was limited to giving his wife her house-keeping money,
and spending very occasional days with the children. For the rest
of the time, he sought relaxation from his hard and often brutal-
ising work in the pub. One of my first recollections, as a young

lecturer working for the Workers' Education Department in Birmingham in the early 1950s, was of the virtual unanimity with which my class at Wednesbury insisted on the ease with which Walter and Gertrude Morel could still be found in the West Midlands, especially in the car industry.

The atmosphere of what would now be called upward social mobility is another aspect of *Sons and Lovers* which makes it invulnerable to any Barthesian suggestion that fiction consists solely of the manipulation of signs. The women and men who moved, as Lawrence did, from the working class to the lower and then to the middle or higher reaches of the professional middle class, did so because of the essentially Protestant passion for self improvement of which Gertrude Morel is the perfect example. *Sons and Lovers* is, in this respect, a work of art which is worth ten sociological treatises. The world of the Catholic working class in *Paddy Clarke Ha Ha Ha* is, in this respect as in others, totally different from the one brought back to life by Lawrence. While Paddy's father may help him with his spellings and his sums, there is no suggestion, as there is throughout *Sons and Lovers*, of a world where there are other preoccupations apart from the football stars who obsess adults and children alike on the Barrytown estate. You cannot, in the world recorded by Roddy Doyle, get out of the working class even if you wanted to do so, and it is quite possible that there is, in this respect, a more general historical significance in the contrast between *Sons and Lovers* and *Paddy Clarke Ha Ha Ha*. The world into which Lawrence was born in 1885 was one in which the existence of vast social inequalities in no way prevented the gifted members of the working class from making a more interesting if not necessarily more profitable way of life for themselves. As a qualified teacher, in Croydon in 1911, Lawrence earned £2 a week; his father, as a miner, could in a good week earn £5. But Lawrence could, and did, rise out of his class. Part of the success of *Paddy Clarke Ha Ha Ha* among the readers of the 1990s lies in the convincing if somewhat depressing portrait which it gives of a society in which this is no longer possible, and in which the working class no longer has members who strive to better themselves.

The contrast in style of narration between *Sons and Lovers* and *Paddy Clarke Ha Ha Ha* also raises the question of what is the best way of depicting the world of childhood. Should one, as Lawrence does, abandon the child's point of view completely, and offer the reader an account of experience in which everything is explained in an essentially rational, adult manner? Or should one limit oneself, as Doyle does, to what a child of ten could reasonably be expected to think, feel and know? When, at the age of eight, George Orwell read *David Copperfield*, he paid Dickens the highest possible compliment by feeling convinced that the novel must have been written by a child. While this could clearly never happen to the reader of *Sons and Lovers*, it is by no means certain that *Paddy Clarke Ha Ha Ha* would be all that irresistible a read to a ten-year-old child either. There are a number of paradoxes to the writing of books which children enjoy reading, and which Michel Tournier thinks are the most difficult to get right. One of these is that the books which are most successful with children – the Alice books, Winnie the Pooh, *The Wind in the Willows*, the stories of Roald Dahl – were written by authors who were rather odd human beings even by the standards set by other great creative writers.[5] Another is that the child should always be able to follow the story without feeling that the adult is consciously bringing himself down to the reader's level. The casual as well as the deliberate cruelties practised on one another by the children in *Paddy Clarke Ha Ha Ha* are totally believable to the adult reader with the literary competence to follow Roddy Doyle's narrative. So would they be to children, were not the technique of narration so obviously intended for so sophisticated an adult audience.

II

The novelty of Proust's treatment of childhood: the child unhappy on its own account, with no blame attached either to adults or to other children. Proust's rejection of Sainte-Beuve's concept of literature as unacknowledged autobiography.

Early in *Paddy Clarke Ha Ha Ha*, the narrator and central character seizes his young brother's nose in order to make him open his mouth so that another boy can put a capsule of lighter fuel in it. The burns inflicted are so bad that for two weeks afterwards, young Sinbad – whose real name is Francis – looks as if he has no lips.

It is not an incident one can imagine happening in Lawrence, in *Le Grand Meaulnes*, or in Proust's evocation of his childhood in

Combray, the opening section of the first volume of *Remembrance of Things Past*. So great is Proust's interest in communicating his own experience to the exclusion of anybody else's that he behaves like the Turk in Pope's *Epistle to Dr Arbuthnot* who 'brooks no brother near the throne'. You would never guess, from *Remembrance of Things Past*, that Proust even had a brother. The total absence of any other children from the world of Combray is nevertheless only part of the movement away from the nineteenth-century vision of childhood which makes Proust such an interesting turning point. Not only does his Narrator enjoy a degree of physical comfort and security equally unknown in the working-class world depicted by Lawrence and in the middle-class society of *David Copperfield*. In his treatment of the other well-known episode in *Swann's Way*, *le drame du coucher* (the drama of the goodnight kiss), it is no longer the cruelty or indifference of adults which make the child unhappy, as they did in Daudet's *Le Petit Chose*, in the opening chapters of *Jane Eyre*, or in the first volume of Jean Vallès's autobiographical trilogy, *L'Enfant*.[6] The roots of the Narrator's unhappiness in the first volume of *Remembrance of Things Past* lie in the child himself. If the adults contribute to it, it is for a reason which Dickens would have found totally incomprehensible: a failure to be cruel enough in the short time to be kind in the long run. But since, in Proust, it is within the child's own nature to make itself unhappy, there is very little that the Narrator's parents can do to save their son from himself.

Every evening, when it is time for him to go to bed, the Narrator in *Combray* is intensely unhappy at the idea that he will now be separated from his mother. He tries to put off this unhappiness for as long as possible by insisting on her keeping coming up to kiss him goodnight, and there is nothing harsh in her reluctance to do what he so desperately wants. It is simply that she has the very sensible ambition of trying to make him slightly less emotionally dependent on her. She might even have succeeded had the crucial incident in which her husband has a sudden access of sympathy for his son, and allows his wife to calm the boy's unhappiness by spending the whole night in his bedroom, not taken place. Yet even if his parents had not had this moment of weakness, the inner cause of the Narrator's unhappiness would not have been removed. This unhappiness would still remain, in a curious way, the child's own fault. He ought, Proust insists throughout the novel, to have developed a greater strength of will by himself, and on his own account. This, as he remarks on a number of occasions, would have enabled him to avoid the emotional disasters of his adult life, and especially the relationship with Albertine. If, to the slightly sceptical adult eye, *Remembrance of Things Past* is about a little boy who never grew up, the way the story is told suggests that this is very much the little boy's own fault.

Part of Proust's modernism lies in the possibility which he offers for his novel to be read outside the framework of semi-auto-biographical fiction in which it seems at first to be so firmly based. Although no point of view other than that of the Narrator is officially allowed to intrude, the reader cannot help asking what would have happened if the young Marcel (Proust finally accepts, threequarters of the way through the book, to give the hero his own name) had been born in Roddy Doyle's Barrytown or into one of the families in Zola's *Germinal*. Proust's frequently quoted statement in the critical essays collected under the title *Contre Sainte-Beuve* that a book is 'the product of a different self from the one we manifest in our habits, in our social life, in our vices'[7] is not, in this respect, a very useful introduction to *Remembrance of Things Past*. While the novel is, in many ways, very much the account of Proust's own life, the book translated as *By Way of Sainte-Beuve* is more a contribution to critical theory. It is, in particular, an anticipation of the structuralist distinction between the man who lives and the author who writes. As its title indicates, Proust's essay is part of an attack on the nineteenth-century conception of literary criticism of which Sainte-Beuve was one of the most famous representatives, a rebuttal of the idea that the work of art itself is only a starting point whose real interest lies in the opportunity it offers to find out about the real person who wrote it.

Proust may have had a number of very understandable personal reasons to be hostile to Sainte-Beuve's idea that the aim of the critic should always be to go behind the work to try to discover the man. He did not particularly like the person he was. He disapproved of his homosexuality, saw himself as lacking in willpower, and acknowledged that he had made his parents very unhappy by his selfishness and inability to grow up. This does not prevent his rejection of Sainte-Beuve's concept of works of fiction as autobiographies which refuse to recognise themselves as such from being perfectly explicable on literary and intellectual grounds alone. Even had he been, like his brother Robert, the model son who dutifully followed his father's example and became an eminent doctor, led a normal life which did not involve sleeping all day and writing all night, married, had children, and served with distinction in the 1914–18 war, he would still have been right to disagree with Sainte-Beuve and the whole tradition which he represented. The value of a work of literature, like the quality of a painting or of a piece of music, is quite irrelevant to the personality of the man or woman who wrote it. Anything which a work of art might tell us about its creator is purely anecdotal, and its aesthetic value has nothing to do with the sincerity with which this creator does, or does not, reveal his personal feelings in it. Strindberg's *The Father* would be just as good a play – or just as bad a one – if the author had been the happiest of husbands or the most successful of parents. What is nevertheless curious is the contrast between the virtual unanimity with which this idea is accepted in literary circles and the immense popularity of literary biographies with the book-buying public.

This is not only because literary biographies such as George Painter's two-volume biography of Proust, or Richard Ellmann's books on James Joyce and Oscar Wilde offer so very good a read. It is also because readers innocent of literary theory remain so firmly attached to the common-sense view that authors do write about themselves. *Remembrance of Things Past* is so obviously an autobiographical novel that it is impossible to see Proust's claim in *By Way of Sainte-Beuve* as applying to himself. The novel describes how the Narrator, like Proust himself, moved from the respectable middle-class society in which he was born, and whose members regarded princesses with great suspicion, to the point where he became an honoured guest in the very closed, aristocratic world of the Faubourg Saint-Germain. It tells how the Narrator, again like Proust himself, becomes the man who gives meaning to his life, and makes sense of his experience, by writing a book. The novel also makes it clear that this book is the one which the reader of *Remembrance of Things Past* is currently reading. Perhaps most important of all, *Remembrance of Things Past* is a novel which, although told in the first person, presents its Narrator in an essentially critical light. It is when the little boy who could not bear to be separated from his mother becomes the man who cannot give their freedom to anyone he loves that Proust gives Wordsworth's remark about the child being father to the man a meaning which is totally different from the one implied in 'My heart leaps up'. What the 1,250,000 words which make up

Remembrance of Things Past tell you in this respect is that your childhood can be a disaster from which you never escape. Every emotional relationship in which Marcel becomes involved ends in failure, with Albertine, the great love of his life, feeling so trapped by his jealous and possessive love that she runs away and is killed in a riding accident. Marcel's discovery that the whole purpose of his life is to write the book which will be called *Remembrance of Things Past* is made possible only by the abandonment of any kind of happiness through normal human relationships.

Although Proust is now regarded as one of the great truth-tellers in twentieth-century French literature, this aspect of his work does not seem to have been particularly important in his eyes. He refers to the parts of *Remembrance of Things Past* which do not describe the bliss of involuntary memory as the equivalent of the paste which holds together the individual jewels in an ornament, and seems to have been unaware of how gloomily realistic his grasp of child psychology was. It is left to the reader, perhaps against Proust's own wishes and certainly without any strong hints from the Narrator, to reflect that the feelings which the infant Marcel suffers from when he is put to bed at night are abnormal and irrational. The value of the psychological realism which characterises the presentation of childhood in *Remembrance of Things Past* nevertheless lies in its reminder of how abnormal and irrational children can be. They need no help from adults in making themselves unhappy.

III

A comparison between Proust and Sartre; Sartre's autobiography as an unexpected illustration of the advantages of normality; a comparison with Kingsley Amis and Thom Gunn; Sartre's theory of commitment in literature; Waugh on Wodehouse.

It is in this respect that Proust offers a movement away from nineteenth-century attitudes to childhood and towards those which we recognise as more characteristic of our own time. Childhood is still the period of life in which the emotions are most intense, the hills are greener and the grass is taller. But it is also the period in which our failure as human beings starts to become obvious as well as inevitable. Sartre's short and accessible essay *Baudelaire*

(1947), like the more difficult *Saint Genet, comédien et martyr* (1952; *Saint Genet, actor and martyr*) suggests that he thought that this was generally the case, an impression confirmed by the study of Flaubert in the impenetrable *L'Idiot de la famille*, a title best translated as *The Fool of the Family*, with the implied reference to the custom of putting such a person into the Church. The closing passage of Sartre's autobiographical fragment, *Les Mots* (1963; *Words*), again stresses the idea that you don't escape from your childhood:

> You can get rid of a neurosis, you can't be cured of yourself. Worn out, barely legible, humiliated, hidden, passed over in silence, all the features of the child remain alive in the fifty-year-old man. For most of the time, they hide away in corners, waiting for their opportunity: the moment I lower my guard, they come back to life, head held high, and enter, disguised, into the light of day.[8]

This is not, however, the only similarity between Sartre and Proust. There is another, equally important one, which is implicit in Proust's obsession with jealousy.

If we are jealous in love, as distinct from being envious of another person's skills, possessions or success, this is because we are afraid that the person we love prefers somebody else. We cannot make another person love us, and a constant theme in Racine's tragedies is the suffering of the love which is unrequited in this way. What we experience in jealousy is consequently, in this respect, what Sartre calls the absolute nature of another person's freedom. However strong the sexual bonds, however fervent the formal vows, the person we love is always free to stop loving us. This is the terrified intuition which runs through the whole of *Remembrance of Things Past*. It links one of the main themes of *Combray*, the infant Marcel's irrational fear that Mama might always prefer the adult company of Charles Swann and her other visitors over the need which her infant son has of her, to the analysis in *Swann's Way* of Swann's own neurotic obsession with the possible infidelities of his mistress, Odette de Crécy. It then leads, in the later volumes, to the panic terror which the technically adult Marcel experiences at the thought that his beloved Albertine might leave him.

For thinkers of the existentialist school, and especially for Sartre and Jaspers, it is not when we are earning our living as teachers or chartered accountants, spending our leisure hours playing Scrabble or enjoying a bottle of claret with our friends, that the human condition reveals itself most clearly to us and that we most clearly discover the kind of person we are. It is, on the contrary, when we are facing torture, despair or death, or when we are in the grip of an emotion as intense as the jealousy which afflicts almost all the male characters in *Remembrance of Things Past*, that we are most fully human. From an existentialist point of view, there is consequently nothing at all regrettable about the inability of Proust's Narrator – or of Proust himself – to lead a normal life. The characters in Proust may not see themselves as particularly free. Indeed, Proust's insistence on the idea that we are as much the creatures of our biological inheritance as of the traumatic experiences of our childhood is another of the features of his work which links him very firmly to the scientific determinism which inspired the naturalist movement of the nineteenth century. But seen from a Sartrian perspective, Proust's analysis of jealousy is yet another indication of the fact that we need a very powerful emotion to make us face up to reality. It is only through an emotion such as jealousy that we are made to recognise that other people are as free as we are. Without it, we should indulge in the characteristically human activity of denying both our own and other people's freedom, and lapsing into bad faith.

What is fascinating and instructive about *Words*, especially for a reader imbued with the English cult of common sense, is the way it calls into question the importance accorded in existentialist thought to the eccentric and the unusual. When Jean-Baptiste Sartre died, in 1907, his wife had no money and no possibility of earning her own living. She thus had no choice but to go back home, relying for her upkeep, as well as for that of her infant son, on a characteristically middle-class family which, as Sartre puts it, 'preferred widows to unmarried mothers, but only just'. Officially, Charles Schweitzer, cousin to the famous Protestant missionary Albert Schweitzer of Lambarene, adored his new grandson, and Sartre returned his love in what he presents in *Words* as a constant comedy of family affection. In fact, as the very legible subtext of *Words* makes clear, Charles was a selfish old man, who invented excuse after excuse to avoid sending Sartre to school. The result of this refusal to share his grandson with the outside world was that Sartre grew up in more or less total isolation from other children.

It was not that he did not see them. Every day, his mother took him to the Jardin du Luxembourg, near the Schweitzer apartment in Paris. Every day, if Sartre's account of his childhood is true, he wandered disconsolately from group to group, constantly excluded from the games in which the other children were so absorbed. He had, as he wrote in *Words*, in 1963, met his true peers, his genuine equals, and their indifference turned him into stone. He was not the wonderful little boy whose brilliance in learning to read by himself, and even in beginning to write his own stories, was such a source of amazement and admiration to his adoring grandfather. He was merely a weedy little lad who did not go to school.

In Kingsley Amis's *Stanley and the Women*, the central character has to listen to the woman psychiatrist treating his son for schizophrenia lecturing him about what she insists is a new approach to education, one in which there is 'much more emphasis on the social function, training the kids to relate to each other and preparing them to take their places in the adult world'.[9] When Stanley very sensibly replies that 'At my school, we got that thrown in, just by being there. We didn't attend classes in it' he evokes exactly the kind of experience which Sartre would have liked to have had, and the enthusiasm in *Words* for this robust, no-nonsense Anglo-Saxon approach to the bringing up of children comes as something of a surprise in an author so frequently and accurately presented as the high priest of atheistic existentialism. Sartre's echoing of Thom Gunn's admiration for

All the overdogs from Alexander,
To those that wouldn't play with Stephen Spender

goes completely against the traditional existentialist view that it is outcasts and misfits like Kafka and Kierkegaard whose insights into experience are most valuable. If, Sartre implies in *Words*, he had had a conventional, well-adjusted childhood, with siblings to teach him to share and friends from whom he could learn what it was to compete with equals, he would never have become a writer. And this, given the inability of the writer to change the world, would have been a very good thing. Proust would hardly have approved of a sentiment which the more philistine of Sartre's readers have been known to applaud.

Immediately after the Second World War, Sartre became the

best-known writer in France, and perhaps, for ten years or so, the best-known living writer in the world. This fame was based on novels and plays as well as on his literary criticism and works of formal philosophy, but it also stemmed from his controversial views about the nature of literature. This, he argued in an essay published in 1947 under the title *What is Literature?* was not to provide the reader with a few hours of harmless entertainment, and even less to construct works of pure beauty and significant form of the type which the Narrator in *Remembrance of Things Past* decides to write. It was to make the reader more conscious of the social and political issues of his time. The long-term aim of literature, once it had contributed to the political changes necessary to solve these problems, was then to become 'the self-consciousness of a society in permanent revolution'. Since, as Sartre argued, literature was possible only in a society in which authors were free to write what they wanted and readers to read it, it followed that the writer could serve no cause other than that of freedom. And this, for Sartre, as for most men and women of his generation, was inseparable from the fortunes of the left, and more specifically of socialism.

Writers often tell the truth about society, as well as about themselves, in a way which they had not consciously intended. From the standpoint of the 1990s, the automatic way in which Sartre identified social and political freedom with the future of socialism is an example of the same kind of illusion which led the economist Thomas Balogh, in 1946, to predict that in ten years time, the dynamism of the Soviet economy would give the USSR an 'absolute predominance economically over Western Europe'.[10] It is not that Sartre or Balogh were foolish. A large number of people thought as they did. But the fact that they were so imbued with the atmosphere of their time meant that they became the unconscious and therefore very sincere witnesses to the way that many of their contemporaries saw the world. What we, in the 1990s, can see as a mistake was fully understandable in the circumstances. The right, for them, meant Fascism. It meant Hitler, Franco, Mussolini, the Salazar who had ruled Portugal since 1922 and the Oswald Mosley who had tried, in the 1930s, to win power in England on a programme of systematic anti-semitism. For the French, it meant the autocratic regime established in 1940 in the wake of their defeat by the Germans, and placed under the authority of the 84-year-old Marshal Pétain.

It was not only European writers who followed Marx and Lenin in seeing Fascism as the logical outcome of capitalism. John Steinbeck's *The Grapes of Wrath*, published in 1939, followed Marx very closely in arguing that 'the farms grew larger and the owners fewer – as in Rome, though they did not know it',[11] and presented an America in which Fascism was becoming a distinct possibility. Dos Passos's *USA Trilogy* described an America whose inability to cope with the problems of mass industrialisation prevented it from establishing a viable democracy, and Ernest Hemingway's decision to go and fight on the side of the Republicans in Spain was not entirely the result of his constant desire for violent physical action. Orwell also went to Spain to join the fight against Franco, and completed his conversion to socialism on the streets and on the battle fields of Catalonia. André Malraux, though never a member of the Communist party, gave his 1939 novel about the Spanish civil war, *L'Espoir* (*Man's Hope*), an ending which presented the discipline imposed by the Communist party as the only means whereby Fascism could be defeated.

Sartre's problem, which he was not alone in being unable to face with complete honesty, was that the left, in continental Europe if not in the British Isles, was falling more and more under the influence of the tyrannical regime established under the name of socialism in the Soviet Union. It was Sartre's inability to come to terms with this problem, as well as with the fact that capitalism had survived and prospered much more efficiently in the post-war world than anyone had expected, which led him to conclude *Words* in the way he did: 'It's my habit and it's also my job', he wrote and continued:

> For a long time, I took my pen for a sword. Now I know how powerless we are. It doesn't matter. I write books and I shall continue to do so. They are needed. They are of some use. Culture saves nothing and offers salvation to nobody. It does not justify. But it is a product of man. He projects himself into it, recognises himself in it. This deforming mirror is alone in offering him an image of himself.[12]

It was a statement which underlined how completely he had lost the optimism about the nature and power of literature which he had so successfully communicated to his readers in 1947.

The closing paragraph of *Words* does not, for readers who found

Sartre's original desire to use literature to change the world a shade overambitious, offer altogether a bad definition of literature. It has analogies with Stendhal's view of the novel as a mirror that one carries along a highway, but is more perceptive as well as more modest. Sartre recognises that anything which the writer tries to tell his fellow human beings about themselves is going to come through the distorting prism of his own personality. If both Proust and Sartre tell us something about childhood, it is because they describe what it was like for them, and leave us free to draw our own conclusions. They do not, as novelists tended to do in the nineteenth century, present their truth as the only one available. Rather surprisingly, considering the importance which Sartre gave to literature at the beginning of his career, and the all-importance which Proust ended by attributing to it, *Words* is quite attractive in its modesty.

The ideal education which Rousseau describes himself as giving to his pupil Emile takes place in a one-to-one relationship between the child and his teacher. There are no other children to provide companionship or rivalry. The idea that children can grow up into healthy adults only if they are brought up in the company of their own kind may be extraordinarily banal. The only other writer in whom I have found it – apart from Sartre – is P. G. Wodehouse, a writer as different from the author of *La Nausée* as one could possibly imagine. 'The three essentials for an autobiography', Wodehouse wrote in 1957,

> are that its compiler should have had an eccentric father, a miserable childhood, and a hell of a time at his public school, and I enjoyed none of these advantages. My father was as normal as rice pudding, my childhood went like a breeze with everybody understanding me perfectly, while as for my schooldays at Dulwich they were just six years of unbroken bliss.[13]

It is perhaps an explanation for the tone struck in the closing peroration of Evelyn Waugh's *An Act of Homage and Reparation to P. G. Wodehouse*, broadcast on the BBC on 15 July 1961:

> For Mr Wodehouse there has been no Fall of Man, no aboriginal calamity. His characters have never tasted the forbidden fruit. They are still in Eden. The Gardens of Blandings Castle are that original garden from which we are all exiled. The chef

Anatole prepares the ambrosia for the immortals of high Olympus. Mr Wodehouse's world can never stale. He will continue to release future generations from a captivity that may be more irksome than our own. He has made a world for us to live in and delight in.[14]

There are clearly some childhoods which men can be very fortunate to have enjoyed. In the case of Wodehouse, it not only led to the idyllic world so appreciated by Evelyn Waugh. It also gave rise, in the last words of 'The Heart of a Goof', to what is perhaps the most appropriate ending to a comic short story in the English language:

He folded her in his arms, using the interlocking grip.

3

Visions of Childhood II: The Child Wicked on its own Account

I

Two novels describing the behaviour of children in Eastern Europe during the Second World War: Agota Kristof's The Notebook *and Jerzy Kosinski's* The Painted Bird; *some comparisons with Voltaire, Orwell and Hemingway.*

In the way she acts throughout the first half of Orwell's *Nineteen Eighty-Four*, Winston Smith's mistress Julia is a realist in the sense which the word has in a non-literary context: she knows what she wants and is brave, skilful and ruthless enough to get it. She has a totally disillusioned view of what the authorities in Oceania require from its citizens, and is determined not to let them have it. But she is also a realist in her total freedom from any illusions about the way children behave. When the guilt-ridden Winston tells her of how he snatched the chocolate from his little sister's hand and ran off to devour it alone in the street, she dismisses his feelings of guilt with the brisk comment: 'I expect you were a beastly little swine in those days. All children are swine'.[1] Not even Julia, however, would have thought children capable of the acts performed by the two nameless twins in the novel which Agota Kristof, a Hungarian writer living in Switzerland, published in French in 1986 under the title *Le Grand Cahier*. Its translation into English under the title of *The Notebook* in 1989 made less of an impression than the original version had in France, and certainly less than a rather similar novel, Jerzy Kosinski's *The Painted Bird*, did in the United States in 1965. *The Painted Bird* sold three million copies, and when later translated was voted by the French critics the best foreign book of the year.[2] Both novels move away from the vision of children as victims to which the 1947

68

The Diary of Anne Frank gives such perfect expression in literary terms. Both of them also cast considerable doubt on the intellectual acceptability of the idea with which Anne Frank's *Diary* ends: 'In spite of everything, I still think that people are good at heart'.

The Notebook and *The Painted Bird* both describe the experiences of children in Eastern Europe during the great disaster of the 1939–45 war, and have a number of qualities not found in previous accounts of childhood. This is not because the horrors inflicted on the world by the twentieth-century experience of totalitarianism were something entirely new. Human history has always been characterised by the suffering of the innocent. The difference lies in the readiness of twentieth-century novelists to show how exposure to horrors of this kind can make children capable of behaving with exactly the same wickedness as adults. This is not a characteristic of pre-twentieth-century fiction, where the expectations of the reader were that children might suffer abominably from this wickedness but would not behave in the same way themselves. Both *The Notebook* and *The Painted Bird* also underline how well-founded Maurice Spandrell's question was, in Aldous Huxley's *Point Counter Point*, in 1928, when he asked Philip Quarles whether he had ever thought that this world might be another planet's hell.[3]

While Kosinski's book is a first-person narrative, Agota Kristof uses a more original technique to show what it could be like for children in the quest for survival in countries such as Poland, Hungary, Czechoslovakia or Romania during the Second World War. Her narrators are twin boys, who agree that each shall check the accuracy of the entries which the other makes in their joint diary. Within the framework of the novel, this guarantees the authenticity of the narrative which describes how the twins, entrusted by their mother to their illiterate grandmother at the beginning of the war, are led to lie, cheat, steal and even murder in order to stay alive. They are highly intelligent children who teach each other the language of the occupying power, before moving on to that of the army which 'liberates' their country. They read the Bible, and learn several passages of it by heart. But when the village priest asks them if they obey the Ten Commandments, they reply that it would be pointless to behave like that in a world where everybody kills. When the priest replies that this is because it is wartime, they ignore what he says and simply ask for more books, 'History books, geography books. Books that tell us true things, not invented things'. They are, in this respect, total realists, who sum up their attitude to language when they describe the 'very simple rules' which must be satisfied if an entry is to be judged good enough to be written down in the note- book: 'The composition must be true. We must describe what is, what we see, what we hear, what we do.' Words that describe feelings, they add, 'are very vague', and they continue:

> it is better to avoid using them and to stick to the description of objects, human beings and oneself; that is to say, to the faithful description of facts.[4]

It is a credo which occurs in a number of twentieth-century writers, among them the French novelist and theoretician Alain Robbe-Grillet, who expressed his ideas in a number of articles defining the ambition of what was known in the France of the 1950s as 'le nouveau roman' (the new novel). It also recalls Hemingway's statement in Chapter XVI of *A Farewell to Arms* to the effect that

> abstract words such as glory, honour, courage, or hallow were obscene beside the concrete names of villages, the numbers of roads, the names of rivers, the numbers of regiments and the dates

and reflects the same suspicion of abstract language. In Camus's *The Plague*, all men's misfortunes are said to stem from the use of unclear language, and George Orwell pointed out in his essay 'Politics and the English Language', in 1945, how much more honest it was to write 'I believe in killing off your opponents if you can get good results by doing so' than to employ sentences such as

> While freely conceding that the Soviet regime exhibits certain features which the humanitarian may be inclined to deplore, we must, I think, agree that a certain curtailment of the right to political opposition is an unavoidable concomitant of tran- sitional periods, and that the rigours which the Russian people have been called on to undergo have been amply justified in the sphere of concrete achievement.[5]

Exact descriptions of the horrors of war have also been a fairly familiar feature of literature. They abound in Voltaire's *Candide*, which also contains a phrase which anticipates one of the central themes in *The Notebook*. For when Candide's beloved Cunégonde asks him, in Chapter IX, how it could possibly have come about that he, the mildest of men, should in the space of two minutes have run his sword through both a Jew and a prelate of the Catholic church, he replies:

Ma belle demoiselle, quand on est amoureux, jaloux, et fouetté par l'Inquisition, on ne se connaît plus (My dear young lady. When you are in love, jealous, and have just been flogged by the Inquisition, you no longer know yourself).

What is new is the fact that the human capacity for violence is clearly placed in the personality of children, not of adults, and there is also another difference between Agota Kristof's twins and Voltaire's hero: they are totally without illusions from the very beginning. Unlike Cunégonde, they express no surprise at the need which people who wish to survive have of the qualities of force and fraud which Hobbes saw as indispensable to mankind in a state of nature. But although the twins are autodidacts in a world in which life is nasty, brutish and short, they occasionally show a rudimentary if brutal sense of morality. When the priest's housekeeper mockingly holds out a piece of bread to a crowd of starving refugees, only to push it triumphantly into her own mouth, they take one of the live cartridges that they have stolen from the occupying army and hide it in the firewood which they know she is going to use in the stove. It explodes and blinds her.

Where the twins lack any traditional sense of right or wrong is where their own well-being is at stake. At the end of the war, their father comes back. He has been a journalist, and is thus highly suspect to the liberators now occupying the country. He has been tortured by them, and is understandably anxious to escape. But the liberators have sealed off the frontier with two barbed wire fences separated by a minefield which is seven yards wide and where, as the twins explain, 'the mines are arranged in zigzags, in W's – if you walk in a straight line, you run the risk of walking on only one mine.' Their father decides to risk it, and they give him the wooden planks he will need to get over the barbed wire. When he sets off one of the mines and is killed, the twins are separated for the first time in their life. One of them takes advantage of the temporary gap made in the minefield to escape.

There are no names in *The Notebook*, either of people or of countries. But although there is no doubt that the action takes place
in one of the countries in central or Eastern Europe which were
occupied during the war by the Germans and after the war by
the Russians, there is no suggestion that any person, any country
or any ideology is to blame. This, Agota Kristof is saying, is how
children behave when the adult world around them has gone
mad. Human nature is infinitely malleable, and the presupposition is that in a society as relatively stable and protective of its
young as the United States or the United Kingdom, the twins
would have grown up with the normal peculiarities of the aver-
agely awful child. But children are no more immune than adults
to the evil evoked in human beings by the way they are treated
by their fellows, and the same is true of the unnamed six-year-
old boy in Jerzy Kosinski's *The Painted Bird*, who is also placed
in 1939 by his parents in what they hope will the safe environment of a village. But the boy is dark and olive-skinned, and
thus incurs all the hostility which the blond and blue-eyed peasants
feel for anyone looking like a gypsy or a Jew. The impact on him
of the events which he witnesses or in which he is involved is
understandably disastrous. When his parents find him again, at
the end of the war, he has become remarkably similar to one of
the twins in *The Notebook*, a little savage who breaks the arm of
his new baby brother in a fight over a toy. He has already, in
one of the many horrifying scenes which recur insistently throughout the novel, murdered a carpenter who had mistreated him by
tricking him into falling into a hole swarming with rats. He then
watches while the carpenter is eaten alive.

The realism in the presentation of children which characterises
both novels is not an entirely new phenomenon. In *Germinal*, Zola
reports as a fact the preference which the miners in Northern
France have for girls who have not yet reached puberty. They
cannot get pregnant. But although Zola also describes how a group
of children ambush and kill one of the soldiers sent to keep order during the miners' strike, realism of this kind was the exception rather than the rule in the nineteenth century, and Zola was
regarded, in France as well as in England, as a very immoral
writer. There was the same reaction in the France of 1950 to Hervé
Bazin's novel *Vipère au Poing*, in which he described how three
brothers were so cruelly treated by their mother that they tried
to drown her. Instead of accepting that she had really rather asked

for it, the eminently respectable readers from the French middle class, with whom I happened to discuss the book on a hitch-hiking holiday in the *massif central* in the summer after it had just been published, could speak of nothing but how abominable and unnatural these children were. The change which came over the expectations of readers as the twentieth century moved towards its close can be seen in the fact that when Agota Kristof described the behaviour of the twins in *The Notebook*, critics and readers alike saw it as more or less par for the course.

Whether *The Painted Bird* and *The Notebook* are good literature, as distinct from highly convincing narratives about what life was like for children as well as for adults when Slav and Teuton clashed in the conflict between Communism and Fascism in the most murderous of all wars, is an open question. The two novels certainly have one advantage which is absent from most forms of committed literature, as well as from some kinds of black or feminist writing. There is no attempt to make the male, middle-class, Caucasian reader feel that it is all his fault. But if either novel is compared to books which have stood the test of time, or to works of the present century about whose quality there is a certain unanimity, there are a number of reasons for saying that they do not qualify as literature of the first order. The comparison with *Candide* or *King Lear* is justified only to the extent that Agota Kristof and Jerzy Kosinski are also describing what happens when the normal order of society breaks down. When children are depicted as behaving as wickedly as their elders, it is unreasonable to describe either the complexity of Shakespeare or the irony of Voltaire. When the facts are as stated, there is no room for a Cordelia or a Kent, and even the black humour of Voltaire is out of place. But there are also qualities in two other books which describe how children behave when the constraints of adult society are removed, Richard Hughes's *A High Wind in Jamaica* and William Golding's *Lord of the Flies*, which offer a reasonable yardstick by which *The Notebook* and *The Painted Bird* can be judged as examples of imaginative literature.

II

Richard Hughes's A High Wind in Jamaica *and William Golding's* Lord of the Flies *as convincingly realistic accounts of how children behave without adults; a comparison with Ballantyne's* The Coral Island; *doubts about the validity of Golding's story as a narrative illustrating the truth of Christianity.*

Julia's remark in *Nineteen Eighty-Four* that all children are 'beastly little swine' is one with which William Golding would have agreed only reluctantly, and which Richard Hughes would have thought rather missed the point. The dominant theme in *A High Wind in Jamaica* is that children are entirely different from adults. They live in a world which is so alien from the moral standards developed by the adult world that the writer can only describe their conduct. He can never judge it. Hughes's own comment that 'one can no more think like a baby than one can think like a bee' recurs in a less poetic form when the lawyer, Matthias, says that he would 'rather extract information from the Devil himself than from a child'.[6] The story in *A High Wind in Jamaica*, first published in 1929, and known in the United States as *The Innocent Voyage*, describes how Emily Bas-Thornton, her brothers Edward and John and her sisters Rachel and Laura are captured by pirates while on their way from Jamaica, where their house has been destroyed by a hurricane, to England, where they are being sent to school. They entirely captivate the pirates, who are a fairly harmless gang of ruffians, and barely notice when the eleven-year-old John is so fascinated by a Nativity Play with real animals in it that he falls 40 feet from the balcony of the theatre in Santa Lucia, breaks his neck, and is killed.

The disaster lying in wait for Captain Jonsen and his crew is foreshadowed when they capture a Dutch ship and tie up its captain, leaving him in the same room as Emily, who is recovering from a wound in her leg. When Captain Vandervoort, in the hope of cutting himself free, tries to get at the very sharp knife which 'some idiot' has dropped in the corner of the cabin floor, Emily thinks he is going to attack her, panics and stabs him so repeatedly that he dies 'not so much of any mortal wound as the number of superficial gashes he has received'. When Captain Jonsen eventually succeeds in what has been his ambition from the start, and hands the children back to the normal adult world, they tell such tales that he and his crew are arrested for piracy and brought to London to stand trial. In spite of the careful coaching she has received from Matthias, Emily totally breaks down in court when being interrogated by the lawyer entrusted with the pirates' defence.

Her hysterical outburst describing how the Dutch captain was 'lying in all his blood' is interpreted as proof that Captain Jonsen and his accomplices deliberately killed him. The Captain, his first mate Otto and the Negro cook are hung for murder. The last words of the novel describe Emily, now at school, making friends with the older pupils. 'Looking at that gentle, happy throng of clean, innocent faces and soft, graceful limbs' writes the narrator, 'listening to the ceaseless, artless babble of chatter rising, perhaps God could have picked out from among them which was Emily; but I am sure that I could not.'

It is an ending which invites the reader to give Rousseau's claim in *Emile* that we should 'leave children to themselves; their wisdom is not our own' a different meaning from the one originally intended. If there is wisdom in an eleven-year-old child such as Emily, it is of so different a kind that it cannot meaningfully be called by the same word. Children, Hughes suggests, are wholly other. They are not miniature adults, but members of a different species. They simply do not have the ideas and emotions which adults project on to them, and are capable only of an unthinking conformity to an adult world of which they have no real understanding.

This is not quite the case in the other novel written by an Englishman which sets out to describe how children behave when the constraints of the adult world are removed, Willam Golding's *Lord of the Flies*. Two at least of the boys who find themselves alone on an island in the Pacific when their plane crashes and no adult survives, Ralph and Piggy, try to do what they know is right. Ralph assumes the responsibilities and risks of leadership, and comes close to paying for them with his life. Only the *deus ex machina* of the sudden return of the adult world in the form of the naval officer and his 'trim cruiser' saves him from being murdered by the other boys. Piggy is killed, partly the victim of his inability to see without glasses, but more directly through the viciousness of Roger, who deliberately releases the boulder which knocks him off the ledge and into the sea. But until he is murdered, Piggy remains sane and sensible throughout, with the irony that Ralph begins to recognise his qualities as a 'true, wise friend' only after he has been killed. He is a rationalist, who can see that the real world of buses, streets and television is incompatible with the existence of the ghosts and monsters which haunt the imagination of the other boys.

Yet this world, as Golding reminds us in the scene in the early

part of the novel in which Roger, throwing stones in the direction of Henry, but never aiming so close as to infringe the 'protection of parents and school and policemen and the law', is in
ruins. The boys are on the island because the plane in which
they were travelling, and which has either crashed accidentally
or been shot down deliberately, was taking them away from the
atomic war which has broken out in Europe. And the reader is
clearly invited to establish a parallel between the failure of Ralph's
and Piggy's attempt to create order and impose rules on the island,
and the inability of the adults in the outside world to live in
peace and harmony with one another. As Golding observed in a
comment on the novel when it was published in 1954, the naval
officer who rescues the boys,

> having interrupted a manhunt, prepares to take the children
> off the island in a cruiser which will presently be hunting its
> enemy in the same implacable way. And who will rescue the
> adult and his cruiser?[7]

In Neville Shute's 1957 novel, *On The Beach*, the outbreak of
unlimited nuclear war in the Northern Hemisphere has done more
than destroy all biological life above the equator. It has also created a cloud of poisonous, radioactive dust which the winds are
carrying down into the Southern Hemisphere, and which will soon
kill everybody there as well. The action of *On The Beach* is set in
Australia, possibly the destination of the aircraft carrying the boys
to supposed safety in *Lord of the Flies*, and a fact which evoked
an ungenerous comment from Ava Gardner, when the novel was
being filmed: that if you had to make a movie about the end of
the world, Melbourne was obviously the place. *Lord of the Flies*
nevertheless belongs to a different category from the 'post-nu-
clear disaster' novels such as *On The Beach*, Isaac Asimov's *A
Canticle for Leibowitz* or Aldous Huxley's *Ape and Essence*. Human
beings, Golding is saying, have always been infected by the evil
which has led to the outbreak of nuclear war, and the existence
of atomic weapons has produced a quantitative, not a qualitative
change. In so far as there is a solution to their problems, it does
not lie in so specific a measure as the banning of a particular
form of warfare. Any solution which might exist lies in the realm
of the spirit, not in that of politics.

At two points in the text, the reader of *Lord of the Flies* is invited to make a comparison with R. M. Ballantyne's 1885 novel *The Coral Island*. This happens first of all in Chapter II, when *The Coral Island* is mentioned alongside *Swallows and Amazons* and *Treasure Island* as a place where boys can 'have a good time', and again at the end when the naval officer who rescues Ralph expresses surprise that the boys, who after all are English, have not behaved more like Ballantyne's heroes. The situation in *Lord of the Flies* is nevertheless very different from that of *The Coral Island* from a purely practical point of view, and this difference casts some doubt on the Christian ideology which Golding is trying to put forward as the best explanation of why things go wrong. Apart from the clothes they stand up in, the only physical object which the boys in Golding's novel inherit from the outside world is a pair of glasses belonging to Piggy. When Ralph is defeated, and all the boys except Piggy choose 'the brilliant world of hunting, tactics, fierce exhilaration and skill' represented by Jack Merridew and his hunters over the 'world of baffled common sense' in which Ralph tries to build shelters and keep the fire going so that they can be rescued, it is partly because he has nothing physical with which to back up the rules. These, he ruefully insists, have to be observed because they are 'the only thing we have'. He is, in this respect, like Colonel Nicholson in Pierre Boule's *The Bridge on the River Kwai*. But while Nicholson's tragedy stems from the fact that he is successful in his aim, but does not understand quite what he is doing, Ralph has a total intellectual grasp of the situation, but lacks the physical force as well as the moral authority to put it into effect.

In *The Coral Island*, the situation is very different. Only three boys are shipwrecked, as opposed to the twenty or so in *Lord of the Flies* – significantly enough, Ralph and Piggy never succeed in counting them, and one disappears without trace on the first evening – and one of Ballantyne's heroes, Jack Martin, is a 'tall, strapping, broad-shouldered youth of eighteen'. He is therefore not really, in modern terms, a boy at all, but a young adult, someone who would have been liable at the time of publication of *Lord of the Flies* to military service, and who would nowadays be entitled to vote. Peterkin, like Piggy, is not a good swimmer. But while Piggy is a solemn little boy whose long illnesses have taught him how to think, Peterkin is a healthy teenager, 'little, quick, and decidedly mischievous'. Ralph, the narrator in *The Coral Island*, is fifteen, as opposed to the Ralph of *Lord of the Flies*, who is only 'twelve years and a few months'. The island in Ballantyne's novel has breadfruit as well as the ordinary fruit which gives the littluns such constant diarrhoea in *Lord of the Flies*, and the three heroes in *The Coral Island* are very much better off for equipment.

They do not, it is true, have the full box of carpenter's tools which Robinson Crusoe has such difficulty in learning to use, but without which he would never have been able to reconstruct civilisation on his island. But they do have an axe, a telescope, some whipcord, a small sailmaker's needle, and the iron end of an oar. Jack cleverly fashions this into a much stronger knife to supplement the 'small penknife with a single blade broken off at the middle' which Peterkin owns, and which is the kind of thing which might have survived in *Lord of the Flies* if Golding had not weighted the scales quite so heavily against his shipwrecked school-boys. For Golding is not making the essentially literary compari-son which Sartre is offering to his reader in *Words*, Joyce in *Ulysses*, Tom Stoppard in *Rosencrantz and Guildenstern are Dead*, or Michel Tournier in his rewriting of the Robinson Crusoe story in *Vendredi ou les limbes du Pacifique* (1971; *Friday*). What each of these authors is doing is to invite the reader to look critically at an earlier lit-erary work or series of works and see how its presentation of the world is different from our experience of it in the twentieth cen-tury. They, like Golding, are exploiting myths, but are doing so without trying to suggest that there was something basically wrong with the beliefs that inspired the authors of romantic autobiogra-phies, pagan epics, revenge tragedies or accounts of how Euro-peans survived on desert islands. With the possible exception of Tournier, their aim was an aesthetic, not an ideological one. They are suggesting a different version of realism, not a different vision of human nature. Golding, in contrast, is out for bigger game, with the muscular Christianity which informs Ballantyne's novel only the first of his targets.

The ideal reading of *Lord of the Flies* would, in this respect, be one which saw it as realistic in the much more ambitious sense of a work which described an essential and inescapable truth about human nature, one which might almost be described as meta-physical. Like Pascal, who claimed that Christianity was true because it provided an accurate account of man's dual nature, as a being fallen from perfection into sin, Golding is writing from an openly religious standpoint. What he is offering his reader is religious fiction in the tradition of Dostoievski, and the similarity between the two authors is heightened by the fact that Simon, the boy whose insights into spiritual reality are presented as offering a correct description of the situation, resembles Prince Myshkin, in Dostoievski's *The Idiot*, by being subject to attacks of epilepsy. When the other boys grow frightened of the beast which they think lives on the island and is about to prey on them, Simon tries to explain to them that the beast is 'perhaps only us'. However, he becomes so inarticulate in trying to present what Golding describes as 'mankind's essential illness' as an explanation for what is going wrong that nobody understands what he is saying. Later in the novel, when Simon discovers that what the boys thought was the beast is a dead airman trapped in the trees by his parachute, and tries to interrupt one of the ceremonies which mark the boys' reversion to barbarism in order to tell them this truth, he is killed for his pains. People are reluctant, Golding suggests, to acknowledge the reality of what a review of Camus's *The Plague* once called 'the plague within us'. They prefer either the excitement of savagery or the neo-Pelagian confidence in man's ability to cope with problems by human virtues alone which breathes through Ballantyne's novel.

It is Simon who is the subject of the statement that however he tried to think of the beast, 'there rose before his inward sight the picture of a human at once heroic and sick' and the phrase again has strong overtones of Pascal's analysis of what is wrong with us. We still, for him, have traces of the glory which was part of our nature before the Fall, and our sorrows are those of 'a king dethroned'. Potentially, we are still capable of infinite good. God made us, and we retain something of His essential goodness. But because of man's first disobedience and our consequent fall from grace, we are the victims of original sin, a notion that Golding carries further than Pascal did by evoking the notion of the Devil. What Simon takes to be the beast is the head of a wild pig that the other boys have killed and decapitated. Fixed as it is in the ground on the end of a stick sharpened at both ends, it attracts the flies which buzz endlessly about it, and speaks to Simon in the tones of Beelzebub, the Devil, the Lord of the Flies. 'I'm part of you',[8] it tells him, 'I'm the reason why it's no go.' It is the Devil, as Huxley argued in more hysterical mode in his 1953 fantasy *Ape and Essence*, who really orders the affairs of this world. If you want proof of this, just look at the way people behave.

The atmosphere of *Lord of the Flies* is only partly an endorsement of W. H. Auden's claim that 'at school, I lived in a Fascist state'. Gresham's School, Holt, where Auden was educated, may have been rough, but at least there was a semblance of order. What characterises *Lord of the Flies* is the complete breakdown of all order, and when the book was first published, in 1954, a friend of mine teaching in a school of the type attended by Jack Merridew and the other members of the choir, told me that he thought Golding had given a somewhat optimistic account of how boys behave when left to their own devices. Golding had spent some years as a schoolmaster, and the only half-ironic comment made by my schoolteacher friend might well have occurred to another teacher turned novelist, Roddy Doyle, whose boys do not even need the isolation from the adult world to behave like savages.

In the 1920s, Bertrand Russell and his second wife set up a school that was totally free of the traditional rules which they saw at the time as unduly restrictive of children's behaviour. But as Russell himself later acknowledged, there were two reasons why the school did not last long. The first was that the progress-ively-minded parents who sent their children there were very bad at paying the fees. The second was the more important one that the absence of rules meant the tyranny of the strong over the weak. This is exactly what happens in *Lord of the Flies*, as it also does in a novel describing an appallingly run Protestant board-ing school, the Pension Vedel, in André Gide's 1926 novel, *Les Faux-Monnayeurs* (*The Coiners*). There, a group of boys led partly by an anarchist, Strouvilhou, but inspired more by one of their own number, the eleven-year-old Ghéridanisol, bring about the death of another boy, Boris, in what he thinks is a fake attempt at suicide, but where they know that the gun is loaded. By the time that Gide wrote this novel, he had fully emerged from the Christianity in which he had originally been brought up, and there is no suggestion that the boys are motivated by anything other than straightforward but ultimately inexplicable evil.[9] Nor is there any need to believe in original sin, in what Golding calls 'man-kind's essential illness' to find the events in *Lord of the Flies* to-tally believable. Children, like adults, can behave well when circumstances are propitious – as they are in *The Coral Island* – and abominably when they are not. The chance survival of just one adult on the island where the action of *Lord of the Flies* takes place, coupled perhaps with one or two of the tools which make life so much easier in Ballantyne's novel, could have made all the difference between the creation of some kind of order and the murderous anarchy which did in fact ensue.

III

W. H. Auden and Cardinal Newman; I'm the King of the Castle and the territorial imperative; Jack London and animals.

Golding's careful selection of the right kind of situation to prove an ideological point does not make him unusual among modern writers. Indeed, if one accepts Roland Barthes's criticism of the whole concept of realism, it makes him into a typical example of the traditional novelist. Such a person, for Barthes and his followers, is someone who only claims to be describing things as they are. In fact, he is using incidents which he has deliberately invented in order to persuade his readers of the validity of a particular point of view. All literature, in Barthes's analysis of realism, is basically rhetoric, and in its permanent endeavour to persuade, *Lord of the Flies* fits this definition very well.

For the reader who accepts the Christian concept of original sin, Auden's claim, in *September 1, 1939*, about the

> Error bred in the bone
> of each woman and each man

which

> Craves what it cannot have,
> Not universal love
> but to be loved alone

offers a highly appropriate comment on the novel. There is, indeed, something wrong about human beings which is not there in the animal kingdom, and which can be explained by the Christian hypothesis. Animals kill only to eat. They do not murder or torture members of their own species, and do not commit suicide. But the Christian hypothesis about original sin, about what Cardinal Newman called the 'terrible aboriginal calamity' which lies at the root of the human adventure, and which Evelyn Waugh saw as being so conspicuously absent from the world of Wodehouse, is not the only means of explaining why human beings should be capable of such wickedness.

A book which suggests an alternative explanation as to why human beings, and more specifically children, behave so badly towards one another is Susan Hill's short novel, published in 1970, *I'm the King of the Castle*. It describes the behaviour of two boys, Edward Hooper and Charles Kingshaw, who are about the same age as Ralph, Piggy and Jack Merridew in *Lord of the Flies*, and who resemble Golding's characters in being English, middle-class, and placed in a situation where the adult world does nothing to help them solve their problems. Because Edmund's widowed father, Joseph, needs a housekeeper, he takes in the widowed mother of Charles, Helen Kingshaw. But although he is convinced that Charles will make a suitable playmate for Edmund, Edmund has other ideas. He is quite happy by himself, and cannot see why he should make room for Charles and treat him as a friend. He is also, as the story shows, a coward, a bully and a liar, and one whose lies are believed by the grownups. Helen Kingshaw is so anxious to escape from her genteel poverty by making Joseph Hooper marry her that she ignores everything her son tells her about the way Edmund treats him. When she falls in with the plan to take Charles away from the school where he is relatively happy and send him to the same school as Edmund, Charles drowns himself. To his mind, what he sees as an endless period of bullying organised by Edmund seems like an eternity of suffering.

I'm the King of the Castle is as much an indictment of parental irresponsibility as it is of what Agata Kristof and William Golding present as the apparently boundless capacity of children for evil. A father less haunted than Joseph Hooper by the sexual failure of his first marriage, what Susan Hill calls the 'elaborate courtesy of the double bed, the cold gap between his permitted behaviour and his desires'[10] would have noticed how badly his son was behaving and put a stop to it. The title of Susan Hill's novel, coupled with the words 'and you're a dirty rascal', which inevitably come into the mind of the native speaker of English, also evokes a more rational explanation of the inhumanity which man has traditionally shown to man, and which children in twentieth-century literature show to members of the adult world as well as to one another. Robert Ardrey's book *The Territorial Imperative* suggests that a good deal of the aggressiveness which animals show towards one another stems from the need which they feel to defend their living space, and one of the reasons why Edmund Hooper behaves so badly is that he sees Charles Kingshaw as an intruder on the space which was his before Charles's arrival.

If *A High Wind in Jamaica*, *Lord of the Flies* and *I'm the King of the Castle* nevertheless offer a more satisfying read than either *The Notebook* or *The Painted Bird*, this may stem from the fact that William Golding and Susan Hill do offer some kind of explanation for the way the children in their novels behave. One may not accept either original sin or the territorial imperative as a satisfactory intellectual framework for analysing human behaviour, but they are there and can be rationally defended. One of the limits of the kind of realism practised by Agota Kristof or Jerzy Kosinski lies in the decision of both authors to refrain from explanation. It is not that their narratives are incredible. It is the feeling which the reader has that some kind of explanation ought to be forthcoming, and that evil cannot be presented as quite such a brute fact as it is in *The Painted Bird* or *The Notebook*. There is also, in *A High Wind in Jamaica*, an irony of tone which places the book in the characteristically English tradition of writers who refuse to exaggerate.

There are limits to what one can say about a group which Western Europeans did not see as having an autonomous existence until towards the middle of the eighteenth century. As the way in which children are depicted in painting suggests, and as is confirmed by a study of children's clothes, they tended to be seen as miniature adults, interesting less for their own sake than for what they might become.[11] One of the curious features of the twentieth century has been the way in which authors have, in a sense, gone back to a pre-Rousseauist view of childhood which sees children as capable of all the unpleasantness of adults, though on a smaller scale. But on an aesthetic plane, W. C. Fields was right. Children may start off by stealing the show, which is why any experienced actor will refuse to share the stage with them. But like dogs, the interest which they offer is eminently exhaustible. Virginia Woolf's 1933 novella *Flush*, which describes the life of Elizabeth Barrett Browning's pet cocker spaniel, has a certain period charm. But for the way animals really behave, one has to turn back to the pre-Rousseauistic world of Jack London's *The Call of the Wild*, or to the ending of his 1908 short story, 'To Build a Fire'. For what happens, when the immense efforts which the man has made to light the fire under the tree have the effect

of warming the snow, is that it melts, falls, and puts out the
fire.

The dog accompanying the man then behaves with a totally
realistic grasp of the situation. As it begins to realise what has
happened, writes London, it

> whined loudly. And still later it crept close to the man and
> caught the scent of death. This made the animal bristle and
> back away. A little later it delayed, howling under the stars
> that leaped and danced and shone brightly in the cold sky.
> Then it turned and trotted up the trail, in the direction of the
> camp it knew, where there were other food-producers and fire-
> providers.

4

Varieties of Realism I: Plays, Intertextuality and Myth

I

The notion of intertextuality and Synge's The Playboy of the Western World; *a mention of Beckett's* Waiting for Godot; *some unflattering reflections on the Southern Irish.*

Not all forms of realism are as depressing as the accounts which certain twentieth-century writers have given of childhood. Some can be comic, and even liberating, in spite of the fact that the immediate target audience may have seen the attempt at liberation as impertinent and even blasphemous. The first night of J. M. Synge's *The Playboy of the Western World*, on 26 January 1907, is a case in point, in that it turned into a riot, and it was not only Irish playgoers who were offended. When the play went on tour in America in 1911, the disturbances in Philadelphia were so great that the entire cast ended up in prison. Resistance to the play, especially in Ireland, remained so intense that one of the greatest interpreters of the role of Christy Mahon, Cyril Cusack, said that *The Playboy of the Western World* did not attain its real dimensions on the stage until 1954, when it was performed at the First International Festival of the Theatre in Paris. This is appropriate in several ways, since it was also in Paris that another play by an exiled Irishman, Samuel Beckett's *En Attendant Godot* (*Waiting for Godot*) had received its first performance only a year before. There are, however, two other features of Synge's play which link it with the internationalisation of literature which is so marked a feature of the twentieth century, and which so often had France, if not Paris, as its headquarters.

The first of these is anecdotal. In 1937, at the appropriate age of 24, Albert Camus took the part of Christy Mahon in his own production at the Théâtre de l'Atelier, a theatrical group which he had founded in Algiers in 1935. No accounts survive of how the play was received at what was, at the time, almost as much a cultural desert as the 'village on the wild coast of Mayo' where the events depicted in *The Playboy of the Western World* take place. Since Camus had still not entirely shaken off the tuberculosis which had almost killed him in 1930, he had the physique for the part, that of the 'slight young man' whose arrival causes such drama. He also had the inner fire which bursts out in Christy Mahon when the womenfolk of the village greet him as an irresistible hero, and it is a shade disappointing that the critics who have approached Camus's work from a Freudian standpoint have not made more of his decision to play the part. For Christy Mahon is a young man who thinks that he has murdered his father in a quarrel sparked off by the old man's insistence that his son marry a widow old enough to be his mother.

The second feature of *The Playboy of the Western World* which has a link with French literature offers a key to the understanding of a notion popularised in the 1970s by Julia Kristeva, and which she and other critics called intertextuality. This is a theory of literature which insists that writers never talk directly about the experience which human beings have of the world. All literature, for Julia Kristeva and the critics who grouped themselves in the 1960s and 1970s around a review called *Tel Quel*, consists of texts, and all texts are reflections or reproductions of different versions of other, pre-existing texts. There is no such thing as the 'raw material' which the realists in the nineteenth and early twentieth century thought they were presenting to their audience. In the theory of literature which dominated French intellectual life in the 1970s, we have no experience of any objective and independent reality. What we call knowledge is nothing but the account which we absorb, through language, of the discourses with which society presents us.

Two of the best illustrations of what intertextuality means in practice can be found in James Joyce's *Ulysses* and Tom Stoppard's 1967 play, *Rosencrantz and Guildenstern are Dead*. By presenting the reader with an alternative version of a text powerful enough to have imposed its own version of reality on to generations of readers, Joyce's novel and Stoppard's play call into question the validity of accounts of experience couched in the established genres of the heroic epic and of classical tragedy. At the same time, both the novel and the play cast doubt on the value systems on which the original works are constructed. Although Joyce clearly did not have the Kristevan concept of intertextuality in mind when he wrote *Ulysses*, and Stoppard's starting point was in his practical experience of the theatre, their rewriting of the myths fulfils the basic ambition of intertextuality by ensuring that neither Homer's *Odyssey* nor Shakespeare's *Hamlet* can ever be read in quite the same way again. Writing becomes, in this context, primarily a reflection on literature itself, and an invitation to the reader to think more critically of the account which novels, plays and poems have given of experience in the past.

The discourses through which members of a society absorb its picture of reality do not always need to be written down. They can perfectly well exist in myths, in oral traditions, in religious beliefs, in the way people talk, in their dreams, ambitions and fantasies. They nevertheless remain, even when imposed by what Marshall McCluhan calls the 'hot' medium of radio or television, rather than through the 'cool' medium of print, essentially verbal constructs, which establish a permanent screen of words, legends and mythical visions between the individual and the society in which he or she lives. But although the nearest that a writer can ever get to what authors of the previous century claimed was a 'slice of life' is to take discourse as the starting point, the words used also have the power to unravel the screen which other words have constructed. Literature consequently becomes a force for demystification and liberation, an instrument for enabling people to see, perhaps not reality itself, but at least a different, a less flattering as well as a less impressive and less imprisoning version of it.

The writer who sets out to undo the myths in which a society enshrouds itself nevertheless runs a number of risks. The fury which the production of *The Playboy of the Western World* set off in the Dublin of 1907 is a perfect example of how a society behaves when the discourses which it holds about itself are called into question by an alternative version presented in a literary text, and tries to censor it. By the end of the nineteenth century, a number of different movements had come together to create a particular discourse in which the Southern Irish were encouraged to make sense of their social and historical experience. The vision of the Ireland of the Saints had merged with the movement known as the Celtic revival to present a vision of Irish society in which men and women were equally respectful of the past and equally fervent in their religious faith. The Irish, so went the firmly held belief, were an essentially mystical and poetic race whose nature and insights had been systematically repressed by the Anglo-Saxon invader and exploiter. This version of their society also insisted that any sexual drives which the Irish women and men might have could be given full and satisfactory expression in the institution of marriage as defined by the Roman Catholic Church.

The portrait of the Irish in *The Playboy of the Western World* bore as much relation to this mythical vision of their society as the Augustinian gloom of *Lord of the Flies* did to the muscular Christianity of *The Coral Island*. The occupying forces of the British Empire are present only in the occasional mention of the 'peelers' who turn a blind eye to the overgenerous interpretation of the licensing laws, who talk 'whispers in the night' to the local girls, but whose basic sanity comes out in the fact that they take a more austere view of murder than any of the native inhabitants, and especially the women. For the reaction of the Irish themselves to Christy Mahon's announcement that he has killed his father with a loy (a spade for cutting turf) is one of undisguised admiration. Pegeen Mike, 'a fine girl of about twenty', and the heroine of what turns out to be a tragedy of disappointed hopes, falls for him immediately. News travels quickly in rural Ireland, and the thirty-year-old Widow Quin rapidly arrives to show her interest as well. So, too, early next morning, do three young girls, each carrying a gift: a pat of butter from one, a brace of eggs from the second, and a little laying pullet from the third.

In his Preface Synge gives great praise to the 'rich and copious' language spontaneously used by the peasantry of Western Ireland, and writes that

> in a good play, every speech must be as fully flavoured as a nut or an apple, and such speeches cannot be written by anyone who works among people who have shut their ears to poetry.

It could equally well be argued that nobody who had not dwelt among them and uncovered their secret dreams could describe the spontaneous glee with which the peasants of rural Ireland react to the arrival of a young man who has murdered his father.

The admiration showered upon him by the womenfolk fills Christy with such boldness and energy that he wins all the races due to take place that very afternoon down on the beach. But just as the reports of his victories are coming in, his father arrives, hale and hearty, full of the lust for vengeance, and steadfast in his refusal to believe that his son, 'that dribbling idiot' should achieve such triumphs. The inhabitants of the Mayo village have nevertheless, as Christy himself puts it, 'made such a mighty man of him by the power of a lie', that when his father threatens to beat him a second time, he turns on him with even greater violence.

To begin with, the fight that ensues, and the apparent second death of old Mahon, has a sobering effect on Pegeen Mike. It teaches her, as she says, that 'there's a great gap between a gallous story and a dirty deed', and she joins the others in turning against Christy. However, just as they are about to drag him off to the peelers to be hanged, old Mahon reappears for a second time. But although he is tougher than anyone in the play suspected, the two fights have changed his relationship with his son. Young Christy is now the master, and the play ends with the two of them going off together 'telling stories of the villainy of Mayo and the fools that are there'. The Irish, the play tells us, like nothing better than a tale of murder; so long as it turns out to be only a tale. Any dreams of sexual and social liberation which may come from the murder of a tyrannical parent are consequently fated to remain dreams, and nothing more. The sexual longings of the women will remain as unsatisfied as the desire to see a change in the power relationships in society, and there will be no relief for anyone's frustration. The only suitor for the high-spirited, sexually assertive Pegeen Mike is her cousin, a man so afraid of what the priest might say that he dare not even stay to keep her company when her father is to be out of the house overnight at a wake. When the play ends, as it does, on one of the great laments of world literature, 'Oh, my grief, I've lost him. I've lost the only playboy of the Western World' the case against the God-fearing, priest-ridden Ireland of the Saints is complete; but not, as will be seen from *Ulysses* and can be verified by a more recent novel about Southern Ireland, Bryan Moore's 1979 novel *The Mangan Inheritance*,[1] completely closed.

All literary judgements are based on personal attitudes, and views as to what does and does not constitute realism are even more subjective than most. What is realism to me, a sceptical agnostic who spent nine happy years among what Pegeen Mike's father, the publican Jimmy Flaherty, called the 'holy Luthers of the preaching north', is blasphemous slander to a devout Catholic or a romantic Irish nationalist. I was also in the Black North when I saw my second performance of Samuel Beckett's *Waiting for Godot*, this time in English. In the Paris of 1953, when Heidegger and Sartre still held sway, and man was cast asunder in a world which an absent God had peevishly abandoned to its absurd destiny, the play was a sombre, metaphysical drama about the hopelessness of the human condition. Played in Belfast, albeit by a company from the Republic, it was a piece of straightforward reportage. Everyone in the audience knew that the Southern Irish spend their time hanging around talking to one another in the vague hope that something more interesting might turn up. All credit, it was felt, to Sam Beckett, born a Protestant and one of the best fly halves ever to play for Portora Royal Academy, for telling the truth, albeit in what was occasionally rather an unusual and slightly worrying form.

If *The Playboy of the Western World* is seen as a piece of comic realism, a play about the gap between fiction and reality, it works on two separate if interrelated levels. There is the general gap between the Ireland of the Saints and the sexual reality which the Widow Quin expresses when she pulls Christy up from the floor and says, 'There's great temptation in a man did slay his da, so we'd best be going, young fellow; so rise up and come with me'. There is, secondly, the inability of the different characters in the play to deal with the experience of seeing their dreams turn into reality. So long as the murder of Old Mahon remains a distant and semi-magical event, Christy is a hero. Once it takes place in their own back yard, he is a murderer who must be dragged off to the gallows. The Southern Irish, O'Casey is telling his audience, would like to be freed from a society in which the old oppress the young, and in which this oppression can take the blatantly Freudian form of trying to make a young man marry a woman who has, literally, suckled him when a child. But since they lack the courage to carry out the necessary murder of the father, everything ends in a mixture of highly entertaining but deeply frustrated story telling.

II

National myths in a naturalistic setting: Ray Lawler's The Doll Trilogy.

Frustration and disappointment are also basic themes in Ray Lawler's *The Doll Trilogy*. It is a series of plays which are naturalistic in content, by virtue of the statements they make about Australian society, as well as in style, in that *The Summer of the Seventeenth Doll* (1958), *Kid Stakes* and *Other Times* all present experience in an apparently direct and unsophisticated manner. The plays are also like *The Playboy of the Western World* in that they deal with the contrast between a particular myth of national identity and the reality which lies beneath it. Australian audiences were more sympathetic to Lawler's portrayal of their society than the Southern Irish had been when Synge's play was performed, while in England the three plays were seen as marking the coming of age of the Australian theatre and the end of what the Australians themselves used to call the cultural cringe.

From the beginning, the visual arts had flourished in Australia, prompted initially by the need to provide an accurate portrayal of the flora and fauna of a strange land where animals used only their hind legs to move, where the trees shed their bark but not their leaves, and where you built your house facing south if you wanted to keep cool. Painters such as Russell Drydale, William Dobell or Sydney Nolan were known throughout the world, as were the poet and short story writer Judith Wright, and the novelist T. H. White. Now, it was the turn of the theatre to show Australians and others what their country and culture were like. If, in the event, the coming of age turned out to be less definitive than appeared at first sight, the plays themselves remain, as does *The Playboy of the Western World*, as evidence of the theatre's ability to deal realistically with national myths.

The first of the themes treated by Lawler was the contrast between the city, where jobs were dull but the fun intense, and the country, where men were men, where real money and genuine prestige were earned by the exercise of physical toughness, leadership and strength under appalling physical conditions, but where the passage of youth – as in the world of Ernest Hemingway, the Salinas valley of Steinbeck's fiction or the French Algeria celebrated in Camus's *The Outsider*, and in his early, lyrical essays – marked the end of the only life worth living. The second was mateship.

The harshness of the Australian climate, coupled with the dependence of the Australian economy on activities which required men to be absent for long periods from their home, meant that the most important relationships were between men. The strength of the bond between the itinerant labourer and his mate, a relationship from which any tinge of homosexuality was so automatically excluded as to make the very mention of it unthinkable, emphasised the relegation of the Australian woman to a far more subordinate role than her American or British counterpart. In the early, heroic days of the history of the United States, the wife would accompany her husband as they set off, as a pair, for the conquest of new territories. She sat next to him in the covered wagon, shared the perils and excitement of the building of the log cabin and the raising of children in what had only recently been a wilderness, and made her own distinctive contribution to the slow establishment of Western style civilisation through the churches and the townships. The account of the opening of the West in the autobiographical novels of Laura Ingalls Wilder is, naturally, idealised by being seen in fond recollection through the eyes of a child. It nevertheless rings true because of the confirmation it provides, through the accumulation of detail, of the physical realities which support and justify the myth. In Australia, the situation was different, and provides the third of the themes which make *The Doll Trilogy* so convincing an account of the Australian experience.

The plot of the first, and best known of the plays, *The Summer of the Seventeenth Doll*, shows two mates, Barney and Roo (short for Reuben), coming down, apparently as usual, to spend their five-month lay-off period in Melbourne, resting when the sun is too hot even for them from the back-breaking work of cutting cane in the blistering heat north of Cairns. But something has changed, in that for the first time in 17 years, there will not be a foursome between Barney, Roo, Nancy and Olive. Nancy has decided, after 16 years of being Barney's mistress (although the conventions of the Australian stage in the 1950s could not directly acknowledge it, there is no doubt that the two had been sleeping together every lay-off and army leave since the 1940s) to marry a bookseller: stable, reliable, but by the Australian macho ethos which is the tragic preoccupation of the trilogy, unbearably dull. Her place is to be taken, theoretically at any rate, by the sceptically-minded widow, Pearl, whose suspicious and disbelieving glance hastens and highlights the collapse of the dream in which Barney, Roo, Nancy and Olive had been living until then.

This dream is symbolised by the kewpie doll, to the informed spectator as well as to the convinced Freudian, an obvious baby substitute, which Roo has been in the habit of bringing to Olive every year as a token of all the good times they have had together. But everything else has changed as well, and Olive has got out just in time. Roo is now over 40, and no longer the leader of the pack. His inability to adjust to the change is the second element, after the departure of Nancy, which puts an end to paradise. It leads to the collapse of his relationship not only with Olive but also with his mate, Barney. The wrecking of Olive's life is symbolised by her destruction of the doll and the tearing down of the decorations which Pearl has seen from the beginning as tawdry, but which, for 17 years, have symbolised glamour, happiness and love.

Kid Stakes and *Other Times*, though performed twenty years later, in 1978, achieved the remarkable feat of following up an original success in an equally moving and incisive manner. By presenting Barney in the wholly credible role of the young stud who had sired two bastards in the space of two months from different women in his home town, it explained why he would have found a stable and conventional marriage to Olive just as impossible a way of life as she would. Her refusal to tie him down in a city job where he would be with her all the time revealed a shrewd appreciation of his character, just as her rejection of the possibility of following him around from one work place to another reminded the audience of the economic and social realities underlying their relationship. *Other Times* looked at the return of Roo and Barney from active service in the Second World War, and offered an equally accurate analysis of another aspect of Australian society, the attitude adopted by most men to authority. Roo, a natural leader, has consistently refused to accept promotion, and for two eminently explicable reasons: it would have separated him from the more slow-witted Barney; and it would have meant endorsing the values of official society. This, ever since the initial establishment of Australia as a penal colony, has always been seen as exploitative, oppressive and unauthentic, not something which a real man would want anything to do with.

In spite of the success of the later production of the trilogy by Jean Mignon in an expressionist mode at the Anthill Theatre,

Melbourne, in 1983, the trilogy remains a triumph of naturalism, and one of the best illustrations of how limited an approach to literature based either on Barthesian semiology or the concept of intertextuality can be. Its theme, like that of *The Playboy of the Western World*, is the contrast between myth and reality. The justified assumption throughout both plays is nevertheless that this is happening to real people, and that Alice's reply to Tweedledum's contemptuous question, in Chapter 4 of *Through the Looking-Glass*, 'You don't imagine that those are real tears?' is an undoubted and unequivocal 'Yes'.

The praise bestowed on Lawler, in his native Australia as well as in England, showed that the society for which he was writing had reached the level of maturity at which it was quite happy to see its myths called into question.

III

Intertextuality and Hamlet: *Tom Stoppard's* Rosencrantz and Guildenstern are Dead *and Anthea Hayter's* Horatio's Version.

There are a number of reasons why Tom Stoppard's 1967 play *Rosencrantz and Guildenstern are Dead* is so useful an example of the concept of intertextuality. One lies in the perfection of Stoppard's English, which is as good an example of how well the language can be written in the twentieth century as Shakespeare's was in the England of the Renaissance. Another is the difference in social, intellectual and moral attitudes, the result of changes to which Stoppard is more keenly attuned than any other English playwright. Guildenstern's summary of Hamlet's famous 'To be or not to be' speech, 'Death followed by eternity ... the worst of both worlds' hits off with absolute precision the metaphysical despair of a world even fuller of doubt than that of Shakespeare and yet able to make a joke about it. Similarly, Rosencrantz's earlier question highlights the extraordinary psychological paradox underlying André Malraux's description of man as 'the only animal which knows it is going to die':

> Whatever became of the moment when one first knew about death? There must have been one, a moment, in childhood when it first occurred to you that you don't go on for ever. It must

have been shattering – stamped into one's memory. And yet I
can't remember it. It never occurred to me at all. What does
one make of that? We must be born with an intuition of mortality. Before we know the words for it, before we know there
are words, out we come, bloodied and squalling with the knowledge that for all the compasses in the world, there's only one
direction and time is its only measure.

The relationship between *Rosencrantz and Guildenstern are dead*
and *Hamlet* is similar in a number of ways to the one between
James Joyce's *Ulysses* and Homer's *Odyssey*. In the case of Joyce's
novel, the contrast between the humble and occasionally hum-
bling experiences of Leopold Bloom and the noble adventures
related in Homer's epic raises the whole question of what one
can or cannot believe of someone who, like Odysseus, is presented as having had experiences totally unlike one's own. The
interest of *Rosencrantz and Guildenstern are Dead* lies in seeing how
the action of one of the world's greatest tragedies can be presented in a comic and consequently a critical light by being looked
at from below, and by two characters who never quite understand what is going on. Their fate is thus, as Guildenstern puts
it, 'to be intrigued without ever quite being enlightened' and what
he appropriately describes as a 'fine persecution' is a highly appropriate image of the human predicament. This, essentially, is
what life is like. We are all trying to make sense of a world of
which we, as human beings, can never have anything but a partial knowledge, and where what the deconstructionists call the
'grand narratives', and particularly the explanatory systems of
Christianity and Marxism, have now lost all intellectual value.

Stoppard is, however, as much a man of the theatre as a writer
intrigued by philosophical questions, and the Player whom his two
anti-heroes have 'o'erraught on the way' makes a criticism of the
world of Jacobean tragedy which must have occurred to many
spectators when he asks, towards the beginning of Act III: 'The
end? You call that an ending? With practically everybody still on
their feet?' In a less immediately literary context, he also puts his
finger on another aspect of the human condition when he comments
that he and his troop are constantly performing events over which
they have no control. Guildenstern, on the ship taking him and his
companion to what the spectator knows is certain death in England,
expresses the same idea in more elegiac tones when he says:

We have travelled too far, and our momentum has taken over;
we move idly towards eternity, without possibility of reprieve
or hope of explanation.

The intertextuality of *Rosencrantz and Guildenstern are Dead* does
more than comment on the plot and atmosphere of *Hamlet*. Its
central theme is the contrast between the constant bafflement which
characterises ordinary experience and the much greater understanding of events enjoyed both by the people in literature to
whom they happen and the reader or spectator who is given
privileged access to them by the traditional text. But it is also a
presentation of the experience of Everyman. The characters in
Hamlet do not, it is true, understand everything which is happening, and Hamlet has particular difficulty in understanding himself. But they know what they want, and have plans that they
wish to bring to fruition. Rosencrantz and Guildenstern, like most
ordinary folk, have few ambitions other than to survive and perhaps make a little money, and they fail in both. Each of these
two men, who are so alike in their own eyes that neither knows
which member of the pair he is, is like Eliot's Prufrock, an 'attendant lord', one who will

> swell a progress, start a scene or two,
> Deferential, glad to be of use
> Politic, cautious and meticulous

and in that respect the perfect incarnation of how inadequate the
twentieth-century Everyman feels himself to be in a world of eloquent and gesticulating princes.

Stoppard's spectator is not only expected to recognise the implied reference to *The Love Song of J. Alfred Prufrock* which runs
throughout the play. He is also assumed to know about Eliot's
remark that what is worrying about Hamlet, as a character, is
that there is no 'objective correlative' to his unhappiness – that
he is, in other words, sadder than he has cause to be.[2] For when
Guildenstern and Rosencrantz are trying to work out what is wrong
with Hamlet by pretending that Guildenstern is the Prince, under-
going a kind of cross-examination at the hands of Rosencrantz,
his friend puts the essence of his problem in a convenient nut-
shell:

To sum up: your father, whom you love, dies, you are his heir, you come back to find that hardly was the corpse cold before his younger brother popped on to his throne and into his sheets, thereby offending both legal and natural practice. Now why exactly are you behaving in this extraordinary manner?

The irony of Guildenstern's reply – 'I can't imagine!' – exactly hits off the way Eliot missed the point. There are other literary references in *Rosencrantz and Guildenstern are Dead* which have the comparable effect of keeping spectators constantly on their toes. Diana Rigg, who was the perfect Dottie in the first production of *Jumpers*, once said that Stoppard expected anyone attending his plays to be perched eagerly forward on the edge of their seat so as not to miss any of the ideas, and their alertness was always rewarded. The Player's rewriting of Miss Prism's famous definition of fiction in *The Importance of Being Earnest* – 'The bad end unhappily. The good happily. That is what fiction means' – hits the nail on the head with even more accurate irony in the definition which Stoppard makes him offer of tragedy:

We're tragedians, you see. We follow directions – there is no *choice* involved. The bad end unhappily, the good unluckily. That is what tragedy means.

In 1972, in a play entitled *Horatio's Version*, Alethea Hayter also applied the concept of intertextuality to the plot of *Hamlet*, though perhaps without quite realising how useful an illustration she was providing for what is often an elusive concept in the work of the French critics who invented it. The action of Horatio's version, like that of Perry Pontac's *Hamlet Part 2*,[3] takes place after Shakespeare's play has ended, and looks at what might have happened afterwards. Horatio is, as Hamlet knew he would be, scrupulous in ensuring that the truth is told about the events leading up to the accumulation of dead bodies on and off the stage with which the play ends. The Court of Inquiry in which he refutes the version put forward by Osric and other former servants of Claudius shows Horatio at his best, and is a splendid piece of imaginative reconstruction on Alethea Hayter's part. But Horatio cannot avoid acknowledging the unease which he feels at the Prince's lack of scruples in treating Rosencrantz and Guildenstern as he does, and *Horatio's Version* does nothing to heighten our admiration for Hamlet as a man.

It also leads us, as the theory of intertextuality says it should, to see both *Hamlet* itself and *Rosencrantz and Guildenstern are Dead* in a new light. We realise more fully just how Stoppard's heroes are realistically convincing heroes in twentieth-century terms, men who are caught up in a situation which they never understand, and whose fate and misfortunes therefore closely parallel our own. In this respect, both *Rosencrantz and Guildenstern are Dead* and *Horatio's Version* have the same effect on us. When we next see *Hamlet*, we leave the theatre feeling considerably sorrier for these two minor characters than we do for the Prince. They have none of the casual cruelty which his privileged position in society has taught him he can use with impunity. And in their fate, but for the grace of living in a different kind of society, we see a portraiture of ours. After Stoppard, it is no longer possible to accept Racine's remark, in his preface to *Bajazet*, in 1667, that we see the heroes of tragedy with a different eye from the one with which we look at our contemporaries. We may continue to see them as belonging to a different world. But we have ceased to believe in the myth of their immunity to the petty meannesses which disfigure the rest of mankind.

IV

Stoppard, politics and the liberal imagination; some comparisons with Orwell and others.

The comparison between *Rosencrantz and Guildenstern are Dead* and Samuel Beckett's *Waiting for Godot* also has the incidental effect of underlining a contrast in styles of writing which constitutes one of the great dividing lines in twentieth-century literature. On the one hand, there is the style which makes no concessions to the middle-class, middle-brow reader, and simply calls upon him to make the necessary effort to understand. This reaches its height in the work of Beckett and of the later Joyce, but is also there in Borges, Kafka, Pound, Eliot and Faulkner, as well as in the French novelist Georges Pérec and the Italian Italo Calvino. On the other hand, there is the more traditional way of writing, especially strong in English and American literature, which from this point of view reaches its peak in Tom Stoppard. Like the work of Aldous Huxley, his plays are full of ideas. They are easy to understand and they are also very funny, often in much the same way that the novels of Huxley or of Evelyn Waugh are funny, as well as having the advantage of being free from the self-pity which so mars the end of Hemingway's 1929 *A Farewell to Arms*:

That's what they did. You died. You did not know what it was about. You never had time to learn. They threw you in and told you the rules and the first time they caught you off base they killed you.

But when this happens to Rosencrantz and Guildenstern, as it happens to Catherine Berkeley, Stoppard takes the view that it does the universe too great an honour to let its cruelty make us cry. The sign of a gentleman is the ability to laugh, and not to cause embarrassment to others by dwelling either on his own misfortunes or even on those of the people he loves. The sign of a good writer, within the aesthetic adopted by Stoppard, is that he expects the reader to be alert enough to see the joke, but not to spend the whole of his life trying to understand it.

This aesthetic is not, however, universally popular. When, in 1982, Michael Steward, writing in *Tribune*, described Stoppard as the 'Great Comforter of the middle class', he was talking primarily about the political implications of his work, and especially of the recently performed *The Real Thing*. 'If', he wrote,

you were upset by the circumstances of Berny Prosser's death, or queried the new powers of the police to restrain your liberty, here is the man with the impeccable credentials of spending the first two years of his life in Czechoslovakia to tell you how much more horrible the KGB is. And he will do more. He can go on to consecrate every petty and craven feature of his adopted class as not merely the best of humanity but the very definition of it. All else is reduced to barbarism.[4]

His remarks, coupled with the attack on Stoppard by another English critic, Neil Sammells, who in 1988 accused him of a 'militant conservatism' which, 'in the way it enlists literary form in its cause, is aesthetic as well as political'[5] draw attention to another curious feature of twentieth-century literature, the equation between progressive thinking and obscurity of expression.

This equation is not constant. Both Pound and Eliot held very reactionary political views and wrote poetry which is very difficult to understand. But Stoppard's defence, in *The Real Thing*, of clarity of discourse has social and political implications as well as aesthetic ones. Ever since Barthes, it has been generally accepted that only sympathisers with the bourgeoisie accept Anatole France's view that the first duty of the writer is to be immediately comprehensible. When, in Act II of *The Real Thing*, Henry claims that

> words are innocent, neutral, standing for this, describing that, meaning the other, so that if you look after them you can build bridges across incomprehension and chaos,

he becomes the anti-Barthes *par excellence*, and the spokesman for a view then strongly identified with the right. For Barthes's view, widely held and put even more widely into practice by structuralists, post-structuralists and deconstructionists, is that

> clarity is a purely rhetorical attribute, it is not a general quality of language, attainable at all times and in all places, but merely the ideal appendix to a certain discourse, the one subjected to a permanent attempt to persuade.[6]

The fact that Lenin is the least interesting of the characters in *Travesties*, first performed in 1974, coupled with an unsympathetic presentation of Marxism, also strengthens the temptation to place Stoppard on what used to be considered the right in British politics. Neil Sammells's remark about his 'militant conservatism' was clearly meant to remind his readers that Stoppard had written a number of other plays, and expressed a number of comparable attitudes, which made him something of a Cold War warrior. In 1977, he collaborated with André Prévin in *Every Good Boy Deserves Favour*, an attack on the habit of totalitarian regimes of the left of locking up their critics in lunatic asylums, and his 1977 television play, *Professional Foul*, dealt with the suppression of political dissidents in his native Czechoslovakia. Like *Jumpers*, first performed at the National Theatre in 1972, *Professional Foul* confronts the problem which English philosophers working in the associated traditions of logical positivism and linguistic analysis have in finding a basis for condemning totalitarian regimes on moral grounds. For if what A. J. Ayer called 'the emotive theory of ethics'[7] is right, and all statements, as Stoppard's George Moore puts it in *Jumpers*, 'implying goodness or badness, are not statements of *fact*, but merely expressions of feeling, taste or vested interest' then it is hard to see what moral basis there is, in Stoppard's own case, for the energy which he puts into his campaign for Amnesty International.

Stoppard's interest in moral philosophy links his work with the problems which I try to analyse in Chapters 7 and 8, as well as with writers such as Sartre and Camus. Where he also adopted a position identified at the time with the right in England was on the issue of free speech, and Neil Sammells quotes him as saying that:

> It's sheer perversity of speech to describe the society I live in as one that inflicts violence on the underprivileged. What worries me is not the bourgeois exception, but the totalitarian norm. Of all the systems on offer, the one I don't want is the one that denies freedom of expression – no matter what its allegedly redeeming feature may be. The only thing that would make me leave England would be constraint over freedom of speech.[8]

At first sight, this statement might seem to place Stoppard on the left, and make it hard to see why Neil Sammells criticises him for having promoted what he also calls 'a conservative message'. Freedom of speech is, after all, like clarity of expression, one of the causes most firmly associated with the left-wing tradition in England and America as well as in Western Europe.

As George Orwell pointed out in 1946, however, in an essay called 'The Prevention of Literature', a change came over the left in the late thirties and early forties, one whose effects were still visible in the sixties, seventies and eighties. It was after the events of 1968 that the National Union of Students, dominated at the time by the 'Broad Left', imposed an effective ban on certain speakers who might otherwise have been invited to British campuses, and bore out the validity of Orwell's remark that:

> Fifteen years ago, when one defended the freedom of the intellect, one had to defend it against Conservatives and against Catholics, and to some extent – for they were not of great importance – against Fascists. Now, one has to defend it against Communists and 'fellow travellers'.[9]

Stoppard's espousal of the cause of free speech, like his attack
on the 'Radical-Liberal Alliance' which takes power at the beginning of *Jumpers* and celebrates its victory by arresting all its opponents, consequently makes him something of a latter-day Orwell.
So, too, does the cult of clarity mentioned earlier in the discussion
of *The Real Thing*, an attitude strongly reminiscent of Orwell's
view that 'good prose is like a window pane'. It also makes him
something of an exception among twentieth-century writers. One
of the most marked characteristics of twentieth-century literature
has been the lack of sympathy which writers have expressed even
for the more successful manifestations of the liberal, pluralist,
industrial society in which most of them have been fortunate
enough to live. Lionel Trilling drew attention to this in 1951 in
The Liberal Imagination, when he wrote that it is

> in general true that the modern European literature with which
> we have an active, reciprocal relationship, which is the right
> relationship to have, has been written by men who are indif-
> ferent to, or even hostile to, the tradition of democratic liberal-
> ism as we know it. Yeats and Eliot, Proust and Joyce, Lawrence
> and Gide – these men do not seem to confirm us in the social
> and political ideas which we hold.[10]

The same is even truer of Beckett, Dürrenmatt, Ionesco, Kafka,
García Márquez, Genet, Sartre and Waugh, and can also be found
in one of the greatest poems of the twentieth century, Auden's
September 1, 1939. For when Auden wrote

> Exiled Thucydides knew,
> All that a speech can say
> About Democracy,
> And what dictators do,
> The elderly rubbish they talk
> To an apathetic grave

there was no doubt what his target was. It was Pericles's Funeral
Speech in Book Two of Thucydides's *History of the Peloponnesian
War*, a passage traditionally regarded as the first great statement
in the history of Western political thought of the democratic ideal.

For other twentieth-century writers, it is industrialisation as much
as democracy itself which is the main enemy. The whole of

D. H. Lawrence's work is shot through with a feeling of loss at the disappearance of the England which he knew as a boy, where the miners at Eastwood still lived close to the countryside, and the most memorable passages in *Sons and Lovers* take place against a rural background. But Lawrence also has the same hostility towards industrialism and urban democracy which characterised the attitude of nineteenth-century writers such as Flaubert, Matthew Arnold, Ruskin, Baudelaire and Mallarmé. It is not simply that Lawrence's excursion into political writing led to the very favourable presentation of a Fascist-style leader in *Kangaroo*. It was that his whole religion of the dark gods was incompatible with the rational, analytical principles on which not only industrialism but also liberal capitalism are founded. Stoppard, in contrast, seems quite at home in this tradition, and adopts a kind of defiant but essentially rationalistic humanism when he makes Septimus Hodge, tutor to the young Thomasina in his most recent play, *Arcadia*, say: 'We shed as we pick up, like travellers who must carry everything in their arms, and what we let fall will be picked up by those behind. The procession is very long and life is very short. But there is nothing outside the march so nothing can be lost to it.' It is a view which is wholly consistent with the defence of freedom of speech and clarity of expression, as well as of support for pluralist democracy, which were regarded as such nefariously right-wing attitudes by left-wing critics during the Cold War.

V

Intertextuality and Wilde: the example of Travesties; *Stoppard, politics and the place for argument.*

James Joyce is reputed to have said of *Ulysses* that 'On the honour of a gentleman, there is not a word of truth in it' and it is tempting to apply his remark to the way Tom Stoppard's *Travesties* raises the same problem of the relationship between literature and reality already underlined by the contrast between *Rosencrantz and Guildenstern are Dead* and *Hamlet*. For in the debate at Zurich in 1917 between Tristan Tzara, Lenin and James Joyce, which confronts the world of the professional revolutionary with that of the traditional patriot, as well with the father of surrealism, it is

Joyce who has the last word. It is, in other words, the artist who tries to tell the truth about human experience who wins over the surrealist, the Marxist and the believer in conventional values.

The plot, as in all Stoppard's plays, is a fascinating and complicated one, with his skill as a dramatist enabling him to overcome his self-imposed difficulty of having the story unfold, at least in part, through the occasionally unreliable reminiscences of Henry Carr, a minor consular official who had fought bravely for his country before being invalided out and sent to represent British interests in Zurich. There, Carr occupies his spare time organising an amateur production of *The Importance of Being Earnest*, and *Travesties* is like *Rosencrantz and Guildenstern are Dead* in that it provides another practical example of the concept of intertextuality. The text and characters of Wilde's play are interwoven into the main action, from which they take on a new meaning at the same time as they illuminate what is happening to the characters on stage. As Alan Bennett also showed in the first act of *Forty Years On*, Wilde is a relatively easy author to parody, and sets a less difficult challenge than the Shakespeare against whom Stoppard chose to measure himself in *Rosencrantz and Guildenstern are Dead*. *Travesties*, first produced in London in June 1974 and triumphantly revived in 1993, is nevertheless like the earlier play in the questions which it asks about the nature of reality and about the different ways in which this can be presented in literature.

In the preparation of the 1917 Zurich production of *The Importance of Being Earnest*, there has been a dispute between Carr and Joyce over the cost of a pair of trousers to be used as part of one of the costumes, and old Carr is reminiscing about how he interrogated Joyce:

> I dreamed about him, dreamed I had him in the witness box, a masterly cross-examination, case practically won, admitted it all, the whole thing, the trousers, everything, and I *flung* at him – 'And what did you do in the Great War?' 'I wrote *Ulysses*', he said. 'What did you do?'

Carr had in fact fought in the war, and provides an eloquent rebuttal of Tristan Tzara's contention that wars are fought solely for economic motives.

My God, you little Romanian wog – you bloody dago – you jumped-up phrase-making smart-alecy arty-intellectual turd!!. . . . I went to war because it was my *duty*, because my country needed me, and that's *patriotism*. I went to war because I believed that those boring little Belgians and incompetent Frogs had the right to be defended from German militarism, and that's *love of freedom*.

It is one of the few statements of conventional values to be made by a character in twentieth-century literature with whom the audience is expected to sympathise, but Stoppard is too even-handed a thinker, too deeply imbued with the values of the liberal society, as well as too good a playwright, to let Carr get away with it. Later in the play, a series of questions and answers between Joyce and Tzara repeats the dialogue form of the question and answer session in the last chapter of *Ulysses*, in which Stephen and Bloom recognise each other as spiritual father and son, and one of the great virtues of *Travesties* lies in the thrust and parry of ideas which runs through the play. Indeed, Tzara's reply to Carr is as convincing a statement of the artist's function as the comparable if briefer riposte put into Joyce's mouth in the witness box:

My God, you bloody English philistine – you ignorant smart-arse bogus bourgeois Anglo-Saxon prick! When the strongest began to fight for the tribe, and the fastest to hunt, it was the artist who became the priest-guardian of the magic that conjured the intelligence out of the appetites. Without him, man would be a coffee mill. Eat – grind – shit. Hunt, *eat* – grind – saw the logs – *shit*. The difference between being a man and being a coffee mill is art.

Travesties is a play about history as well as one of the most effective dramatisations in twentieth-century literature of a clash between values. Like the real Somerset Maugham, Stoppard's fictionalised Carr is in a position where he might perhaps have stopped the Bolshevik revolution of 1917 from taking place. Had he followed the order from his Minister to 'prevent Mr Ulyanov leaving Switzerland at all costs', which arrived immediately after the congratulations addressed to him by telegram on the excellence of his performance as Algernon Moncrieff, the whole history of the twentieth century might have been different. By reminding the audience of the essential contingency of historical events, it heightens the criticism of Marxism which links *Travesties* with Stoppard's more obviously political plays such as *Every Good Boy Deserves Favour* or *Professional Foul*.

5

Varieties of Realism II: Censorship, the Novel and the City; the Use of Myths in Joyce and Tournier

---

I

Censorship as an indication of the nature of a society; the case of Lady Chatterley's Lover *and the ambiguity of the verdict; more about Southern* Ireland; Angels in America *and the end of censorship.*

It is often through their objections to the demolition or rewriting of their myths that societies reveal their true nature. From the moment that the Soviet Union instituted censorship, a few months after the revolution of October 1917, it was obvious that something had begun to go badly wrong. It is true, for supporters of censorship, that there is something odd about a society in which Hubert Selby's *Last Exit to Brooklyn* can not only be openly published but made into a film, in which Howard Brenton's *The Romans in Britain* can be produced at the British National Theatre, or in which Tony Kushner's *Angels in America* wins almost every literary prize in sight in the early 1990s. There nevertheless remains a great deal to be said for the benefits associated with the virtually total freedom of expression which characterises Western society. The readiness of such a society to accept that no kind of sexual behaviour is regarded as offering unsuitable subject matter for literary expression is one of the surest signs which it can offer of the confidence which it feels in its own stability.

The virtual disappearance of censorship from the industrial

107

democracies of the West is partly a result of a general change in the attitude towards the law. In the days when censorship was regarded as the norm, the law was not expected to content itself with punishing offenders whose actions caused actual harm to real people. By suppressing books, whose contents could harm only the feelings of those prepared to open them and able to understand their contents, it also proclaimed that certain ideological values deserved the same protection as the life, liberty and property of living human beings. The belief that it was the proper province of the law to defend the official ideology of a society in this way lay behind its use by the churches to punish heresy, as well as by the state to limit the ability of writers to express ideas which it saw as a threat to what people were expected to believe. Even after the view had come to be accepted that all ideas deserved free expression, writers still found themselves liable to prosecution if they described certain activities which particular groups saw as dangerous. Since these activities were almost invariably of a sexual nature, and not therefore capable of being shown in a court of law to have harmed those adults who had freely chosen to indulge in them, the law was consequently still being used to proclaim the sacred or quasi-sacred nature of certain values.

The disappearance of literary censorship marks an important step in the process by which the behaviour of a democratic society is brought into line with its official principles. The province of the law is to punish offenders, not to protect beliefs or defend myths, whether these involve religious beliefs or the view of what is or what is not acceptable sexual behaviour between consenting adults. This change has also, however, come about through the tendency of those who tried to use literary censorship to defend certain ideas to make fools of themselves by the arguments they presented. The fact that two of the most important works in the whole of French literature, Flaubert's *Madame Bovary* and Baudelaire's *Les Fleurs du Mal*, were both prosecuted in their year of publication, 1857, as works offensive to public morality, is not only instructive as to the nature of the regime installed in France by Louis Napoleon's *coups d'état* of 1851 and 1852. It is also seen as a typical example of how the law gets it wrong when it tries to legislate on literary matters. Baudelaire lost his case, and was not finally rehabilitated until 1950, by which time his poems had become basic texts for literary study in all French schools. And while Flaubert won, this was not because his judges recognised the literary quality of his book. It was because the skill of his lawyer persuaded them that the detailed account of Emma Bovary's extra-marital activities was a highly moral version of the advice provided in Arthur Hugh Clough's *A New Decalogue*:

Adultery do not commit
Advantage rarely comes of it.

In England, it was not until 1959 that the argument that the publication of works of literature with sexually explicit scenes was permissible if it could be proved that the work in question is justified 'as being for the public good on the ground that it is in the interests of science, literature, art or learning, or any other object of general concern,' and even then the arguments actually used in the first case to be contested were not free of a certain casuistry.

The policy of Penguin Books, founded in 1936 as the first serious house to produce good quality paperbacks, had always been to provide its readers with a full and unexpurgated text. In 1960, they decided to test the new law by publishing the full version of D. H. Lawrence's *Lady Chatterley's Lover*, a novel which had been banned in all English-speaking countries since its first apppearance in Paris in 1928. It was not the first time that this particular law had been used. In 1959, Frederick Shaw had been sent to prison for nine months for bringing out a guide to London prostitutes entitled *The Ladies Directory*. The argument that anyone buying such a publication would already be pretty corrupt anyway was not accepted as an adequate defence, and at no time in England or America do books seem to have been prosecuted because they advocated, described or endorsed violence. What has always been seen as much more important, and more dangerous, is their tendency to encourage people to have sex, whether of an orthodox or an eccentric variety.

Lady Chatterley's Lover was a book which had already had a checkered history even when published in a fairly expensive hardback edition, having been banned from entry into England between its original publication until the time when it began to be placed, almost as a matter of course, on the syllabus at various universities. The decision of Penguin Books to produce a paperback edition at 3/6d, less than one tenth of the price of a bottle of whisky at the time, gave rise to another of those scenes which Lord Macaulay evoked when he commented that he knew of 'no spectacle so ridiculous as the British public in one of its periodic fits of morality'.

Counsel for the prosecution, Mr Griffiths-Jones, asked the jury if this was a book that they would let their wives or servants read. The Bishop of Woolwich, following the lead provided by the critic and sociologist Richard Hoggart, who under some quite vigorous cross-questioning, stuck to his definition of Lawrence as a puritan, described *Lady Chatterley's Lover* as 'a book all Christians should read', while the Reverend Donald Tyler was made to agree that a long quotation from Lawrence's essay *A propos de 'Lady Chatterley's Lover'* was 'a most impressive statement of the Christian view of marriage'. It was a phrase which came as something of a surprise to anyone who had read both the marriage vows set out in the Prayer Book of the Church of England and Lawrence's novel. For while the marriage vows contain the explicit promise to be faithful 'in sickness and in health, for richer for poorer'[1] there is an equal and opposite absence of ambiguity in *Lady Chatterley's Lover*. Sir Clifford Chatterley has been made impotent by a war wound; an occurrence which, as Jake Barnes observed in Hemingway's 1926 novel, *The Sun Also Rises*, 'is supposed to be very funny'. The ironically named Constance begins by having a series of love affairs with men of her own and her husband's social class before falling deeply and passionately in love with the gamekeeper on Sir Clifford's estate, Arthur Mellors. Their love-making is described in some detail and often very poetically. The novel ends with her becoming pregnant by Mellors and leaving her husband to lead a new life with her lover.

Nobody will ever know whether the jury which considered the case in October 1960 dismissed the charge against Penguin Books because it thought that Lawrence's book was a celebration of Christian marriage, and therefore a totally moral work of art in the traditional sense of the word, or because it thought that any possible effect which its essentially pagan message might have on the morals of the young was counterbalanced by its literary merit. It is even harder to say whether the possibility of buying *Lady Chatterley's Lover* for the same price as a packet of cigarettes was a factor in the outburst of sexual activity which is said to have characterised the 1960s. The availability after 1965 of the contraceptive pill is likely to have had a more direct impact, especially since it was already becoming difficult, even among students from University Departments of English Literature, to find anyone who had actually read Lawrence's novel. Other, more significant cases followed the 1960 decision, which had the incidental effect of allowing *Lady Chatterley's Lover* to be legally imported and sold in the United States. The victory on appeal of *The Naked Lunch* in 1966 marked the last instance of a work of literary merit being prosecuted for obscenity in the United States, and it was clear by the 1970s that literary censorship had to all intents and purposes disappeared from the United Kingdom as well.

Matters nevertheless remained relatively unchanged in the Irish Republic, where in Dublin itself it was still difficult in 1970 to buy a copy of James Joyce's *Ulysses*, and where in 1957 a number of copies of the weekly journal *Woman's Own* had been impounded by the customs authorities as soon as it was discovered that one of the issues contained an article on family planning. It was an intervention which would not have surprised Leopold Bloom, the chief character in *Ulysses*, whose monologue on seeing his friend Dedalus's daughter outside Dillon's auction rooms is also a meditation on the theme which David Lodge was to use to such brilliantly comic effect in *The British Museum is Falling Down* in 1967 and *How Far Can You Go?* in 1980:

> Must be selling off some old furniture. Knew her eyes at once from the father. Lobbing about waiting for him. Home always breaks up when the mother goes. Fifteen children he had. Birth every year almost. That's in their theology or the priest won't give the poor woman the confession, the absolution. Increase and multiply. Did you ever hear of such a thing? Eat you out of house and home. No families themselves to feed.[2]

The reception still awarded to *Ulysses* in Joyce's city almost ten years after the Lady Chatterley case suggests that little had changed in Ireland since 1907, when the riot which accompanied the first performance of *The Playboy of the Western World* reached its peak towards the end of Act III as Christy declaimed that:

> It's Pegeen I'm seeking only and what'd I care if you brought me a drift of chosen females, standing in their shifts themselves, maybe, from this place to the Eastern World.

It was the word 'shift' that did it, apparently. It is not something which one could imagine happening in the American theatre in the 1990s, where the first part of Tony Kushner's *Angels in America*, 'Millenia Approaches' has hardly been going for twenty minutes, and the word 'fuck' used only thirteen times, when Prior Walter says to Louis Ironson, 'You don't notice anything. If I hadn't spent the last four years fellating you I'd swear you were straight.'[3] No wonder Joyce had to leave Ireland if he wanted to depict not only how the human mind really worked but what sexual dreams occupied perfectly ordinary men and women.

II

Ulysses and the problem of censorship; a further illustration of the concept of intertextuality and the use of myth; some similarities between Ulysses *and* The Waste Land; *references to Orwell and Tom Stoppard; myth and fatherhood in* Ulysses *and elsewhere.*

There are, from this point of view, two closely related ways in which the word 'myth' is used in connection with Joyce's work. In a purely literary sense, he uses the myth of Ulysses to explore the nature of modern society and to suggest what similarities and differences exist between Homer's period and our own. But it proved possible for him to do this in a satisfactory manner only in a society in which certain myths about the nature of human sexuality, and especially about the virtual non-existence of female sexuality, had ceased to be regarded as sacrosanct. He had to write, in other words, in Zurich and Paris, not in Dublin, London or New York.

Ulysses was published in Paris by Sylvia Beach's Shakespeare and Company in 1922, the same year that T. S. Eliot's *The Waste Land* appeared in London. Later in the same year, in the United States, Margaret Anderson was fined for publishing extracts of it in *The Little Review*, and in June 1923, 499 of the 500 copies imported into England were seized and burned by the customs authorities in Folkestone. The ban remained in force in the United States until 1930, when Random House printed a full version, and two judges, Federal Judge John M. Woolsey, supported by Supreme Court Judge Hand, dismissed the charge that the book was obscene. It was, said Judge Hand, 'a book of originality and sincerity of treatment', which 'does not have the effect of promoting lust', adding that 'works of art are not likely to sustain a high position with no better warrant for their existence than an obscene content'.[4]

No formal legal judgment was ever made of *Ulysses* in the United Kingdom, where it was gradually accepted as a book deserving serious study, and where George Orwell, having finally obtained a copy in the summer of 1933, told his sister a year later that he 'rather wished' he had never read it. 'When I read a book like that' he continued,

> and then come back to my own work, I feel like a eunuch who has taken a course in voice production and can pass himself off fairly well as a bass or a baritone, but if you listen closely you can hear the good old squeak again.

At first sight, it is a surprising judgement from a writer who gave such importance to clarity of expression. It is his earlier comment, in June 1933, that *Ulysses* 'sums up better than any book I know the fearful despair that is almost normal in modern times'[5] which fits in better with the image which Orwell gave of himself as a plain, straightforward Englishman. A man who, like Orwell, listed 'industry, courage, patriotism, frugality and philoprogenitism' as 'the qualities by which any society can be sustained'[6] is unlikely to find much comfort in Joyce's novel. Leopold Bloom may well long for another son to replace young Rudy, who died when he was only eleven days old. But the rest of the novel is scarcely a defence of family values.

Orwell's initial reaction is one which underlines the similarity between *Ulysses* and *The Waste Land* which Dame Helen Gardner noted when she wrote that both books were 'richly allusive' and that both boldly juxtaposed 'a modern world described with a most complete realism and a world of romance, epic and high tragedy'.[7] In *Ulysses*, as in *The Waste Land*, it is the treatment of the city which best illustrates this idea. Eliot's admiration for Baudelaire was one of the factors which led him to move poetry from its traditional preoccupation with the countryside to an evocation of the way in which people live now. It is still very difficult, once you have read *The Waste Land*, to walk across the Thames and into the City over London Bridge without Eliot's adaptation of Dante –

Unreal City
Under the brown fog of a winter dawn,
A crowd flowed over London Bridge, so many,
I had not thought death had undone so many –

coming into your mind. Similarly, once you have read *Ulysses*,
Dublin will always be Joyce's city, the city of Mark Digman's
funeral, of Buck Mulligan and Stephen Dedalus, of the Citizen,
the bars, and the Liffey flowing sluggishly into the snot-green
sea. But these are not noble images, evocative of the hero whose
boast was that he 'knew men and cities'. They are images of the
city as we know it, with its constant juxtaposition of the noble
and the beautiful with the tawdry and depressing.

On the level of characterisation, the comparison is less straightforward. There is no means of knowing whether or not one is doing
the right thing in seeing Mr Bloom as an ironic parody of Odysseus,
or as a modern version of him which is at one and the same time
more human and more humane. Unlike Odysseus, Mr Bloom does
not go around killing people, and he does not seduce women
only to abandon them as soon as he remembers that he ought
really to be going home to his wife. Unlike Ulysses, he has no
social inferiors to sacrifice to his own well-being, his sexual peculiarities do harm to nobody, and he is far more tolerant and
open-minded, as well as much more interested in ideas, than
anyone is allowed to be in Homer's world. There is also little in
common between the return of the original Odysseus to Ithaca,
an event which leads to a battle in which he and Telemachus
slaughter not only the importunate suitors but also the women
who have slept with them, and the peaceful arrival of Stephen
Dedalus and Leopold Bloom at 7, Eccles Street in the small hours
of the morning. Mr Bloom makes Stephen a cup of cocoa before
going upstairs to make his wife Molly wonder what has happened by asking her to bring him a cooked breakfast in bed the
next morning. Nothing particularly wrong about that. As with
the comparison between *Rosencrantz and Guildenstern are Dead* or
Horatio's Version with the text of *Hamlet*, one of the advantages
of intertextuality is that it provides the opportunity, unusual in
twentieth-century literature, of thinking that our behaviour might
in some ways be better than that of earlier generations.

This is not, however, the only way of reading the novel. Homer's
hero was a man whose sexual exploits had a healthy if some-

times brutal and selfish directness about them. There is consequently a marked contrast with Bloom's action in masturbating
while watching Gerty MacDowell, Cissy Caffrey and Edy Boardman
in the evocation of the Nausicaa episode in Chapter 13. Just as
Eliot, in *The Waste Land*, deliberately juxtaposes the affair between
the typist and the 'young man carbuncular' with the atmosphere
of moral sanity in *The Vicar of Wakefield*, and with the splendid if
disastrous loves of Antony and Cleopatra or Tristan and Iseult,
so Joyce sometimes gives the appearance of suggesting that his
readers will be struck first of all by the idea of how far humanity
has fallen since those noble days.

From one point of view, this is especially so in the case of
Molly Bloom, whose difference from Penelope makes her a less
obvious model for her sex. The 20-year-long absence during which
the original Odysseus was away from home, first at the siege of
Troy and then in his wanderings, may well be paralleled by the
impotence which seems to have afflicted Mr Bloom in his relationship with his wife since the death of their son. But since the
original Penelope remained faithful to her husband for the full
20 years of his absence, keeping the suitors at bay by undoing at
night the tapestry which she had woven during the day, it is less
appropriate for the story line of Joyce's novel to be punctuated
by news of the impending arrival of the latest in Molly's series
of 25 lovers, Blazes Boylan. On the other hand, the novel ends
with a long monologue which asserts not only the triumph of
life but the power and importance of female sexuality.

Ulysses does not have a plot in the same sense that *Pride and
Prejudice* or *Anna Karenina* do. In that respect, it carries on from
the innovation introduced by *Remembrance of Things Past*, and
neither novel keeps the reader's attention by inviting him to wonder
what happens next. What story line there is, apart from the mention
of the imminent arrival of Blazes Boylan, is what the reader of
the *Odyssey* recognises as the Telemachus theme. Bloom is unconsciously seeking for a replacement for Rudy, and finds him in
Stephen Dedalus, who has rejected his own biological father and
all he stands for. In so far as *Ulysses* makes an emotional impact
on the average male heterosexual reader, it is in the reflection
which it offers of Roy Cohn's remark, in *Angels in America*, that

The father–son relationship is central to life. Women are for
birth, beginning, but the father is continuance. The son offers

his father his life as a vessel for carrying forth his father's dream[8] or of the parallel which it offers to Steinbeck's *East of Eden*.

Joyce might well have been surprised to be judged in these terms, since Stephen Dedalus, the character in the novel who most resembles him by background and ambition, declares that 'Fatherhood, in the sense of conscious begetting, is unknown to man. It is a mystical estate, an apostolic succession from only begetter to only begotten' and claims that the only natural link between father and son is 'an instant of blind rut'.[9] But as G. K. Chesterton once said, the aim of literary criticism was to tell the author something which would make him jump out of his boots. Like Sartre, Joyce may well have had a paternal instinct which he diligently suppressed in the words he put into the mouth of his apparently most autobiographical figure.[10]

IV

Ulysses on the French and English; and on Catholicism; more thoughts on censorship, and some examples, past and present, of its absence; more on Mr Bloom.

It is perhaps unfortunate, in the light of the fact that it was published in Paris and the ease with which it still fits into a number of different ideas originally developed in France, that *Ulysses* should contain the uncharitable remarks which it does about the French themselves. These are not, it is true, as harsh as the comments made about the British, who

> believe in rod, the scourger almighty, creator of hell upon earth and in Jacky Tar, the son of a gun, who was conceived of unholy boast, born of the fighting navy, suffered under rump and dozen, was scarified, flayed and curried, yelled like bloody hell, the third day he arose again from the bed, steered into haven, sitteth on his beam end till further orders whence he shall come drudge for a living and be paid.[11]

Nor are they as funny and well-directed as the irony at the expense of the beliefs entertained by the Roman Catholic Church in the passage where Father Conmee reflected on the providence of the Creator who had made turf to be in bogs where men might dig it out and bring it to town and hamlet and make fires in the houses of poor people

and thinks of 'that tyrannous incontinence, needed however for men's race on earth, and of the ways of God which are not our ways'.[12]

The presentation of the French in *Ulysses* is nevertheless not complimentary. 'Excellent people, no doubt', John Eglington remarks on learning that the French subtitle for *Hamlet* was 'Le Distrait' or the absent-minded beggar, 'but distressingly shortsighted in some matters', while the character known as the Citizen is even more forthright:

> Set of dancing masters! Do you know what it is? They were never worth a roasted fart to Ireland. Aren't they trying to make an entente cordiale now at Tay Pay's dinner party with perfidious Albion? Firebrands of Europe and they always were?[13]

The Citizen is not, of course, an entirely unprejudiced witness, in spite of being credited with the parody of the Lord's Prayer quoted above, a passage which would still do credit to any undergraduate satirical publication. He is a rabid Irish nationalist, and the parallel with Cyclops, the one-eyed giant whom Odysseus blinds completely, is not a flattering one.

The 50-page inner monologue which concludes the book, and in which the reader is given privileged access to Molly Bloom's stream of consciousness, was one of the reasons why *Ulysses* was originally considered pornographic. It is relatively mild by modern standards, especially when placed by the side of Alfred Clayton's description, in John Updike's *Memories of the Ford Administration*, of an incident in his liaison with Genevieve Brent:

> my perfect love partner tucked back her black hair so that a gleam of face showed in the faint light from the streets and found my prick with her mouth and despite my squeamish, chivalrous, insincere efforts to push her off ruthlessly sucked and hand-pumped me into coming, into helplessly shooting off (like fireworks in a chaste fifties movie as a metaphor for sex) into a warm wet dark that was her tiny little head.[14]

It is not, for the informed reader, an altogether expected passage to find in an Updike novel. From the publication of *Couples*, in 1965, through the Rabbit series, he has accustomed his readers to contemplating both the enjoyable realities of sex and its frequently unfortunate consequences, especially the 'legal action involving realtors, judges, mellifluous lawyers, abandoned children' mentioned as a counterpoint to its delights in the *Memories of the Ford Administration*.[15] But it is a shade more surprising when even a writer as entertaining, perceptive and fastidious as Alison Lurie can make her heroine Emily Stockwell Turner, in *Love and Friendship*, tell her lover, Will Thomas, 'I like it at the end when you get bigger and I can feel myself slowly exploding and nothing can be done about it'.[16]

In the absence of the efficient contraception which allows Emily not to worry too much about getting pregnant – Will uses condoms with the evocative name of 'Trojans'; we are not told the brand of French letter which Molly knows that her husband keeps in his wallet – Joyce's heroine is more concerned about the possible results of sex:

> must have eaten oysters I think a few dozen he was in great singing voice no I never in all my life felt anyone had the size of that to make you full up he must have eaten a whole sheep after whats the idea making us like that with a big hole in the middle of us like a Stallion driving it up into you because thats all they want out of you with that determined vicious look in his eye I had to halfshut my eyes still he hasn't such a tremendous amount of spunk in him when I made him pull it out and do it on me considering how big it is so much the better in case any of it wasn't washed out properly the last time I let him finish it in me nice invention they made for women for him to get all the pleasure[17]

One of the most obvious gaps in the attempts at realism which caused so much controversy in the nineteenth century was the absence of any direct reference to contraception, to menstruation, or to any need which the characters in fiction might have to empty their bladder or evacuate the contents of their bowels. It is a taboo broken early on in *Ulysses* when Mr Bloom, having enjoyed his breakfast kidney, sits reading an old number of *Titbits*, restraining himself, the first column and, yielding but resisting, began the second. Midway, his last resistance yielding, he allowed his bowels to ease themselves quietly as he read, reading still patiently that slight constipation of yesterday quite gone.[18]

Aldous Huxley comments in *Point Counter Point* on how rarely novelists talked about the effect which being constipated or in the midst of menstruation might have on the mood of a character in fiction. He was, however, held back by the conventions of his time from following out all the implications of his comment, and there is nothing comparable to the scene in *Memories of the Ford Administration* in which Ann Coleman 'squats on the cold-lipped chamber pot, relieving her bladder in a stream whose pungence rises to her nostrils with the sharpness of horse stale'.[19] There is also a slightly surprising piece of information in Milan Kundera's 1984 novel *The Unbearable Lightness of Being*, where he notes how the hero, Tomas, 'washed and urinated into the washbasin (standard practice among Czech doctors)'[20] as well as an apt reminder, in Tom Wolfe's *The Right Stuff*, of how human beings remain subject to their bodies even when they are involved in the most daringly conceived scientific experiments. When, on 5 May 1961, Alan Shepherd was strapped into the capsule which was to make him the first American in space, he had to wait so long for take-off that his bladder almost burst. The only solution to the problem, which nobody seemed to have foreseen, was for him to allow his tight-fitting space suit to become the first star-trek wet suit in history.

Huxley's 1932 novel *Brave New World*, one of the few really successful attempts to write science fiction, does contain references to the need for the girls to keep themselves in constant readiness for enjoyable but infertile sex by wearing a 'Malthusian belt', but the reader is spared any details of precisely what type of contraceptive it contains. It was not until the publication of Sartre's short story *Intimité* (*Intimacy*) in 1939, and the appearance of *Les Chemins de la Liberté* (*The Paths of Freedom*) immediately after the Second World War that another author carried on where Joyce left off. The text leaves no doubt about the fact that Mathieu Delarue, the main character in *The Paths of Freedom*, has made his mistress pregnant by not withdrawing in time and, as Marcelle puts it, 'letting himself come in me like a boy having a wet dream'.[21] From this point of view, Sartre's fiction contains more human interest than his reputation as a somewhat gloomy philosopher might lead you to expect. Nobody in his novels and short stories ever makes love in the hope of having children, and they all rely solely on *coitus interruptus* as a means of contraception. It is a detail which throws an interesting if involuntary light on the frustrations which must have accompanied a great deal of sexual experience in France before the pill, the coil, the cap and the sheath were finally legalised in that country in 1967.

What is remarkable, in this respect, is not that Joyce and Sartre should have made the references which they did to *coitus interruptus*. If you are setting out to tell the truth about the human condition, a good deal of reference to the possible consequences as well as to the pleasures and frustrations of sex is inevitable. What is odd, in retrospect, is the fact that authors in the past who were writing ostensibly realistic fiction should have been so mealy-mouthed about the question of how their characters managed to have so much sex and yet avoid any pregnancies not strictly required by the plot.

This coyness was not a characteristic of all the fiction written before the nineteenth century. In Laclos's 1782 novel *Les Liaisons dangereuses*, the Vicomte de Valmont proudly informs the Marquise de Merteuil that he has taught Cécile de Volanges 'everything except the precautions', so that the later news that Cécile is pregnant is as much an indication of Laclos's realistic treatment of sex as an essential element in the plans which the Marquise has to ruin Cécile's reputation before her marriage to Gercourt. It also seems to have been possible, in the seventeenth and eighteenth centuries, to use the stage to remind audiences of the fact that sex is not always limited to straightforward bonking. In 1682, in *Venice Preserved*, Thomas Otway makes Antonio, 'a fine Speaker in the Senate' visit the courtesan Aquilena and pretend to be her dog so that she can whip him. There is, in a broader historical context, little that seems genuinely new in either Joyce, Genet, Joe Orton's 1964 *Entertaining Mr Sloane*, or David Mamet's 1976 *Sexual Perversions in Chicago*.

If realism is defined as the desire to tell the whole truth about human experience, with no holds barred in the mention of physiological details, the examples of Joyce and Sartre are as much a harking back to the more robust traditions of the past as genuine innovations in what literature can offer its readers. Rabelais describes how Gargantua, when pestered by the inhabitants of Paris

to offer them some recognition of the welcome they had afforded
him,

> unfastened his noble codpiece and lugging out his great pleasure-
> rod, so furiously bepissed them that he drowned two hundred
> and eighty-six thousand four hundred and eighteen persons,
> not counting the women and children.[22]

Swift was also sufficiently interested in how people's bodies actually behave to make Gulliver experience great difficulty, on his
arrival in Brobdignag, in explaining his need to defecate, eventually being enabled to hide himself between 'two leaves of sorel
and there discharge the necessities of nature'. The supposedly
realistic Flaubert, in contrast, can have Emma travel round the
city of Rouen for seven hours in a cab with her young admirer
Léon without either of them needing to get out for any purpose
whatsoever.

Later on, during the passionate love affair which Emma enjoys
with Léon, and which is one of the major factors leading to her
downfall, she manages to pay him regular visits by claiming to
have a monthly piano lesson in Rouen. One of Mr Bloom's mon-
ologues brings out the problems that might arise in practice for
the comfort of any lovers following strictly calendar arrangements
of this type when he reflects:

> How many women in Dublin have it today? Martha, she. Some-
> thing in the air. That's the moon. But then why don't all women
> menstruate at the same time with the same moon, I mean? De-
> pends on the time they were born, I suppose. Or all start from
> scratch then get out of step.[23]

In so far as Bloom is a kind of Everyman, it is reasonable and
realistic to lend him thoughts of this kind. Some of his own sexual
tastes inevitably bring a smile to the reader who does not share
them, as when his sado-masochistic tendencies merge with a touch
of foot fetishism in the long dream sequence in Chapter 15. This
takes place in what seems to be a brothel, and has analogies with
the episode in Homer's poem in which the witch Circe turns all
of Odysseus's followers into pigs. Mr Bloom is not so immune to
temptation as was Odysseus himself on that particular occasion,
and evinces the same kind of terrified delight in the presence of

The Honourable Mrs Mervyn Talboys and Mrs Yelverton Barry
as Christopher Isherwood's hero does in the presence of the
redoutable, whip-wielding Anni in *Mr Norris Changes Trains*. Bloom
then 'murmurs lovingly':

> To be a shoefitter in Mansfield's was my love's young dream,
> the darling joys of sweet buttonhooking, to lace up crisscrossed
> to kneelength the dressy kid footwear satinlined, so incredibly
> small, of Clyde Road ladies.[24]

The absence of passages of this kind from the supposedly realistic fiction of a Flaubert or a Zola is not a sign of ignorance on
their part. If Flaubert's correspondence is often a good deal more
interesting than his novels, it is because he could write in private
with a lack of inhibitions that the various myths about sexuality
current in nineteenth-century society did not allow in public. These
myths were essentially puritanical in nature, and an illustration
of the thesis that a society in the process of rapid industrialisation has to sacrifice immediate and even medium-term sexual
gratification to the strict discipline required by the industrial process. Since powerful taboos against sexual activity outside marriage seem to characterise all societies which carry out nineteenth-
century style industrialisation, it is hard to believe that it is merely
a coincidence that these taboos should have disappeared as Western
societies have moved into what is widely described as a 'post-
industrial phase'. The exploration of myths in imaginative literature in the middle and later years of the twentieth century
consequently takes on a different form as the taboos of the nineteenth century fade into the past.

V

Michel Tournier on myth; the rewriting of Robinson Crusoe *and of
the legend of the Erl King.*

Joyce's aim was not to produce the kind of camera-ready realism
which Christopher Isherwood gave as his aim, and which helps
to make *Mr Norris Changes Trains* so irresistible a read. He was
aiming more at a higher order of realism, the one where it at-
tains the level of mythical, described by T. S. Eliot as

simply one way of controlling, of ordering, of giving shape and significance to the immense panorama of futility and anarchy that is contemporary history.[25]

Michel Tournier is less pessimistic than Eliot and Joyce about twentieth-century civilisation, being one of the few French writers not to see capitalism as finished, and he uses myth in a way which is significantly different from that of his Anglo-American and Irish predecessors. He has a detached attitude to myths, seeing them as an anthropologist would, stressing the idea that the essential characteristic of a myth is that it should be a story which recurs in otherwise different cultures, but which cannot be attributed to a particular author. But if Tournier uses myth to comment on his own society, it is without the note of didactic disapproval which informs Eliot's treatment of the Graal legend and the story of the fisher-king in *The Waste Land*.

Thus in the book by which Tournier became immediately famous in 1967, *Vendredi ou les limbes du Pacifique* (*Friday*), he deals with the myth given permanent expression by Defoe, that of the European recreating civilisation virtually from scratch on a desert island. This is what happens in *Robinson Crusoe*, the only work of fiction which Jean-Jacques Rousseau would allow to his pupil Emile to read, and at first sight there seems to be a fairly specific ideological target in Tournier's rewriting of the myth: the faith in applied science and the attitude of Europeans towards societies different from their own. Indeed, one way of reading the book is as an attack on the attitude which looks upon the whole world as a garden to be cultivated and brought under control by Europeans. In this respect, Tournier's attitude is very similar to that of the Conrad of *Heart of Darkness*, or even of *Nostromo*, with the criticism of Europe taking an ecological rather than a more specifically political form. Not all cultures, he suggests, have the all-conquering attitude to nature embodied in the verses in Genesis 1:26 which give man 'dominion over the fish of the sea, and over the fowl of the air, and over the cattle, and over the earth, and over every creeping thing that creepeth upon the earth;' especially not the one to which Robinson Crusoe's Man Friday belongs.

Friday is nevertheless not an ecological tract, and its treatment of the myth of Robinson Crusoe and Man Friday has an openness to it which matches the intellectual tolerance of the open society which Tournier so admires. To the reader sceptical about the claims of the ecological movement, and consequently inclined to admire the ability of Western man to bring nature under control, there is something very comforting in the first part of Tournier's narrative, which remains intact in spite of the unexpected ending of the book. Here we have the triumph of the Protestant work ethic, the use of science to render the world inhabitable, even to the point where Robinson exploits the hostility between the black and the brown rats to make the two tribes kill one another and thus free the island of this particular vermin. But just as the mind of such a reader is filled with admiration for the ingenuity and persistence with which Robinson has built up enough food stocks to last him for years, and totally tamed the wilderness he found waiting for him on his arrival, Friday ruins it all. He disobeys his master's injunction not to smoke the pipe which Robinson insists is the privilege of Western man, and does so near the cave where Robinson keeps his gunpowder. A spark causes an explosion which destroys the whole of Robinson's equivalent of the surpluses produced by the Common Market Agricultural Policy, and leads him to carry out a fundamental revision of his world view. Instead of taking advantage of the arrival of the schooner to go back to England, Robinson decides to stay on the island, with which he has established a new kind of communion.

Friday, however, who has by now taken over the place of Robinson as hero of the book, decides on the contrary to take ship for Europe, and at first sight his action seems rather surprising. Why should he, whose example has apparently helped Robinson to see the error of his ways, and the dangers of plethoric production, go back to the Europe whose representative had initially had no thought but to enslave him? There are, however, two reasons to explain his action, the first psychological, the second with more philosophical and even political overtones. Whereas the Robinson of the middle part of the novel was a tellurian creature, deeply rooted in the land, Friday has always been a creature of the air, fascinated by everything that is light enough to fly. What he finds irresistible in the schooner is the grace and elegance of its rigging, the impression which it gives of being about to fly as it sets sail. But it is also, when one moves away from Friday's own immediate and personal motivation, a decision which pays tribute to Western technology. Friday is choosing, in the final analysis, to ally himself with the culture which

can use and exploit nature in a way which he had never previously thought possible.

It is the possibility of interpreting his rewriting of the Robinson
Crusoe–Man Friday myth in several different ways which helps
to make Tournier's work so appropriate and encouraging an expression of the spirit of late twentieth-century liberal democracy.
All ways of looking at a myth are valid, and none should be
discouraged either by the external constraints of society or the
ideological prejudices of the reader or writer. It may well be that
Friday's fuller experience of European society will be disappointing. He may arrive in Europe only to discover, like other immigrants from the Third World who have followed his example,
that he might have done better to stay at home. It is a theme
treated by Tournier in a later novel, *La Goutte d'or* (*The Golden
Droplet*), in 1986, one of the few successful attempts to deal in
fiction with the problems of the North African immigrant in France,
and a book which could well be read as a sequel to *Friday*. But at
least Friday will have found out about a society different from
his own, and seen its advantages as well as its drawbacks.

The same possibility of what Barthes would call a 'lecture
plurielle' characterises Tournier's best-known and most successful novel, the 1974 *Le roi des Aulnes* (*The Erl King*). Its central
character, Abel Tiffauges, is at one and the same time the terrifying, child-stealing ogre of the legend and, more prosaically, a
sexually and socially inadequate left-handed French garage mech-
anic. The physical link between the two sides of his personality
is provided by Tiffauges's minute genitalia, and the historical link
by what happens to him when he is captured by the Germans in
the defeat of 1940. Just as Mr Bloom is at one and the same time
the Greek hero whom Joyce admired above all others and a small-
time advertising agent, Abel Tiffauges has a dual personality which
is simultaneously richly comic and emotionally terrifying. When
he gallops round the countryside of Eastern Prussia in order to
steal children from their parents, he takes on all the attributes of
the traditional ogre. Since the children in whom he is interested
are those who have exactly the right cranial measurements to be
selected for the experiments in supposedly scientific breeding
carried out by the Nazis in the camps known as Nappolas, he
also becomes the incarnation of the absurd confidence in itself
which characterised the pseudo-science of the Nazi regime. But
at the same time, he never ceases to be what he is in a more

mundane political context: a not particularly bright French prisoner of war who has found himself a cushy billet.

Tournier's use of myth hits exactly the right note here. To begin with, he expresses one of the peculiar horrors of twentieth-
century history, the sacrifice of children as well as grown-ups to
the lunatic ambitions of the totalitarian dream. The celebrations
for Hitler's birthday, April 23, involved all the ten-year-old boys
in Germany taking a public oath to sacrifice themselves to his
glory. Tiffauges's enormous appetite for raw meat is the physical
symbol for the way the Nazi regime showed the same hunger
for devouring those whom it had the duty to protect as it did for
destroying its enemies. But at the end of the novel, Tiffauges is
given another role, and one which makes the symbolism of *The
Erl King* even more complex. As the Third Reich collapses around
him, Tiffauges begins to change. He becomes possessed by the
desire to save some of the Jewish children who would otherwise
have been murdered by the Nazis, and his personality is transformed into that of Saint Christopher, the patron saint of children who carries them to safety on his shoulders. As the last
child he lifts up becomes so heavy that Tiffauges sinks beneath
his weight into the mud and mire which are the natural elements
from which the ogre, like the Nazi regime, ought never to have
emerged, the novel becomes a reminder of where the roots of
the Nazi movement really were. In so far as it was the last jacquerie,
it was the product less of Prussian militarism than of the primitive forces embedded in the mountains of Southern Germany.

The interest of Tournier's exploitation of the myth of the Erl
King is nevertheless not limited to its applicability to German
politics. As is shown by the autobiographical essays collected in
the volume called *Le Vent Paraclet*, Tournier is one of the best as
well as the most sceptical observers of his own country, and *The
Erl King* is a work of literature which shows the twentieth-century
writer dealing with the concept of myth in the sense which the
word has when applied to the view of Ireland deconstructed and
satirised by Synge in *The Playboy of the Western World*. One of the
views about the German occupation of France during the Second
World War which attained mythical status in the years immediately after the liberation was that this occupation elicited a spontaneous reaction of horror and refusal by all members of the French
nation apart from a few self-interested politicians. What *The Erl
King* shows is that there were some people who managed, often

at a very humble level, to do quite well out of it. With one side of his character, the aspect which makes him a rather endearingly ineffectual member of the French working class, Abel Tiffauges becomes exactly that. It is a tribute to the ability of the more literate sections of French society to see their recent history in perspective that the publication of *Le Roi des Aulnes* provoked little of the controversy and attempts at censorship which greeted the appearance of *Ulysses* and *The Playboy of the Western World*.

6

Varieties of Realism III: Naturalism, Tragedy and the Unconscious

I

Popular literature and the role of the critic; some examples of realism: Truman Capote, In Cold Blood, *Tom Wolfe,* The Bonfire of the Vanities; *their link, if any, with Barthes; a whiff of tragedy and a difference in critical attention.*

If the novels of Danielle Steel, Barbara Cartland, Jilly Cooper or Barbara Taylor Bradford are discussed by literary critics, it is as objects for sociological analysis. The same is true of best-selling male authors such as Ian Fleming, Frederick Forsyth or Stephen King, and from this point of view the situation has not changed since the publication in 1932 of Q. D. Leavis's *Fiction and the Reading Public*, or Richard Hoggart's *The Uses of Literacy* in 1957. Since popular fiction is generally held not to ask the questions which authors such as Camus, Joyce, Proust or Thomas Mann raise in so interesting a form, this neglect is understandable. Literary criticism is appropriate as well as enjoyable when it forms part of an on-going dialogue about aesthetic, ethical, political or social values. It is almost a defining characteristic to say of fiction which is popular in the way that the novels of Barbara Cartland, Jilly Cooper or Danielle Steele are popular that it does not raise essentially contested concepts.

This is not, however, true of books belonging to the genre which Truman Capote wanted to establish as a serious new literary form: the Non-Fiction Novel. Although these books tend to become bestsellers, they raise the same kind of questions as the fiction which tends to reach a smaller audience, something especially true of the book which Truman Capote published in 1966 under the title *In Cold Blood*. It was as different as possible from his

128

earlier novels, such as the highly poetic *Other Voices, Other Rooms*, or the long short story *Breakfast at Tiffany's* whose adaptation to the cinema provided Audrey Hepburn with one of her best roles. *In Cold Blood* was the reconstruction, most of it from official records and interviews with the people concerned, of the particularly brutal murder, on the night of 15 November 1959, of Herbert William Clutter, his wife and two teenage children, by Richard Eugene Hickock and Perry Edward Smith. It describes all the events, from the day before the crime to the early morning of 15 April 1965, when after more than 2000 days in the condemned cell, Hickock and Smith were finally hanged. Its interest from a literary point of view, apart from the fact that once you start to read it you can't put it down, lies in the contribution which it makes to the peculiarly twentieth-century debate about the nature of realism.

One of the key notions in Barthes's critique of the notion of realism lies in what he calls *l'effet du réel*, a term whose meaning is best rendered as 'realistic effects'. When Dickens makes David Copper-field tell us about Mr Murdstone's 'shallow black eye', or the 'square-ness about the lower part of his face, and the dotted indication of the strong black beard he shaved close every day', he is not making his favourite character describe a real person. He is using a number of traditional descriptive techniques to introduce the reader as soon as possible to Mr Murdstone's cruel and sinister nature. When Truman Capote describes the healthy early morning breakfast of Herbert Clutter – 'an apple and a glass of milk were enough for him; because he touched neither coffee nor tea, he was accustomed to starting the day on a cold stomach' – and contrasts this with the 'three aspirin, cold root beer, and a chain of Pall Mall cigarettes' with which Perry Smith begins the day, he is talking about two men who did behave in exactly that way.[1] What they ate and drank really did correspond to the way they were.

Had *In Cold Blood* been a novel, the reader alert to Barthes's criticism of the artificial nature of supposedly realistic literature would have been fully justified in dismissing the details of Clutter's and Perry's diet as carefully coded examples invented specifically to illustrate one of the main themes in the book: the contrast between the stable, healthy, prosperous, hard-working, somewhat Puritanical life-style of the Clutters and the feckless, inadequate and unhealthy way in which Perry Smith and Eugene Hickock drifted and cheated their way through life. In Camus's 1942 long 'récit', *The Outsider*, Meursault notices that Raymond Pérez, the

pimp whose shady dealings play a major part in leading him to
end his life under the guillotine, has very hairy arms. These cause
Marie, Meursault's girlfriend, to make a faint gesture of disgust
when she sees Pérez getting ready to swim, so we are even more
certain that we were quite right to feel all along that Pérez has
been up to no good. But since there never was a real Pérez, it
was a detail that Camus invented to make us think precisely that.
When Harold Nye, one of the four FBI men helping the fourth-
generation Kansan Alvin Adams Dewey to investigate the Clutter murder, sees Perry Smith for the first time, he is fascinated
by the fact that although Perry is sitting in a chair, 'his legs were
so short that his feet, as small as a child's, couldn't quite make
the floor'.[2] As Balzac wrote on the frontispiece of *Le Père Goriot*,
'All is True'; except, this time, that it is. The oddly sinister detail
is not made up to prove a point. This is the way Perry was.

　　The facts in *In Cold Blood* are nevertheless carefully arranged
to tell a story. Even without the quotation from Villon on the
front page –

> Frères humains qui après nous vivez,
> N'ayez les cuers contre nous endurcis,
> Car, se pitié de nos povrez avez,
> Dieu en aura plus tost de vous mercis.

> (Men and brothers who live after us, harden not your hearts
> 　against us. For if you take pity on us poor wretches, God
> 　will be swifter to have mercy on you.)

– the events as narrated raise the whole question of whether or
not capital punishment is ever justified. The crime committed by
Smith and Hickock was stupid, cruel and pointless. But the fact
that they were stupid, cruel and pointless people is presented
throughout as only partially their fault. Like most criminals, they
were the victims of their background. Born into the Clutter family, they could have grown up into just as admirable a pair of
adolescents as the two Clutter children they murdered. This does
not excuse their crime, but it does raise the whole question of
how society should deal with its criminals. However invulnerable an author may make his story to the charge that it is not
realistic because he made it all up, he cannot – even if he wished
to do so, which Truman Capote clearly did not – disguise the
moral attitude which lies behind his narrative.

In Cold Blood is not the only example of the Non-Fiction Novel.
Solzhenitsyn pointed out in his preface to *The First Circle*, in 1968,
that what he was talking about really happened, and that the
names of the characters in his book were the names they had in
real life. As Thomas Kenneally said in the 'Author's Note' at the
beginning of his 1982 *Schindler's Ark*, he also had tried to 'avoid
all fiction . . . since fiction would debase the record' as well as to
'distinguish between reality and the myths likely to attach themselves to a man of Oskar's stature'.[3] The result was the totally
convincing account of how a man, who started off with no clearer
ambition than to use the Nazi system to make money, ended up
risking his own life to save Jews from the gas chamber. Kenneally's
contribution to what Truman Capote called 'the establishment of
a new literary form: the Non-Fiction Novel' has since been made
available to millions through the 1993 film *Schindler's List*, a more
faithful adaptation than Tom Wolfe's *The Bonfire of the Vanities*
enjoyed at the hands of Brian de Palma, Tom Hanks and Melanie
Griffiths in 1991.

Whereas Truman Capote began with fiction before turning to
the 'reportage' of *In Cold Blood*, Tom Wolfe began with journalism. It was only after he had described a wide variety of phenomena, including the attitude of fashionable lefties in *Radical Chic* –
a term he coined himself, and which is almost as useful a phrase
as 'Catch 22' – and the exploits and personality of the pilots who
flew the first space missions in *The Right Stuff*, in 1979, that he
turned his hand to fiction. *The Bonfire of the Vanities* is nevertheless only apparently an example of 'reportage' and of the 'Non-
Fiction Novel'. It even has a mistake in it, since the reference to
the gold-indexed bond, the Giscard, on which Sherman McCoy
hopes to make his biggest killing, is wrong.[4] This bond was issued when Giscard d'Estaing was finance minister during the
Presidency of Georges Pompidou (1969–74), not when he was
President himself (1974–81). It is agreeable to catch Tom Wolfe
out in this matter, since on everything else – shoes, shirts, cars,
food, wine, furniture, fireplaces, criminal proceedings, New York
politics, journalism, the habits of English exiles in New York, sex,
cigarettes – he is so obviously well-informed. Indeed, it is this
which led one of the critics, the syndicated columnist George F.
Will, to evoke the world of nineteenth-century naturalism by using the term 'slices of life' to describe his technique.

The Bonfire of the Vanities nevertheless differs from *In Cold Blood* by the fact that while the slices are all cut from a contemporary reality which Wolfe knows like the back of his hand, he had far more freedom than Truman Capote in choosing where to cut them from and how to serve them to the reader. Like John O'Hara's 1934 *Appointment in Samara*, a novel which it resembles by the knowledge which the reader has, from the beginning, that the hero is doomed, *The Bonfire of the Vanities* tells a story of how one small mistake ruins a whole life. Scott Fitzgerald commented of John O'Hara that he lived 'in a perpetual state of just having discovered that it is a lousy world', and the truth of his remark is born out by the fact that from the moment that Julian English, in *Appointment in Samara*, yields to the impulse which many other men have had, and throws a glass of whisky into the face of a man who is boring him to death, the reader knows that his fate is sealed. The same sense of doom invades the narrative from the moment that Sherman McCoy, in *The Bonfire of the Vanities*, is caught in the stream of traffic on an American freeway and can't make the turning he wants. The fates begin to close in upon him, and the rest of the novel depicts a descent into horror which seems at times as remorseless as the doom which overcomes Oedipus. In that respect, one of the questions raised by *The Bonfire of the Vanities* then becomes whether some novels can have a deeper realism about them, that of tragedy.

John O'Hara gives the tone for what is going to happen to Julian English by prefacing his novel with the traditional Arabic tale of the merchant who goes down into the market square and is frightened to see Death, who proceeds to make what looks like a threatening gesture to him. Thinking that Death is coming to get him at home, the merchant runs away to Samara, only to find Death waiting for him there. 'But why' he asks before he dies, 'did you warn me by this morning's threat?' 'That was no threat' replies Death, 'it was surprise. For I knew that I had, this evening, an appointment with you in Samara.' Sherman McCoy has no such supernatural premonition. Like Oedipus, he starts off with all the confidence of what he himself terms a 'Master of the Universe', looking forward to earning a million dollars a year on the bond market by the time he is 40. But when, accompanied by his mistress, he misses the Manhattan turning and finds himself in the Bronx, a series of events leads him to become what he himself terms a 'professional defendant', a man whose whole life is spent defending himself against some charge or other in a court of law.

The comparison with Oedipus is more appropriate than admirers of classical Greek tragedy might immediately admit. There is, admittedly, little nobility about Sherman McCoy. He is greedy, pompous, and a rather inefficient adulterer. But there is, to the modern eye, not much about Oedipus which is noble apart from his rank as King of Thebes. He does, it is true, solve the riddle of the Sphinx, rightly guessing that the animal which walks on four legs in the morning, two legs at midday and three legs in the evening is man. But Sherman, until his personal worries overtake him, is very good at guessing which way the bond market is going to move, which is a good deal more difficult than remembering that babies crawl and old men use a stick to walk with after they can no longer stand as upright as they did in the prime of life. Sherman may well be so flustered that he rings his own number when he is trying to get through to his mistress, and begins his downfall by getting his wife on the other end of the phone. But he is not prone to the violence which leads Oedipus to kill an old man in a quarrel about who has right of way. Both, however, are victims of *hubris,* Sherman in his vision of himself as Master of the Universe, Oedipus in his proclaimed conviction that he and he alone holds the key to the mystery of who murdered old Laios. And both men are punished in a way which seems, to the modern, agnostic reader, grossly out of proportion for what they have done.

It is always a surprise to be reminded that Sophocles's play was performed as part of a series of religious ceremonies. The Gods who decide, before Oedipus is even born, that he will kill his father and marry his mother, seem so gratuitously cruel that there can be no reason to worship them other than the superstitious terror which we all feel in the face of an ultimately unknowable universe. Sherman's downfall is not caused by the Gods, or even by the mysterious Oriental fates which intervene in the American Mid-West of the 1930s to decide the death of Julian English. If Sherman had not taken the wrong turning, nothing would have happened. If, after the incident with the two black boys who tried to hijack his car, he had followed his own instinct and gone to the police straight away, he would have had an awkward half hour explaining to his wife what he was doing in the car with Maria Ruskin. But he would have had little difficulty in proving self-defence, and thus avoiding the disaster which causes him, as he becomes conscious of how inescapable it is, to

wake up from a dream he couldn't remember, with his heart flailing
at his chest's wall, and realise that it is 'the drinker's hour, that
hour in the dead of night when drinkers and insomniacs suddenly wake up and know it's all over, this sleep dodge'.[5]

Again, if he had kept his nerve when detectives Martin and
Goldberg came round making a routine check on all Mercedes-
Benz with a number plate beginning RF, and calmly invited them
to glance at his undamaged vehicle, he would have been home
and dry. But he didn't, and it wasn't only lust that made him
agree with Maria not to report the incident to the police as soon
as it had happened. When the Mercedes hit Henry Lamb, Maria
was driving. And Sherman, at least at that stage in his life was
as much of a gentleman as Paul Pennyfeather in Evelyn Waugh's
1928 novel *Decline and Fall*. Because, as Margot Beste-Chetwynne's
son Peter remarks, 'You can't imagine Mamma in prison, can you?',
Paul accepts the sentence for the white-slaving trading which he,
poor innocent, had not even realised she was conducting. As elsewhere in twentieth-century literature, there is no reward for those
who attempt to practise the conventional virtues.

The place of the Gods, in the world of Sherman McCoy, is taken
by society, and more particularly New York. It is a more aggressive city than the Dublin of *Ulysses* or the London of *The Waste
Land* and it is its denizens, from the rabble-rousing Reverend Bacon
to the parasitic English journalist Peter Fallow, who bring about
his downfall. None of the few characters – Judge Kovitsky, the
Irish detectives Martin and Goldberg – who try to uphold some
semblance of decency and justice can do anything to help Sherman,
and the same criticism can be made of *The Bonfire of the Vanities*
as of the traditional realism of the nineteenth century: that the
author likes nobody, that the main character is too obviously
doomed from the outset, and that there are far too many bad
characters than good ones. What nevertheless sticks in the mind,
and is realistic in a way which is again reminiscent of certain
features of the tragic vision, is the disproportion between what
Sherman did and what happens to him. When you consider the
venial nature of his offence, it is as though he were one of the
flies killed for their sport by wanton boys. What most characterises the society described by Tom Wolfe is its injustice and inequality. In the way that Sherman McCoy is made to suffer, he
almost assumes one of the central roles of early tragedy, that of
scapegoat. The only difference lies in the fact that for all the ill-

luck which brings about his final downfall, his wounds also belong to the category which is most difficult to bear: the self-inflicted.

II

Barthes, Eliot, Wimzatt and Beardsley on the gap between the man who lives and the author who writes; an application of this to Albert Camus; the concept of unconscious realism; some disadvantages of awareness.

One of the many gaps which separate popular and learned taste lies in the contrast between the immense interest which readers take in the lives of writers, and the universal assumption among literary critics that there is a watertight compartment between the man who lives and the author who writes. This idea was expressed early in the century by T. S. Eliot when he wrote in 1922 in *Tradition and the Individual Talent* that

> Impressions and experiences which are important for the man may have no place in his poetry, and those which become important in his poetry may play quite a negligible part in the man, his personality.

The same idea was put forward more forcibly in 1946 by two American critics, Wimzatt and Beardsley, in an article called 'The Intentional Fallacy'. What they argued was that there was no way in which any statement which the author made about his text had any bearing on the meaning which this might have for the reader. In 1968, Roland Barthes was even more vigorous in his announcement of what he called 'The Death of the Author', and this approach to literature can be a very fruitful one. When Albert Camus wrote *The Outsider*, for example, he had a number of conscious intentions in mind: to depict, as he said when acknowledging the influence of Ernest Hemingway, a man with no apparent awareness of what was going on; to describe what Sartre recognised, as soon as the novel was published in 1942, the 'universe of the absurd man'; to show that a story could be written in French without using the traditional narrative tense of the past definite; and to provide, for readers from Northern Europe, an insight into what he saw as the superior life-style to be found on the shores of the Mediterranean.

What Camus also did, however, was something different and quite unintentional: he provided an insight into the attitude which the Algerian Frenchmen of his generation had towards the Arabs who were, theoretically at least, their fellow citizens. A theme which runs through Camus's work with such insistence that it is easy to agree with his description of it as an obsession is that of capital punishment. It dominates the political message of *The Plague*, where the great criticism against the totalitarian systems of both right and left is the use which they make of legalised murder, and in 1957, the year in which he became, after Kipling, the youngest writer to win the Nobel Prize for Literature, his *Réflexions sur la guillotine* appeared in the same volume as Arthur *Koestler's Reflections on Hanging*. Another of Camus's intentions in *The Outsider* was to show the inhumanity of the death penalty, and the means he chose was to present an amiable if slightly eccentric young man who was, as he himself put it, sentenced to have his head chopped off because he had not wept at his mother's funeral. Realising, however, that not even French bourgeois society is so steeped in sin as to do that, Camus had to make this hero, Meursault, commit an actual crime. The solution he came up with was to make him shoot an Arab. The fact that Meursault did so under the broiling heat of the midday sun had the additional advantage of underlining the ambivalence of nature, with the sun which has given him such pleasure also causing his downfall, and it is an indication of how powerfully Camus had expressed his conscious intentions that it was 13 years before any of the many critics who wrote about his work spotted the racialist implications of its plot and descriptive technique.[6]

This was partly because Camus had been, throughout his life, so consistently on the side of the angels. He was the son of an itinerant agricultural labourer who had been killed at the battle of the Marne, in August 1914, when Camus was barely a year old. The apartment which Camus then lived in with his widowed mother, his grandmother, his elder brother Lucien and a semi-literate uncle, had only three rooms, no electric light and no books. Camus nevertheless overcame this poverty, as well as the tuberculosis which almost killed him when he was 17, and became a journalist. He then immediately devoted his best efforts, in the Algeria of the 1930s, to trying to improve the living conditions of the native Arab population. This made him so unpopular with the French authorities in Algiers that he was unable, in 1940, to get a job, and was forced to come to Paris. He took part in the resistance movement, and in the newly liberated France of 1944 his editorials in *Combat* expressed all the hopes born of the struggle against fascism. He steadfastly refused to accept any compromise with Franco's Spain, and resigned from UNESCO in 1952 when Spain was admitted as a member. In 1947, he used his position in the French press and reputation in the literary world to draw the attention of the French government to the tragedy brewing in Algeria, but without success. In his long philosophical essay *L'Homme révolté* (*The Rebel*) he criticised Soviet Communism when it was very unusual for a man of the left in France to do so, and was violently attacked by Sartre and others for expressing such an unfashionable attitude. If ever there was a man whose generous humanism ought to have shone through everything he wrote, it was Albert Camus.

When, however, both *The Plague* and *The Outsider* are looked at in the context of the portrait they provide of French North Africa, the impression which they give is rather different. In the opening pages of *The Plague*, the journalist Rambert is very concerned about the living conditions of the Arabs in Oran, and wishes to use his newspaper to condemn them completely. However, after the conversation in which he explains this ambition, the Arabs disappear completely. None is reported as falling ill or as taking part in the struggle against the plague. Oran becomes, instead, not a town with a serious problem of inequality between the races, but a slightly exotic background for a series of Eurocentric debates about the nature of man's struggle against the injustice of God and the limitations to be placed on the use of violence in politics. Similarly, in *The Outsider*, all the Europeans have names, and their physical appearance is described in considerable detail. The Arabs, in contrast, are an anonymous mass, poor players with walk-on parts in a drama which is important only in so far as it affects the Europeans involved.

Had Camus not yielded to the very French habit of giving interviews and writing prefaces to explain the meaning of his works, *The Outsider* would not have been vulnerable to the criticism of being a text that reveals an unconscious racialism on the part of Camus himself. The fact of being told in the first person would have made it, like James Hogg's *Portrait of a Justified Sinner*, an essentially ironic first-person narrative whose realism was heightened by the narrator's total lack of awareness of the kind of person he really was. This, Camus could have been interpreted as saying, is how young Frenchmen see the world if they have been brought up, as Meursault was, in a society in which a *de facto* apartheid leads Europeans to see themselves as fully human and Arabs as only partly so. But since Camus insisted, in his 1955 preface to the novel, that Meursault was a martyr to truth and 'the only Christ whom we deserve', it is hard to maintain that he intended his hero to be seen in so critical a light. On the contrary, what Camus provided in *The Outsider* – and, to a lesser extent, *The Plague* – was a portrait of himself which was unconsciously realistic in the sense of revealing an aspect of his personality which he did not even know existed.

It is only because of the contrast which it offers between what Camus was like as a man and some of the unconscious attitudes which reveal themselves in his work as an imaginative writer that the charge of racialism has any bearing on the literary value of *The Outsider* or *The Plague*. The great argument in favour of the approach to literature recommended by Barthes, Eliot, Wimzatt and Beardsley is that it clears the ground, and enables us to make a clear distinction between the anecdotal value of literary biographies, which is high, and their relevance to the aesthetic or intellectual merit of the works under discussion, which is generally fairly low. So long as a clear distinction is maintained between Camus the committed humanist and Camus the creative writer, *The Outsider* gains from the highly realistic portrayal which it offers of how Europeans viewed the world in a colonial context. It is an example of a very interesting type of realism – quite different from the kind practised by Truman Capote or Tom Wolfe – the type produced when the author does not quite know what he is doing.

Had Camus been conscious of the extent to which his vision of the realities of Algerian life was as partial as the vision of rural Ireland called into question by Synge in *The Playboy of the Western World*, his fiction would have been very different. It would not, however, necessarily have been better. Indeed, it might not even have been written at all. One potential disadvantage of the concept of intertextuality, as of Barthes's vision of fiction as the exploitation of a number of codes, is that it inhibits spontaneity. The concluding line in Philip Larkin's poem 'MCMXIV', evoking the England of before the outbreak of the First World War – 'Never such innocence again' – can apply equally well to the process of literary creation. The opening volume of *Remembrance of Things Past* would have been a very different book if Proust had read Freud; so, too would *Sons and Lovers* if D. H. Lawrence had had the same experience. It is scarcely believable that his creation of Gertrude Morel would have made her quite so vulnerable to the charge of being a Jocasta figure if Lawrence had realised what a feast he risked offering to the Freudians.

III

Realism and naturalism. The examples of Thomas Mann and Steinbeck.

An attempt was sometimes made in nineteenth-century literary theory to distinguish between realism and naturalism. While the former was the accurate, supposedly neutral and generally disillusioned account of ordinary life, especially as experienced by people who did not have much money, naturalism used the same technique in order to prove the essentially philosophical view that human beings were the products of their heredity and environment. 'Vice and virtue' claimed the nineteenth-century critic Hippolyte Taine in 1863 in his *Histoire de la littérature anglaise*, are products like 'sulphuric acid or sugar', and should be studied with the same recognition of their inevitability and moral neutrality. The idea that human beings have no control over what happens to them is fundamental to Zola's depiction of what happens to the various members of the Rougon-Macquart family, and inspired a number of novels written in English in the latter part of the nineteenth century. Enough of the idea was still around in the early years of the twentieth century to be visible in the novels of Sinclair Lewis, and to inspire one of the few works of fiction to use nineteenth-century determinism in a Freudian context – Erskine Caldwell's 1930 novel, *Poor Fool*.

In German literature, Thomas Mann's *Buddenbrooks* (1901) shows an almost Zola-like obsession with the inevitability of physical decay, as the energy of the founders of the family gradually gives way to a sickly and less vigorous race. The process is hastened by the marriage of Thomas Buddenbrook to the beautiful and artistic Gerda, with Mann's typically *fin-de-siècle* belief in the ultimately destructive nature of the aesthetic impulse already playing a major role in his first novel. This recurs in a different form in Mann's best-known shorter novel, *Death in Venice*, with the austerity which characterised Ashenbach's former life being so undermined by the mysterious beauty of the boy Tadzio that he stays by the Adriatic long enough to catch the plague and die. The dark forces which he had so long sought to repress in himself, and which included a rigorously suppressed tendency towards homosexuality, thus triumph over the Northern Protestant work ethic, and the publication of the story in 1913 seemed to prefigure in an indirect and mysterious way the collapse of the whole culture of which Ashenbach, like Mann himself, was so eminent and conscious a representative.

The sense of imminent doom which characterises so much of Mann's work does not, however, take the scientific turn which it did in Zola or Maupassant. Like other European writers, and especially André Malraux, Mann was obsessed by the idea that the whole of Western civilisation was entering into a phase of final collapse, and he recognised the truth of the remark which Paul Valéry made in 1920, in the immediate aftermath of the First World War:

Nous autres civilisations, nous savons que nous sommes mortelles (What characterises our civilisation is that it knows it is mortal).

The idea of the inevitable breakdown of civilisation runs through the whole of *The Magic Mountain*, and reflects the impact which Oswald Spengler's long essay, published in two parts, in 1918 and 1923, under the title *Untergang des Abendlandes* (1923 and 1926, *The Decline of the West*), had on intellectuals in the interwar years and after 1945.

Spengler's thesis was that all civilisations inevitably decline in accordance with a predetermined and predictable 'historical destiny', and that there was no reason to see our own civilisation as in any way immune. The laws of history were as immutable and irresistible as those of physics and chemistry, and there was no way of preventing what Spengler depicted as an age of soulless, expansionist Caesarism from destroying both the Christian and the humanist tradition. This theory, like its adaptation by the English historian Arnold Toynbee, seemed increasingly plausible as dictatorships were established in Russia in 1917, Italy in 1922, Portugal in the mid 1930s under Salazar, Germany in 1933 and Spain on 1 April 1939 with the victory of Franco in the Spanish civil war. It provided a gloomy and possibly influential back-drop for the literature of the mid-century, though not in a way which confirms the thesis that literature is a reflection of the social and political atmosphere in which it is written. The much more optimistic thesis put forward by Francis Fukayama in his 1989 essay, *The End of History*, may well express a justified delight at the ability shown by democratic liberalism to beat off the twin challenges of Fascism and Communism. But neither Fukayama's thesis nor the victory of the West in the Cold War seems likely to inspire the imaginative authors of the West to write more cheerful books.

The setting of the action of *The Magic Mountain* in a sanatori-um emphasises the obsession with physical illness that recurs so frequently in Mann's work. Only in the comic novel, *The Confessions of Felix Krull*, whose appearance in 1954 marked a new note in Mann's work, is this obsession treated ironically, and the history of Germany during Mann's lifetime offered little cause for laughter. Mann's first novel after the great catastrophe of 1939–45, *Doktor Faustus*, published in 1947, was in this respect as in others a symbolic indictment of what had just happened. When the artist Adrian Leverkuhn makes his pact with the Devil in order to cure himself of the sterility which is preventing him from embarking on any new creations, it brings about a series of catas-trophes which mirror what happened to Germany when it thought it had found a solution to the problem of its decline in the vig-our of the Nazi party.

The way Mann's preoccupation with decline and decay changes in the course of his career reads at times like a history of the concept of fate as mirrored in the writings of twentieth-century authors. The view of the nineteenth century, according to which man might be held prisoner by his physiological temperament, but could still find liberation through science, depended upon a vision of history as being ultimately providential. As the twen-tieth century progressed – or, as it seemed in the middle years, declined – faith in any kind of progress seemed increasingly im-possible, and was replaced by a sense of impending catastrophe. This showed itself in American as well as in European literature with Faulkner's *Sanctuary* and *Light in August* (1935) being just as doom-laden as Steinbeck's 1937 short story *Of Mice and Men*. If Lennie is doomed to murder Curley's wife, and to escape the gallows only by being shot by his friend George, the fault lies in a predestination that is inscribed in the ways of a hostile universe in a way which is beyond human comprehension. There is, Steinbeck is saying, something in the world itself which will always prevent human beings from achieving their dreams, and there is a metaphysical pessimism in this aspect of his work which strikes a very different note from the pagan cheerfulness informing his account of life in *Cannery Row* in 1945.

In *Of Mice and Men*, it is not even society which is at fault, as it is in *The Grapes of Wrath*, where the Joad family is the victim of economic laws which only appear to be immutable. For although the danger of the system which sends the Joads on their disastrous trek to California had been denounced as early as 1612 by the British lawyer Sir Edward Coke, when he wrote in *The Case of Sutton's Hospital* that: 'Corporations cannot commit treason, nor be outlawed nor excommmunicated, for they have no souls' the whole point of Steinbeck's novel was, at least in theory, to show that there was nothing inevitable about the working out of economic laws. Business may be, as the text says, 'a curious ritualized thievery', and the banks 'machines and masters all at the same time'. Indeed, the elaboration of this idea in an image which replaces religion by biology shows how differently men think in a non-religious age. The banks, one of his friends tells Tom Joad, 'breathe profits; they eat the interest on money. If they don't get it, they die, the way you die without air, without side-meat.'[7] But although the Joads, like thousands of other families, are reduced to penury by a system in which no individual can be held responsible for what happens, Steinbeck's novel rejects the idea that this is the result of some kind of metaphysical fatality over which men have no control. The various episodes in which the Joads come into contact with representatives of the Federal Government, and thus with the philosophy of Roosevelt's New Deal, suggest precisely the opposite, and the novel is naturalistic only in the sense of providing a direct account of experience, with no holds barred. Although the novel ends with the Joads reduced to even greater penury than when they left their farm in the dust bowl of Oklahoma for the promised paradise of California, there is the feeling that they will nevertheless survive, and that the system is still amenable to improvement. In so far as *The Bonfire of the Vanities* is as clearly a book about the 1980s as *The Grapes of Wrath* is about the 1930s, any reply to the question as to whether or not the improvement has taken place is bound to be a political one. Poverty and injustice abound in the world of *The Bonfire of the Vanities*. Indeed, that is one of the central themes in the book. But they are the poverty and injustice of a society which is on the move. The world of *The Grapes of Wrath* was one where everything, except for the flow of migrants and growth of tyranny, was slowing down.

7

Moral Certainties and the Problem of Determinism: The Example of the Literature of Cowardice

I

The absolute condemnation of cowardice from the nineteenth century onwards compared to the attitude of earlier periods; a possible parallel between Sartre and Kipling; W. H. Sheldon's concept of physiological determinism; Falstaff and the Good Soldier Svejk; Somerset Maugham, Ernest Hemingway and the notion of indirect realism.

The existence in the twentieth century of a number of plays, novels and short stories about cowardice has the advantage of providing specific examples of just how fully the ethical standards of one age can differ from those of another. Although no culture has treated cowardice as a virtue, it is rare before the nineteenth century to find it presented with the same horror which leads Thomas Hughes to describe the hero of *Tom Brown's Schooldays*, in 1857, as seeing it as 'the incarnation of all sins'. In the twentieth century, the attitude of agnostic or atheistic writers as different from one another in other ways as Sartre, Somerset Maugham, Brecht and Ernest Hemingway did nothing to attenuate the condemnation already there in the empire-building, muscular Christianity of Hughes. If there are excuses for cowardice, they are mentioned by twentieth-century writers only in order to be dismissed.

Although the human adventure begins, in the Judeo-Christian tradition, with a typical example of male cowardice – Genesis, 3:12: 'the woman thou gavest to be with me,/she gave me of the

144

tree and I did eat' – the Old Testament makes it very clear that Adam is punished not for cowardice but for disobedience. In the moral teaching of Christianity itself, cowardice is not one of the seven deadly sins, and Dante does not regard it as a sufficiently serious offence for him to reserve a place for cowards in any circle of his Inferno. For him, the worst possible offence is treachery to one's lord and master, a view which causes the reader of Shakespeare's *Julius Caesar* some surprise when he finds the noblest Roman of them all, Brutus, chained upside down and side by side with Cassius, suffering the same torments as Judas Iscariot in the very depths of the ninth circle. Cowards, in contrast, are merely in Purgatory, where their fate is to be stung by bees and – appropriately enough – to be kept perpetually running.

Nor was the situation very different in pagan times. Not even in Sparta was cowardice punished by the death penalty, and the heroes of the *Iliad* run away with a fine disregard for what people might think of them. When, in Book XVI, Hector prepares to flee, he is taunted by Glaucus with the words that 'your splendid reputation hides a coward after all', but he has his answer all ready. We are all, he says, 'puppets in the hands of aegis-bearing Zeus, who can make a brave man run away and lose a battle, but the next day will spur him on'. It is not an excuse that anyone can imagine such eminently twentieth-century fictional heroes as Bulldog Drummond, Simon Templar or James Bond having to make, or which would have satisfied Jean-Paul Sartre. In his early philosophy, Sartre insists that since we are always free, we are always responsible for our actions, and can never excuse any lapse into cowardice which leads us to betray our principles, our friends or ourselves. This is what happens to the most unattractive character in Sartre's most famous play, the 1944 *Huis Clos* (*In Camera*), a journalist and pacifist called Garcin. He has based the whole of his life on the idea that he would, when the chips were down, be a brave man and stick defiantly to his principles. But when war breaks out, he tries to run away and is shot. Sartre has no time for the equivalent of Hector's bland acceptance of the idea that the Gods can sometimes make a man into a coward without depriving him of all future claim to manhood. When Garcin pleads as an excuse for his conduct a 'temporary physical weakness' – something which, in the world of the *Iliad*, the Gods might visit upon anyone – one of his companions in hell, the sceptically-minded Lesbian, Inès, laughs the idea out of court.

As will be seen in Chapter 11, Brecht takes a similarly austere view of the cowardice which leads Galileo to betray his sacred trust as the founding father of modern science, and it may well be that the harshness of his judgement, like that of Somerset Maugham in the 1931 story 'The Door of Opportunity' or of Ernest Hemingway, in *The Short Happy Life of Francis Macomber*, reflects a change in attitudes which can be linked to the fact that we are living in an almost wholly secular age. A central feature of traditional Christianity was the doctrine of forgiveness. However badly we acted, all was not lost, since God, whose mercy was infinite, would pardon and absolve us for all our sins. Now that God is dead, in the sense of having disappeared as an object of real belief, there is no one left to forgive us except our fellow men. And even if they show a charity to which experience teaches us that they are normally little inclined, this is not a source of any great comfort. As Clamence, the narrator in Camus's 1956 *novella*, *The Fall*, remarked, 'they may well forgive. But they will not forget'.

Like Kipling, Sartre expects men to have the willpower to stand up against the weakness of their bodies. Even when we are being tortured, he argues, we never lose our freedom, since it is still we and we alone who decide when the moment has come when we can bear the pain no longer. It is very much what Kipling preaches in *If* when he writes that

> If you can keep your heart and nerve and sinew
> To serve your turn long after they are gone
> And so hold on, till there is nothing in you
> Except the Will that says to you: 'Hold on'.

One of the criticisms made of Sartre's philosophy is that he accepts as absolute the Cartesian separation between body and mind. This leads him to argue that since the mind is a pure and spontaneous spirit, nothing physical can affect it, and this is clearly a view open to a number of objections. But although Brecht's treatment of cowardice takes more obvious account of Galileo's physical constitution, so much so that *The Life of Galileo* seems at times to be as much about physiology as about physics, it is to reject any suggestion that Galileo's physique provided an excuse for his cowardice in yielding to the Inquisition. If, like Maugham and Hemingway, Brecht almost gives the impression of having read the work of the American physiologist W. H. Sheldon before settling down to write his play, it is to reject any use of Sheldon's ideas. However much we may be influenced by our physiological make-up, this can never provide an excuse for a man's failure to stand up for what he thinks is right.

There is, significantly enough, only one woman coward in twentieth-century literature: the young wife Sandy in Albee's *Who's Afraid of Virginia Woolf?* Women, as Kipling maintained in *The Female of the Species*, can be relied upon to be braver than men, as well as more cruel, because it is upon their readiness to stand the pangs of childbirth that the survival of the race depends.

In Sheldon's view, all human beings are made up of a combination of three basic physical types: the mesomorph, with soft, ample flesh, and a large gut; the endomorph, with solid muscles and strong bones; and the ectomorph, with thin, light bones, a smallish gut and nerves very close to the skin. Each physiological type is associated with certain psychological characteristics. The typical endomorph, someone like the fictional Mark Antony, Bulldog Drummond, Dmitri Karamazov, Rawden Crawley or Roderick Spode – or like the Henry Cooper of the boxing ring or the Billy Beaumont of the rugby football field – is totally at home in the world of masculine aggression. The ectomorph, in contrast, is not keen on physical contact, and is relatively indifferent to the pleasures of the table. In real life, he is like Shelley or Aldous Huxley, while his models in imaginative literature would include the Augustus of *Antony and Cleopatra*, Ivan or Alyosha Karamazov, and traditionally – if you ignore Gertrude's ungenerous remark about his being 'fat and scant of breath' – Hamlet. While the endomorph is quite happy to fight his way through life, and the ectomorph excels at making himself unhappy with his own thoughts, the mesomorph – Falstaff, Billy Bunter, Brecht's Galileo, Maupassant's Walter Schnaff, the Good Soldier Sjevk – has the characteristics of what Sheldon calls the viscerotonic. He is the man who – like Brecht with his goose, Falstaff with his sack and Billy Bunter with his cream buns – finds consolation for the problems of life in food. He is too fond of his physical comforts to be very keen on thinking, and he has even less enthusiasm for fighting.

Imaginative writers did not wait for Sheldon to point out the relationship between physical traits and psychological constitution. It was the fat Falstaff, the 'great tub of lard', who ran 'bellowing like a calf' at Gad's Hill, and whom Shakespeare made dismiss as meaningless the concept of honour in *Henry IV, Part 1*. But his cowardice does not seem to have been regarded as a very serious fault either by Shakespeare's audience or, if legend is to be believed, by Queen Elizabeth herself, at whose prompting Shakespeare is said to have brought the fat buffoon back to life in *The Merry Wives of Windsor*. Even nowadays, his statue stands with those of Hamlet, Lady Macbeth and Prince Hal as one of the four most famous Shakespearean heroes in the garden at Stratford.

The other model coward in world literature, the eponymous hero in Jaroslav Hasek's *The Good Soldier Svejk and his Fortunes in the First World War* (1920), is also a fat man, though his reluctance to fight is based on reasons which are different from those of Falstaff. While it does matter to Falstaff that Henry Percy's rebellion is defeated, even if he personally makes no contribution to the victory, Sjevk takes the view that the First World War is such a stupid affair, and the Austro-Hungarian empire so absurd an organisation, that he is fully justified in devoting the whole of his efforts to keeping away from the battlefield. There is a fair chance that Kafka, who knew the same society from close to, and may have taken its bureaucracy as a model for what happens in *The Trial* and *The Castle*, would have agreed with him.

There is an obvious contrast here with Brecht, as well as an equally clear instance of how political opinions can influence moral judgements. As a Marxist, Brecht had the same disapproval of the 'cowards that flinch' as the author of *The Red Flag*, and as the equally left-wing Sartre. Their weakness meant that they would let down the Cause just as easily as the traitors that sneer. Hemingway, who disliked cowards even more, had a more individualistic ethic, and one with which Somerset Maugham would probably have agreed. Courage, wrote Hemingway, was

> a matter of dignity and pride. A coward said that this pride was of no importance. Perhaps it was. But it was of great importance to whoever had it.[1]

In a world in which there is no God, and where history has no purpose, the only value is that of the self-esteem which a man can feel at what he himself has achieved. Cowardice, above all else, is the fault which makes any kind of achievement impossible, whether in response to the challenges of nature or in our relationships with our fellow men.

Together with their strong disapproval of cowardice, Hemingway and Maugham nevertheless share with Brecht, as they share with Shakespeare, an instinctive feeling that there is something to be said for Sheldon's view that the way we behave reflects the way our body works. It is not that their cowards are necessarily fat men, though it is perhaps significant that Pablo, the revolutionary who loses his nerve in Hemingway's 1940 novel about the Spanish civil war, *For Whom the Bell Tolls*, should be going physically to seed. What is more striking is that both Alban Torel, the central male character in Maugham's short story 'The Door of Opportunity', and Hemingway's Francis Macomber, are what Sheldon calls ectomorphs. Alban has 'a fine head, set on a rather long neck, with a somewhat prominent Adam's apple',[2] is not good at football, but can make the big, beefy men whose physique fits them admirably for contact sports look very silly on the tennis court. Francis Macomber is of a very similar type 'well built if you did not mind the length of bone, dark, his hair cropped like an oarsman, rather thin-lipped and was considered handsome',[3] and is very good at what Hemingway calls 'court games', presumably squash, rackets, tennis or badminton, where you do not have to risk hurting yourself by deliberately barging into your opponent or having him barge into you. Significantly enough, however, neither Maugham nor Hemingway makes these points about their heroes in order to invite the reader to think of them more sympathetically. Like Brecht, who insists upon Galileo's corpulence only to depict him, at the end of the play, as seeking the same comfort in a roast goose that Billy Bunter found in a cream bun, Hemingway and Maugham acknowledge that some men may have a physiological tendency to behave as cowards. But both Hemingway and Maugham are as reluctant as Sartre to accept the plea that the kind of body we have prevents us from acting courageously. In the totally non-Christian world in which Sartre, Brecht, Hemingway and Maugham are all writing, there is no excuse for failure. If a man is not the master of his fate and the captain of his soul, it is his own fault. Just as there is no God to whom he can turn for forgiveness, so there are no forces which he can invoke as being out of control.

Since both Torel and Macomber show the white feather, critics who think that writers describe their characters in a particular way because they have noticed how real people behave, and who are sympathetic to the kind of excuses provided by determinism, will praise Maugham and Hemingway for their powers of observation. Structuralists, who see literature as rhetoric, will be more likely to argue that both authors are exploiting a set of fictional codes, using ready-made conventions which interpret thin bones – or fat stomachs, in the case of Falstaff or Brecht's Galileo – as a sign of a tendency to shirk physical danger, just as conservatively minded semiologists see long hair as expressing moral turpitude as well as an open sympathy for the left. Although Hemingway's and Maugham's stories are good examples of how you can use a specific text to understand the critics who base their approach on semiology, both go further than this. Each illustrates the way that the unconscious presuppositions of authors tell us something important about their society, and perhaps about themselves, which they did not immediately have in mind when composing their text.

II

'The Door of Opportunity' *and the ethic of Bloomsbury; its contrast with that of the Raj; a possible autobiographical reading of the story.*

There is no doubt about the basic meaning of Somerset Maugham's 1933 short story, 'The Door of Opportunity'. Alban Torel is a District Officer in what were then known as the Federated Malay States, and therefore responsible for keeping order in his area of the Raj. One lunchtime, news arrives of a riot that has broken out in a nearby plantation. The Chinese coolies have killed the manager, Prynne, and are setting fire to the buildings. But although it is clearly Alban's duty to intervene, he refuses to do so, arguing that with only eight native policemen and one sergeant, he can do nothing. He therefore sends down river to Port Wallace for reinforcements, and waits a week for their arrival. When they come, he goes with them to quell the riot, only to discover that the job was done on the day after it had taken place. A neighbouring Dutchman, Van Hasseldt, had simply walked in, shot the ringleader, and put the rest of the rebels to flight.

Had Alban pushed the door of opportunity, which proverbially swings open only once, he would not simply have done his duty. He would have proved that his value system, which was that of a man who loved art, music, literature and ideas, did not preclude effective action in the ordinary world. But as it is, as his wife Anne, tells him, he has confirmed all the prejudices which the British ruling class, especially in the colonial service, had about highbrows and intellectuals:

> We called them Philistines. We despised them and we had the right to despise them. Our justification was that we were better and nobler and wiser and braver than they were. When the crisis came, you slunk away like a whipped cur with his tail between his legs. You of all people hadn't the right to be a coward. They despise *us* now and they have the right to despise us. Us and all we stood for. Now they can say that art and beauty are all rot; when it comes to a pinch, people like us always let you down.[4]

There are a number of reasons for thinking that Anne – who would undoubtedly have done the right thing if she had been in her husband's place – is expressing Maugham's own opinion. A minor one is that Maugham's years at King's School, Canterbury, were sufficiently unhappy for him to try to make himself acceptable in after life to the bloods who had bullied him when he was at school by putting forward an exaggerated version of what he saw as their ethos. Another possible explanation lies in one of the criticisms most frequently levelled against him: that he never developed a consistent set of values of his own, that as Noel Coward said, he had one illusion about people. He thought they were no good. This led him to be particularly suspicious about those who, like Alban, might let down the literary and intellectual values which he himself shared. But the most important reason for the value system of 'The Door of Opportunity' is summarised in George Orwell's remark that English intellectuals, in the interwar years, 'sniggered at the Union Jack and regarded physical courage as barbarous'.[5] Maugham's target audience lay essentially among people who were very firm in their rejection of this view. What 'The Door of Opportunity' told them was that he had no time for attitudes which put the Raj in danger.

  Orwell's remark thus places 'The Door of Opportunity' very firmly in a specific historical context, and one with which Maugham was extremely familiar. Alban was very much one of those who shared the values of the Bloomsbury group, whose attitude Maynard Keynes summarised in his essay 'My Early Beliefs' when he wrote that nothing mattered except states of mind not associated with action or achievement. They consisted in timeless, passionless, states of contemplation and communion, largely unattached to before or after.[6]

The interest of 'The Door of Opportunity', as a short story which catches a particular historical mood, lies in the contribution which it makes to what was, at the time, a peculiarly English debate. The insistence in the story on Alban's slightness of build is not intended as mitigating circumstances. It was, Maugham implies, his responsibility to overcome what may have been a tendency to cowardice, and thus to vindicate both his values and himself.

Although Maugham may well have had more than an inkling of the light which 'The Door of Opportunity' shed on how attitudes to cowardice had changed since classical times – in the *Iliad*, Helen is not at all put off by the fact that Paris has just run away, and makes love to him quite passionately after one occasion when he has shown the white feather[7] – it is extremely unlikely that he would have seen how applicable the anecdote in this story might have been to his own conduct. Maugham was widely known to be a homosexual, and is said to have laid himself open to an unkind witticism by the excuse which he once gave for leaving a dinner party early. For when he said 'I must go now, or I shall lose my youth', his hostess replied: 'Oh, Mr Maugham you should have brought him with you. We should all have been delighted.'

Had Maugham agreed to give the very small support which was asked of him during the 1950s campaign for a change in the laws forbidding homosexuality, he might well have found, like an Alban Torel who had dared to go and quell the riot by himself, that the rewards were considerable and the risks very slight. If Alban had shown himself capable of acting with the courage required of a British colonial administrator, his undoubted intelligence would have enabled him to rise very rapidly, and even become Governor. Anne would have then been able to make the official residence at Port Wallace (= Kuala Lumpur) an anticipation of Jackie Kennedy's White House, and highbrow values would have been vindicated. Similarly, had Maugham publicly stated that he himself was a homosexual, and therefore supported the campaign led by Ludovic Kennedy, what he saw as the great injustice of the relatively low esteem in which his novels and short stories were held in fashionable literary circles could well have disappeared overnight.

III

The Short Happy Life of Francis Macomber *as the opportunity for a Barthesian* lecture plurielle: *it can, in other words, be interpreted in a number of different ways.*

The Barthesian idea of the Death of the Author seems particularly inappropriate when applied to Ernest Hemingway. His interest in killing, as well as in drink and sex, is visible throughout his work, and he was not averse to making it clear to his friends that his life had been as full of violence as his books. But his remark in 1950, in a letter to Albert Mizener, that he had been 'wounded 22 times and killed 122 sures beside the possibles'[8] does not give the impression of a man at ease with himself. The genuinely brave are as modest about their achievements as the really rich are reluctant to talk about their money, and Hemingway's suicide at the age of 63 suggests an obsession with the fear of losing his physical powers which goes beyond the norm. The attitude adopted towards cowardice in *The Short Happy Life of Francis Macomber* is potentially as severe as anything in Sartre or Maugham, and heightens the temptation to see this story, like 'The Door of Opportunity', as a piece of unconscious as well as conscious autobiography, as well as another and different type of realism: while talking about the problems of one individual, it has the indirect and apparently accidental effect of telling you something of wider interest about the society in which that individual lives.

For like 'The Door of Opportunity', *The Short Happy Life of Francis Macomber* shows Europeans in a non-European setting, and offers a comparable analysis of how European and American males used to think it was natural for them to behave. Francis Macomber, a rich American, accompanied by his wife Margo, is big-game hunting in Africa, and the story begins with the tense atmosphere created by the fact that he has just shown himself 'very publicly' to be a coward by running away from a lion. He has been saved by the firepower carried by the white hunter, an

Englishman called Wilson, who blows the lion's head off with a
.505 Gibbs that he describes himself as a 'damned cannon'. For
all her beauty, now just beginning to fade, Margo Macomber is
less kind to poltroons than Helen of Troy. She avenges herself
for the humiliation inflicted on her by her husband's display of
cowardice by spending the night with Wilson.

On the following morning, Macomber and Wilson go out to
shoot buffalo. The text hints that if he successfully kills one of
them, he will have obtained the right score of dead animals to be
seen as a big-game hunter, and he is soon caught up in the thrill
of the chase. When he shoots but only wounds a bull buffalo,
Margo announces, 'full of anticipation' that it is going to be 'just
like the lion'. Macomber disagrees. For the first time in his life,
he is totally without fear. It is the most exhilarating feeling he
has ever known, and Wilson, a man of experience who has no
reason to look kindly on him, recognises that he has indeed
changed. Although Hemingway does not say so specifically, it is
clear that this is what Macomber has been looking for all his life,
putting himself through a series of experiences to try to prove
that the cowardice which he feels within himself is only an illusion, and that he really is a brave man.

As Macomber goes into the undergrowth to finish off the
wounded buffalo, his heart is pounding and his mouth is dry,
but this is with 'excitement, not fear'. Suddenly, the buffalo charges,
Macomber faces him, shooting and aiming carefully, totally free
of the terror which had made him flee from the lion. He shoots
again,

> with the buffalo's huge bulk almost on him and his rifle al-
> most level with his oncoming head, nose out, and he could see
> the little wicked eyes and the head started to lower and he felt
> a sudden white-hot, blinding flash explode inside his head and
> that was all he felt.

What has happened is that his wife has shot him, and her motives for doing so give the story an ambiguity and a quality which
make it much more than a very moving study of courage and
cowardice.

As its title indicates, *The Short Happy Life of Francis Macomber* is
primarily about the idea that some men can be really happy only
when they are totally free from fear. Since this happens only once

to Macomber, who is immediately killed, the reader's curiosity is moved from reflecting on the brevity of his one moment of real happiness to thinking about the reasons for his death. Was it an accident, in that Margo was aiming at the buffalo and missed? Or did she do it deliberately, managing to hit a small target at a range of about 30 yards with a skill unsuggested by any earlier clues in the story? And if she did do it on purpose, why? Was she afraid that the husband whom she had cuckolded when he had shown himself a coward might find some way of punishing her now that he had found his courage? Might he divorce her for adultery, leaving her to fend for herself in a world where she would no longer have his money and in which her beauty would be a less valuable asset than it was in the past? Or are there more complex reasons, which show her to have been, in a curious way, a better person than the other events in the story suggest?

As the question which Wilson asks her shows – 'Why didn't you poison him? That's what they do in England' – he thinks she did it deliberately, and is only sorry that she did not have the respect for appearances which characterises life among the English upper class. But the reader is not required to see Wilson as a privileged witness. He has clearly served in the British army in the 1914–18 war, and his 'flat, blue, machine-gunner's eyes' inevitably evoke the slaughter in the trenches. His Gibbs .505 enables him to avoid any real danger to himself, and his earlier action in saving Macomber from the lion was just part of his job. When Margo follows up her remark that he 'really is very impressive killing people' with the question 'you kill anything, don't you?' she could well be talking about marriages as well as lions.

The remark which Hemingway made to an interviewer in 1953 is a perfect example of the dangers of thinking that what the author wanted to do, or said he wanted to do, is the ultimate authority for deciding on the meaning of a work of literature. 'Francis's wife hates him because he's a coward', Hemingway said, adding that 'when he gets his guts back she fears him so much that she has to kill him – shoots him in the back of the neck'.[9] It is an interpretation underwritten by three American male critics, Edmund Wilson, Charles Poore and Theodore Barnack, with Barnack writing that 'At the end of the story, when Macomber recovers his courage (and manliness) Mrs Macomber shoots him rather than lose her dominating role'.[10]

If this is how educated, literate Americans see their womenfolk, it is not surprising that some of the writing in the American women's movement should have the shrill note of protest which runs through a book such as Marilyn French's 1972 novel *The Women's Room*. If Margo wanted her husband dead, all she needed to do was stand there and let him be killed by a charging buffalo. Wilson clearly thought that Macomber had now acquired the courage to deal with the situation himself, and was not going to intervene as he had done when the lion was charging. And even if she had shot her husband deliberately, the fear of being dominated by him may not have been the only motive. As Hector remarked, a man can be brave one day and run away the next. Better, perhaps, ensure that Macomber die happy, rather than run the danger of another collapse of morale on his part and subsequent humiliation for both of them.

The possibility of reading *The Short Happy Life of Francis Macomber* in a way which goes against the meaning which Hemingway gave to the story in an interview given fifteen years after it was written suggests some of the advantages of following D. H. Lawrence's advice to 'trust the tale, not the teller'. If the tale lets itself be read in a number of different ways, all the better. It heightens the claim of literature to make us more aware of the complexities of the human condition, and of the different values which human beings adopt to make sense of their existence. For if the shame attached to cowardice is so great as to lead a woman to kill her husband in order to enable him to die in his one moment of happiness, then it is indeed the 'incarnation of all sins'; and there are some attitudes which survive untouched from the second half of the nineteenth century into the twentieth. But like 'The Door of Opportunity', *The Short Happy Life of Francis Macomber* is also a piece of realistic fiction with strong historical overtones. Just as it was the norm, before the Second World War, to expect Englishmen to be brave in order better to bear the white man's burden, so there seem to have been no ecological objections to Americans proving their manhood by killing members of an already endangered species.

8

Moral Dilemmas I:
Religion, Ethics
and some Incidental Truths

I

The moral certainties of some early twentieth-century writers; anti-semitism as a recurrent attitude in the same period; some unfortunate phrases from Claudel, Aldous Huxley and Jean-Paul Sartre; the writer and politics; some advice from Yeats.

In spite of the certainty with which cowardice is condemned by twentieth-century writers, it is unusual for them to declare, in the tones which T. S. Eliot uses in the choruses from *The Rock*, in 1930, that

> However you disguise it, this thing does not change:
> The perpetual struggle of Good and Evil.

Even if the question of how we ought to act is put in the secular terms of a contest between right and wrong, rather than with the religious overtones implied by the words Good and Evil, the answers suggested by most of the playwrights and novelists of the twentieth century are ambiguous, uncertain and often ironic.

Another writer chronologically in the twentieth century, G. K. Chesterton, could indeed speak in the same tones as T. S. Eliot, and declare an unflinching belief in what thinkers in earlier times would have referred to as the eternal verities. At the very moment when Gabriel Syme, the poet turned detective in the 1913 extravaganza *The Man Who Was Thursday*, is about to enter the private room in which the anarchists are planning their next explosion of a bomb in a busy street, he hears in the street outside a barrel-organ suddenly 'spring with a jerk into a jovial tune'. It makes him feel 'the ambassador of all those common people in

157

the street, who every day marched into battle to its music', and there clangs in his mind what Chesterton calls that 'unanswerable truism' in the Song of Roland:

> Paiens ont tort et Chrétiens ont droit (Pagans are wrong and Christians are right),

which in the old French has what Chesterton describes as 'the clang and groan of great iron'.[1]

It is partly because the idea of any superiority of Christianity over other religions represents the height of political incorrectness that such words are unlikely to be found in a writer who belonged intellectually and not just chronologically to the twentieth century. But it is also, and more importantly, because we have lost the intellectual certainty which also underpins the reply which Father Brown, Chesterton's priest turned detective, makes to the master criminal Flambeau at the end of the short story 'The Blue Cross', and which reflects all the moral self-confidence of the traditional Catholicism to which Chesterton converted in 1922:

> You can imagine any mad botany or geology you please . . . Think that the moon is a blue moon, a single elephantine sapphire. But don't fancy that all that frantic astronomy would make the slightest difference to the reason and justice of conduct. On plains of opal, under cliffs cut out of pearl, you would still find a notice board: **Thou shalt not steal**.

But by his own admission, Chesterton looked back for his moral as well as for his social ideas to the Middle Ages. Like his friend and ally Hilaire Belloc, he thought that everything had started to go wrong in Europe – neither author paid any attention to what happened anywhere else – as soon as the Reformation of the sixteenth century had destroyed the social and spiritual unity of medieval Christendom. Neither Chesterton nor Belloc had any time for capitalism and industrialisation. In that respect, if in no other, they were twentieth-century writers in the same sense of the word as Lawrence, Eliot, Sartre or Yeats. But their solution to the social problems of the modern world never had the slightest chance of being accepted. What they proposed was a return to a primarily agricultural England – again, no other country counted – in which men tilled the land, women wove cloth and bore children, the priests offered guidance and instruction to the rulers, and the Marxist concept of the class struggle was proved false by the grouping together of all those who worked in the same profession into a single, united Corporation, on the model of the medieval guilds. Significantly enough, although only Belloc lived to see it, living as he did until 1953 while Chesterton had died in 1936, it was the same philosophy which the Vichy government tried to introduce in France in 1940, after the victory of the Germans had enabled the French right wing to abolish the Third Republic. The world view of what was referred to as the 'Chester–Belloc' was also marked by the same anti-semitism which the Vichy government legalised in France.

Chesterton and Belloc were nevertheless not the only twentieth-century writers to speak of the Jews with the automatic and open hostility which was common practice before the discovery of the Holocaust, and which inspired Leopold Bloom to make his famous riposte to the Citizen: 'Mendelssohn was a jew and Karl Marx and Mercadante and Spinoza, And the Saviour was a jew and his father was a jew. Your God.'[2]

Even the gentle Aldous Huxley, who devoted the last 26 years of his life to preaching pacifism and the mystical doctrine of Non-Attachment, found no difficulty in his earlier career in writing about 'grinning blackamoors' and 'repulsive German Jews'. He also explained the refusal of Francis Chellifer, the hero of *Those Barren Leaves*, to take a job in business by the fact that he did not want to work 'in order that Jewish stockbrokers may exchange their Rovers for Armstrong-Siddeleys' and as late as 1947, in a letter to his cousin Gervase, he commented on the unfortunate necessity, when working in Hollywood, to defer to the 'all-powerful Jewish gentleman in charge of distribution'.[3] Nor did the charity traditionally associated with Christian beliefs prevent T. S. Eliot from showing comparable prejudice, writing in his 1920 poem *Burback with a Baedeker: Bleistein with a Cigar*:

The smoky end of time
Declines. On the Rialto once.
The rats are underneath the piles
The jew is underneath the lot.
Money in furs. The boatman smiles.

Ezra Pound, Eliot's acknowledged mentor, was even less

inhibited. After Eliot had converted to Anglo-Catholicism and denounced the modern world and all its works in the collection of
essays published in 1934 under the title *Under Strange Gods*, he
wrote that the author of *The Waste Land* had not come through
his experiences 'uncontaminated by the Jewish poison',[4] and it is
not surprising that the only way in which Pound could avoid
being prosecuted for offering treasonable support to Mussolini's
Italy through his wartime broadcasts was to choose to be de-
tained in a lunatic asylum.

Perhaps more than at any previous period, writers in the twentieth century have tried to find an answer to the question of right
and wrong by involving themselves in politics. Except for George
Orwell, Arthur Miller and Albert Camus, they have rarely done
themselves much credit or their readers much service, with those
who committed themselves wholeheartedly to one side in Eliot's
'perpetual struggle of Good and Evil' coming out particularly badly.
The French Catholic poet Paul Claudel, whose plays achieved such
success in the productions by Jean-Louis Barrault in the German-
occupied Paris of the 1940s, was already too old for military service
when the First World War broke out in 1914. This did not prevent him, as the true nature of the war became obvious, from
writing in June 1915 a poem in which the refrain

> Tant que vous voudrez, mon général, O France tant que vous
> voudrez (As many as you want, General, as many as you want,
> Oh France)[5]

encouraged further slaughter.

Claudel survived the First World War, as he did the Second,
and received the signal honour of a State Funeral when he finally
died in 1950. Politically, this showed that the France of the Fourth
Republic was catholic as well as Catholic in some of its tastes,
since Claudel was one of several writers who had moved without much difficulty from praising Marshal Pétain when the Germans were winning to writing enthusiastically about General de
Gaulle once the tide had definitely changed. But although Claudel
resembles Kipling, Chesterton and Belloc in being a writer who
was chronologically rather than intellectually or spiritually of the
twentieth century, the remarks which he made in 1915 show the
same indifference to human life as the phrase by which the very
self-consciously twentieth-century Jean-Paul Sartre encouraged

rebellion against all colonial regimes in his 1961 preface to Franz Fanon's *Les Damnés de la terre* (*The Wretched of the Earth*):

> In the first stage of rebellion, killing is essential. To shoot a European is to kill two birds with one stone, eliminating an oppressor and a member of the oppressed race at one and the same time. What remains are a dead man and a free man. The survivor feels, for the first time, a *national* soil beneath his feet.[6]

Both Sartre and Claudel, equally involuntarily, and however different the ideology inspiring their work, suggest how right Yeats was when he wrote, on being asked for a war poem,

> I think it better that at times like these
> A poet's mouth be silent, for in truth
> I have no gift to set a statesman right;
> He has had enough of meddling who can please
> A young girl in the indolence of her youth
> Or an old man upon a winter's night.

II

Claudel contrasted with Graham Greene; moral ambiguities in The Heart of the Matter *and a defiance of conventional standards in* Brighton Rock; *some parallels with Machiavelli and Kierkegaard; a glance at Mauriac, Anthony Powell and others.*

Claudel had been converted to Catholicism after reading a collection of prose poems entitled *Les Illuminations*, written at the age of 17 by the French poet Arthur Rimbaud (1854–91), who then gave up literature in favour of gun-running in Abyssinia. A plaque set in the floor of Notre Dame records the actual date at which the conversion took place as Christmas Day, 1885. The conversion of the English novelist Graham Greene took place in a less spectacular manner, in less impressive surroundings, and for more prosaic reasons. Greene wanted to marry a Catholic, Vivienne Dayrell-Browning, and followed the advice of one of his atheist friends, the journalist, Claude Cockburn – founder of *The Week*, the pre-war ancestor to *Private Eye* – to take the religion of his future wife.

The conversion, however sincere its original motives, gave rise
to a body of work as different as can be imagined from that of
Claudel, and one whose ambiguities and uncertainties correspond
far more closely to the way the majority of twentieth-century
readers see the world. The tone for Greene's novels was nevertheless given by a quotation from another French Catholic poet,
Charles Péguy, which Greene put at the beginning of what is
perhaps his best novel, *The Heart of the Matter*, in 1948. 'Nobody'
Péguy had written in 1905, 'is closer to the heart of Christianity,
than the sinner. Nobody, unless it be the saint.'

There are two main ways in which Henry Scobie, the central
character of *The Heart of the Matter*, is a sinner, though not one
whose sins cause either himself or anybody else any pleasure: he
breaks the seventh of the Ten Commandments, 'Thou shalt not
commit adultery'; and he consciously defies the total condemnation which the Catholic church, like other Christian sects, has
always placed upon suicide. Scobie is the Deputy Commissioner
of Police in what was then the British colony of Sierra Leone,
where Greene himself served in military intelligence during the
Second World War. He is married to Louise, one of the most
unsympathetically presented female characters in world literature,
whose unhappiness at having no friends in the small English colony
is compounded at the beginning of the novel by a feeling of humiliation at the news that her husband has once again been passed
over for promotion to Commissioner. In order to enable her to
escape from the colony and go to South Africa, Scobie places himself
at the mercy of the Syrian trader Yussef by accepting the offer of
a loan of £200, quite a large sum in the 1940s.

It is not, however, this breach of professional ethics and failure to live up to his nickname of 'Scobie the Just', which brings
about his downfall. Indeed, by a characteristic stroke of irony, it
is at the very moment that he is lying to his superior, Colonel
Wright, about his relationship with Yussef, that Scobie makes so
favourable an impression that he is promoted, too late in the day,
alas, to the rank of Commissioner. Scobie's fall comes about through
what is presented, throughout the novel, as his dominant characteristic, an overdeveloped sense of pity. It is this which ties him
to Louise, and it is this, rather than any feelings of lechery, which
leads him to have an affair, during his wife's absence in South
Africa, with a 19-year-old widow, Helen Rolf, whose husband
had died when their ship was torpedoed, and who had spent 40

days in an open boat, clutching her stamp album as her only comfort.

Louise, who has heard about the affair, discovers that her duty has always been to be at her husband's side, and comes back from South Africa. She then insists that Scobie, who had converted to Catholicism in order to marry her, fulfils his religious obligations by accompanying her to mass. Although for him to do so while continuing his affair with Helen would place him in a state of mortal sin, he cannot make the necessary break, being by now tied to his mistress by the same sense of pity which had earlier led him to sacrifice his honour as a policeman in order to get the money to help Louise. The only solution which he can envisage is to opt out of the dilemma by committing suicide. In order to make his death of some use to at least one of the women to whom he is bound, he embarks upon an elaborate subterfuge in order to make it appear that he has died of an attack of angina. This, at least, will enable Louise to receive the money due on his life insurance. It will also free him from the need, as Greene puts it, to 'strike God in the face' by continuing to eat His body when in a state of mortal sin.

Predictably enough, in a novel in which all the characters spy upon one another, the entries in his diary where Scobie inserts earlier references to the chest pains caused by his supposed angina are discovered to be fakes. Louise's judgement on him is characteristically harsh, alleging as it does that he loved nobody, and it is left to Father Rank to tell her, with some exasperation: 'For goodness' sake Mrs Scobie, don't imagine that you – or I – know a thing about God's mercy.'[7]

It is a comment whose truth might have been called into question by theologians of an earlier generation, and is barely consistent with the traditional teaching of the church. This is even more the case with Scobie's view that Hell is 'primarily a permanent sense of loss', an opinion which would have been dismissed as the height of heresy by the priest whose sermon on the unquenchable fires in which the damned burn throughout eternity so terrified the young Stephen Dedalus in James Joyce's 1914 autobiographical *Portrait of the Artist as a Young Man*. Scobie, it is true, emphasises what he means by explaining that you 'have to have lost something really important', and it would be hard to find a modern theologian who thought that Hell was anything other than the permanent awareness that one has rejected the

love of God. Indeed, so reluctant are modern theologians to condemn anyone to eternal damnation that the accepted view now
seems to be that while Hell may exist, it is highly unlikely that
there is anybody there.[8]

If this view is nowadays so widely accepted, it is another illustration of the link between developments in literature and movements which have taken place in other disciplines such as
philosophy, politics and theology, where the absence of any reliable evidence to sustain one theory rather than another means
that prestige depends solely on the ability of those who practise
those disciplines to manipulate language. The idea that there are
no fixed standards in politics goes back at least to Machiavelli,
and perhaps even to Thucydides. For both writers, a man who
was virtuous in his private life might well find himself, when
entrusted with the welfare of his fellow citizens, required to behave
in a totally immoral manner in order to protect their interests. It
is, in contrast, difficult before the twentieth century to find authors
saying, when describing characters in literature with whom the
reader is expected to sympathise, that 'in human relations, kind-
ness and lies are worth a thousand truths'.[9]

It is true that this remark, which Greene makes when talking
of Scobie, has echoes of the main theme in Ibsen's 1884 play, *The
Wild Duck*. It is much better, the play argues, that people should
be encouraged in what Ibsen calls 'the life lie', the illusion which
enables them to get through the day without making either themselves or other people too unhappy, than that they should be
compelled to face up to the truth about themselves and compel
other people to come to terms with it as well. What this parallel
also shows is the modernity of Ibsen, one of the first writers before the twentieth century to call into question the eternal truths
of which Claudel, Chesterton, and T. S. Eliot were so certain.

From a non-religious point of view, there is only one person
whom Scobie harms in *The Heart of the Matter*. This is his ser-
vant, Ali, whom he half-knowingly sends to be murdered by the
'wharf rats' who do Yussef's dirty work for him. But within the
central framework of the novel, this is a side issue compared to
Scobie's relationship to Louise, to Helen and to God, and in this
context he is first and foremost a man who does the wrong deed
for the right reason. The hurt which he does to Louise, for example,
is real only because she finds out about his suicide, and judges
his motives by the very narrow-minded Catholicism which fits

so well into her character. Had the spy, Wilson, not detected the forgeries in Scobie's diary, Louise would have entered into possession of the insurance money. This would not, given her character, have made her a merry widow. But she would have been one who had enough to live on, together with the memory of a husband who had, for all his faults, been after all destined for promotion to Commissioner. In a non-religious context, and without the accidental discovery of the truth about his faked suicide, Scobie might have become the very embodiment of the man who succeeds by his use of immoral means – lying about his heart condition – in attaining an unambiguous good.

To judge the ethical framework of *The Heart of the Matter* in this way, however, and to give priority to the attempt which a man makes to provide someone he loves with a modicum of ordinary human happiness, is to go against the whole temper of Greene's work, and especially against a distinction which he made in an earlier novel, *Brighton Rock*, in 1938. There, the young gangster Pinkie, who murders a man in a gangland feud in Brighton, is also a Catholic, though one born into the Faith, not a convert like Scobie. He therefore knows that his actions are not only wrong in the sight of men, but also evil in the sight of God, and it is this knowledge which places him on a different plane from the barmaid, Ida Arnold. She, an unbeliever, and the character in the novel who eventually tracks him down, lives only on the horizontal plane of the secular distinction between right and wrong. Pinkie, like the eponymous heroine of François Mauriac's 1927 novel *Thérèse Desqueyroux*, satisfies the criterion suggested by the quotation from Péguy which Graham Greene put at the beginning of *The Heart of the Matter*. The attempt which Thérèse makes to poison her husband makes her a criminal in the eyes of the law, and she also knows herself to be a sinner in the eyes of God. It is this awareness which places her, as it places Pinkie, in a different and possibly higher category than those protected by what Péguy also called 'la toile cirée de la conscience moderne' (the waterproof sheet protecting the modern mind). Through the cracks created by sin, the knowledge which all men have of God and of His love may filter through.

From a commonsense point of view, the Péguy–Greene–Mauriac hypothesis, which can also be found in Georges Bernanos, T. S. Eliot and Evelyn Waugh, is very vulnerable to the objections of common sense. In *Cold Comfort Farm*, Stella Gibbons speaks with

great accuracy of people who ruin your favourite stamp album
and then spend the rest of their life trying to atone for it, when
you would much rather have kept your stamp album in the first
place. Her comment is one of the minor but universal human
truths which occur from time to time in the literature of the twentieth century, as when Nicholas Jenkins remarks, speaking of
Widmerpool in Anthony Powell's·*A Dance to the Music of Time*,
that 'the illusion that egoists will be pleased, or even flattered,
by the interest taken in their habits persists throughout life'.[10]

Such remarks, however, with their reminder of the level on
which most people prefer to live, are not very frequent. Some hit
home immediately, as when Miss Shelly Thomas, the girl with
brown lipstick for whom Larry Kramer lusts so intensely but so
unfruitfully in Tom Wolfe's *The Bonfire of the Vanities*, thinks ruefully
to herself that the trouble with men in New York is that 'Every
time you go out with one, you have to sit there and listen to two
or three hours of My Career first'.[11]

Holden Caulfield's remark, in *The Catcher in the Rye*, that in
every school he had ever been to, the athletic bastards always
stuck together, strikes home with even greater force, while there
is an element of sadness in Steinbeck's comment, in Chapter XI
of his 1945 *Cannery Row*, on the need for someone to

> write an erudite essay on the moral, physical and aesthetic ef-
> fect of the Model T Ford on the American nation. Two gener-
> ations of Americans knew more about the Ford coil than about
> the clitoris, about the planetary system of gears than about the
> solar system of the stars.

The comparative rarity of such mundane notations is a reminder
of the fact that twentieth-century writers tend to put common
sense where the American philosopher Blanch Blanshard said that
it should be in any philosophical investigation: never on the judge's
bench, only rarely in the witness box, and most frequently in the
dock. As the Nigerian novelist Chinua Achebe observed, 'Writers
don't give prescriptions. They give headaches', and the presupposition shared by a totally atheistic writer such as Sartre and by
fervent if anguished Catholics like Graham Greene or François
Mauriac is that there is something wrong about wanting to lead
an ordinary, untroubled life. The chorus of the Women of Canterbury, in Eliot's *Murder in the Cathedral*, who 'do not want anything

to happen', are typical in this respect of the target audience which the characteristically twentieth-century writer is trying to hit where it hurts most.

This audience may not always like what it is told, or even understand it. In Malcolm Bradbury's *Stepping Westwards*, one of a number of the entertaining novels which British academics have been inspired to write by their experience of teaching in the United States, the central character has difficulty in explaining to his students the concept of irony in Swift's *Modest Proposal*, the book which argues that the problem of overpopulation in rural Ireland could easily be solved by the serving of children as a main course on the tables of the rich in England.

> Miss Linstrum shook her head in confusion. 'You mean he didn't want people to eat children at all?' Students all around her began saying 'Yes' and 'that's right' and her face grew flushed. 'Well I don't understand it', she said. 'Supposing someone had taken him seriously and they had. Then he'd be responsible, wouldn't he? Anyway, I don't see why writers have to be so smart. Why can't they say what they think right out, 'stead of going around and confusing people.'

Mr Jobalinksi, a football player, agrees with her, asking 'why these literary guys have to be so confusing' and adding: 'Why do they have to make things so difficult? Why don't they just accept things the way they are?'[12]

The objection is not an unusual one, certainly to the teacher of literature outside Oxbridge, the Ivy League and Stanford, but rather misses the point. Greene and Mauriac are not simply suggesting that there is something inadequate about the moral judgements that we normally make. They are giving literary form to the general problem of finding a satisfactory basis for moral judgements. It is, the characteristically twentieth-century writer feels, part of his duty to prevent people from thinking that ethical problems don't really exist.

The general difficulty of finding a secure basis for moral judgements is something which recurs in both Christian and atheistic existentialism, and which links this movement to the style of philosophical thinking popularised in English-speaking countries by the associated movements of logical positivism and linguistic analysis which so worry George Moore in Stoppard's *Jumpers*.

Thus one of the theses put forward by the nineteenth-century Danish writer Søren Kierkegaard was that there was an 'infinite and qualitative difference' between God and man, and that this showed itself most clearly in the domain of ethics. By human standards, Kierkegaard argues, nothing could be more repugnant than God's commandment to Abraham, in *Genesis* 22, verses 1–3, to sacrifice his son Isaac. But, Kierkegaard maintains, it is precisely because this commandment goes against all traditional concepts of right and wrong that Abraham knows it to be divine and the reward which he receives for his faith comes in two forms. First of all, God changes His mind at the last moment, and substitutes a kid for the sacrifice. Secondly, by his readiness to obey the commandments of God without questioning them, Abraham wins the right to be the first in the line of the prophets who announce the nature of God in the Christian revelation. It is not necessarily because they have read Kierkegaard that the authorities who order the service of Nine Lessons and Carols in the choir of King's College, Cambridge, every Christmas Eve begin with the reading from Genesis 22, verses 1–18. The text is, after all, a central one in the beliefs of all Christian denominations. But it is a decision which highlights how justified the Christian existentialists are in their rejection of any attempt to adjust the Christian message either to the rational, secular morality on which most ordinary people try to base their lives, or to the bland requirements of the modern ecumenical movement. It is not just because of his liking for black humour that Evelyn Waugh makes Mr Prendergast's career end so tragically in *Decline and Fall* (1928). By becoming a 'non-denominational clergyman', Mr Prendergast is trying to avoid the reality of human wickedness. This catches up with him with a vengeance in Dartmoor Prison when a lunatic saws off his head. Squadron Leader (ground staff) Denis Barlow, in contrast, gives the impression of being a more streetwise cleric. When he too, at the end of *The Loved One* (1947), decides to adopt the same calling as poor old Prendy, one feels sure that his career as a liar, blackmailer and conniver in suicide will make him an eminently successful practitioner in any profession, secular as well as ecclesiastical.

The difficulty of distinguishing right from wrong, and sorting both out from good and evil, runs through twentieth-century literature in the same way that the words 'Brighton Rock' show themselves every time you cut through a piece of the confectionery bearing that name. Greene's choice of these two words as the title of his 1938 novel is a clear hint to the reader that he should look for a deeper meaning in what might, in the first instance, read like a rather sad love story set in the world of razor gangs and racecourse touts. Wherever you look at human experience, he suggests, you will find the same contrast between those who live and work in the secular world of right and wrong, like the barmaid Ida, and those who live and suffer on the spiritual plane of good and evil, like the gangster Pinkie. You will, moreover, find that the characteristically human experience of finding it difficult to distinguish between good and evil – or even tell the difference between right and wrong – has been made more difficult in a world in which religion itself has lost the moral certainties of which traditional writers such as Claudel or Chesterton were so unshakably convinced.

9

Moral Dilemmas II: Philosophy, Free Will, and some Visions of the Future

I

Anthony Burgess, Huxley and Orwell: violence, committed literature and the impact of science.

In virtually all the societies depicted in novels about the future, the state has become even more powerful than it is today. While this is most obviously true in George Orwell's *Nineteen Eighty-Four* (1949) and Aldous Huxley's *Brave New World* (1932), it is equally noticeable in two novels by Anthony Burgess, the 1969 *A Clockwork Orange* and the less well-known 1962 earlier fantasy, *The Wanting Seed*, as well as in Margaret Atwood's *The Handmaid's Tale* (1985) and P. D. James's 1993 novel, *The Children of Men*. In so far as most of the predictions made by futurologists have tended to be wrong, there is perhaps some comfort to be drawn from the fact that novelists who write about the future all tend to say the same thing. Perhaps they will all be shown to have been as unnecessarily gloomy as Orwell now seems to have been.

In many ways, *A Clockwork Orange* is the perfect example of science fiction. It is fairly short. Novels about the future require more suspension of disbelief than most ordinary fiction, and the author should not require too much of his audience. It is set in an environment which is like our own but recognisably worse, a quality capable of inspiring self-satisfaction and fear in well-balanced quantities. We are all right at the moment, but things could easily get worse. Unlike almost all other portraits of the

170

future, it accepts that language can change as thoroughly as it has done in the past, and consequently offers an intriguing linguistic challenge. This is easily overcome, and there is no need to look at the glossary provided at the end of the book to understand the first-person narrative in which Alex describes his adventures. With a little perseverance, it all falls into place. But most of all, *A Clockwork Orange* raises philosophical questions shared by all human societies, past, present and future.

The plot is a simple one. Alex, a 15-year-old thug with a passion for Beethoven, commits a murder. He is offered a choice between a long prison sentence and a course of treatment which will recondition him to the point where he is incapable of acting in an evil manner. This course, however, has the side-effect of also making him incapable of appreciating Beethoven. He has ceased to be a living thing – the orange of the title – and has become a machine, a piece of clockwork. Human beings, Burgess is saying, are all of a piece. Destroy the capacity to choose between good and evil, and you also destroy the ability to appreciate art and beauty. It is a dilemma which is central to Huxley's *Brave New World*; as well, very probably, to the human condition itself.

A Clockwork Orange is set in an England even more dilapidated than that of the late 1960s, where it immediately became a cult book, and in 1972 was made into a brilliant and highly successful film. This, again, raised another intriguing question: should society adopt a different attitude towards the possible censorship of what Marshall McLuhan called the 'hot' medium – the cinema, television – than it had towards the cold medium of print? For while anybody capable of reading and understanding *A Clockwork Orange* had *ipso facto* made himself immune to any danger that he might behave like Alex and his friends, the same was not true of the young men who went to see the film. The white boiler suits, black bowler hats and black walking sticks which constituted Alex's fighting gear were rapidly adopted as a style of dress by young hooligans as disaffected from the English society of the 1970s as Alex was to the society of his day.

A number of towns consequently banned the film, an action of which Burgess later expressed approval. It was, indeed, a decision which seemed eminently justified by a conversation which took place when a group of hooligans broke into a house and proceeded to behave exactly like Alex and his friends. When the woman, terrified at the way her husband was being beaten up, and only too aware of what was going to happen to her, asked the attackers why they were behaving like this, she received the half-pitying reply: 'Lady, haven't you seen the movie?'

In Orwell's *Nineteen Eighty-Four*, violence has become the exclusive privilege of the state. In this respect, as in many others, the novel was immediately recognised as an account of the totalitarianism which had been defeated in Germany but was still very much alive in the Soviet Union and its newly acquired empire in Eastern Europe. Indeed, Orwell's target was so immediately identifiable that when Frederic Warburg received the typescript of *Nineteen Eighty-Four*, one of his first comments was that its publication would be worth 'a cool million' votes for the Conservative party.[1] This was not, however, because the British Labour party was at the time particularly well disposed towards the Soviet Union. Clement Attlee had never had much time for the Russians, and the Foreign Secretary, Ernie Bevin, had more than once let Molotov have the rough side of his tongue. It was more that Frederic Warburg recognised that *Nineteen Eighty-Four* was a book that could have considerable influence on public opinion generally, and would certainly help to discourage any tendency to appease the Soviet Union. Warburg had already saved the fortunes of his publishing firm by accepting *Animal Farm* after it had been turned down by Jonathan Cape, probably in response to some occult threat from the Ministry of Information, and T. S. Eliot had rejected it for Faber and Faber on the grounds that it did not seem to him 'the right point of view from which to criticise the political situation at the present time'.[2]

Nineteen Eighty-Four proved to be just as much a bestseller as *Animal Farm*, perhaps precisely because it deserved the strictures laid upon it in 1992 by Alfred Clayton's teenage son Bugsy in *Memories of the Ford Administration* when he complained to his father that 'the stuff they make you read is so dumb – *Animal Farm* and like that, showing how lousy Communism is'.[3] When Isaac Deutscher anticipated this criticism in 1950, describing *Nineteen Eighty-Four* as 'a kind of ideological weapon in the cold war', and a book responsible for 'teaching millions to look at the conflict between East and West in terms of black and white' and encouraging readers to 'see a monster bogy and a monster scapegoat for the ills that claim mankind'[4] he was quite right to underline that Orwell's target was the Soviet Union. The best proof of the accuracy of Orwell's diagnosis is the unanimity with which writers who had lived under the Soviet Empire spoke of how completely the description of Oceania fitted the facts of their society. The climate of terror and suspicion, of leader worship and food shortages, of censorship, endless propaganda and continual changes of the party line were exactly as Orwell described them.

His immediate target audience in 1949 consisted of readers who had a very clear recollection of earlier changes, and knew immediately what Orwell was talking about. They could remember how the Soviet Union began, immediately after 1917, by refusing all contact with political parties in the West; how it changed, between 1920 and 1933, to supporting organisations which endorsed its policies, but damning even left-wing parties which dared take a different line; how, after Hitler's seizure of power in 1933, it changed again, and supported the Popular Front policy of uniting all democratic parties against Fascism; how, on the evening of 23 August 1939, this policy was reversed in the twinkling of an eye by the announcement of the non-aggression pact between the Soviet Union and Nazi Germany; how this pact led to the policy, between 1939 and 21 June 1941, of denouncing the war against Hitler's Germany as an imperialist conspiracy; how this changed again with the news of the German invasion of Russia, when it became everyone's duty to fight against Fascist aggression; and how, with the ending of the war against Germany, the United States ceased to be the noble ally and became once again the bastion of imperialist aggression.

In October 1948, when he was writing *Nineteen Eighty-Four*, Orwell commented in a letter to Julian Symons that 'after the Russians have recovered and have the atomic bomb', war would become inevitable.[5] If a third world war was avoided, this may have been because Orwell's novel encouraged a hawkish attitude in the West which led to the defeat by the 1948–9 airlift of the first Soviet attempt to force America, Britain and France out of West Berlin; the establishment of NATO in 1949; the clear sign sent to the Soviet Union by the rapidity with which the United States intervened when South Korea was invaded by the Communist north on 25 June 1950 that it would do the same in a comparable situation in Western Europe; and the refusal by President Kennedy in October 1962 to allow the Soviet Union to install nuclear missiles in Cuba.

Works of imaginative literature which help to bring about a major change in the way people think rarely do so through subtle arguments and fine distinctions. Not all slave-owners were as bad as Simon Legree and not all working-class boys in Victorian England worked as chimneysweeps. But Harriet Beecher Stowe and Charles Kingsley would not have influenced public opinion as they did if they had written prose as nuanced as that of Henry James. There is a brutal directness about *Nineteen Eighty-Four* which is explicable by Orwell's obvious anxiety to warn his fellow-countrymen of what might happen if they adopted the same policy of appeasement towards the Soviet Union which had been so popular and yet so disastrous in Great Britain's dealings with Nazi Germany in the 1930s. But although *Nineteen Eighty-Four* was not the only novel published in English during the Cold War to recommend that anyone supping with the Russians should take a very long spoon, it was the most successful. The fact that the others are no longer in print points to another aspect of committed literature.

In 1960, Constantine Fitzgibbon's *When the Kissing Had to Stop* argued that if a left-wing government committed to unilateral nuclear disarmament took power in Britain, a Russian take-over would very rapidly follow. In 1983 the same thesis was put forward by the military historian General Sir David Fraser in *August 1988*, but neither novel made the same impact as *Nineteen Eighty-Four*. Although *When the Kissing Had to Stop* did make it into paperback, *August 1988* sank without trace. If Kingsley Amis's portrait of England in *Russian Hide and Seek* were not by the same man who wrote *Lucky Jim*, it too would probably be out of print as well, and this is not entirely because the literary world is, in general, highly unsympathetic to works of fiction which endorse the policies which conservatively minded critics see as having enabled the West to win the Cold War. It is that once a novel as powerful as *Nineteen Eighty-Four* has expressed a particular point of view, the job does not need doing again. Committed literature has two major drawbacks: because it dates very quickly, it needs to be like Orwell's novel and raise a large number of other, more hypothetical questions, if it is to remain readable; if it works, the target it destroys doesn't need to be attacked again.

Although the state in Huxley's 1932 *Brave New World* has given up the use of physical violence as an instrument of social control – if a riot does occur, it is dispersed by spraying the rioters with a mildly euphoric gas – its power can no more be challenged than that of Orwell's Oceania. If any of the Alpha Plus intellectuals who run it wishes to lead an independent life and think for himself, he is allowed to go and do so on an island. But there is no opportunity for him to change a system in which people's physical constitution and intellectual make-up are determined from birth through the treatment to which they were subjected while still in the test tube in which they were bred. When Pavlovian conditioning so associates discomfort with intellectual activity or aesthetic pleasure that there is no question of 'lower-caste people wasting the Community's time on books', there is no danger of any new ideas being developed from below. There is not even any need for firemen to go around burning books, as they do in Ray Bradbury's *Fahrenheit 451*, a title designating the temperature at which paper burns. In *Brave New World*, the potentially disruptive power of the printed word has been destroyed far more effectively. Books are harmless because nobody wants to read them. There are no challenges to a state whose authority rests on universal consent.

The date at which the events take place in *Brave New World* makes Huxley's novel invulnerable to one of the criticisms most frequently addressed to *Nineteen Eighty-Four*: that since 1984 has come and gone, Orwell got it wrong. The date of A.F. (= After Ford) 632 situates the action at about AD 2595, 632 years after the birth of Henry Ford in 1863. We have some way to go before finding out whether Huxley got it right or not. Ford's introduction of mass production techniques into the manufacture of motor cars, Huxley suggests, brought about a fundamental change in human history. It made possible a much more rapid creation of wealth, and it also required much greater uniformity on the part of human beings. A factory could work well only if men subjected themselves to the rhythm imposed by the machine, and ceased to act as individuals. Once the crucial step had been taken which enabled human beings to obtain mastery of the physical universe by applied science, the next logical step was to use the biological and behavioural sciences to bring human beings themselves, together with the society they lived in, under equally complete and equally rational control. In *Brave New World*, the problem of overpopulation, an obsession with all the Huxleys, has been solved by the abolition of physical childbirth. Test tube births produce exactly the right number of people society needs at the time it needs them.

Prenatal conditioning also ensures that people's bodies and minds are exactly fitted to the work they will have to do. Pavlovian conditioning destroys free will – as it does in *A Clockwork Orange* – and social stability is ensured by plenty of sex, by the distribution of a harmless drug called soma, and constantly available mechanical amusements. What gives an extra, philosophical dimension to Huxley's novel is that the price of this paradise is – again as in *A Clockwork Orange* – the disappearance of everything which previously made human beings human. The family has disappeared, as has the concept of romantic love. There is no such thing as one human being who is uniquely valuable in the eyes of another. There are merely infinitely exchangeable sexual partners and the terms 'mother' and 'father' have become mildly embarrassing swear words. There is no literature, no philosophy, and nothing but canned music. Scientific enquiry for its own sake no longer exists. There is only the applied science needed to keep the machines working. But together with the horror which Huxley sought to inspire in his readers at the sight of a world brought wholly under rational control, there is also a question: might it not, given man's proclivity for slaughtering his fellows and his ability to make himself very unhappy, be a good idea to stop being human in the way that men and women have been in the past?[6]

Like most societies depicted in novels about the future, *Brave New World* has a rebel. Or, rather, it has two, the Alpha Plus intellectual Bernard Marx, and a young man called the Savage. Partly because he is rather smaller than his peers – the rumour runs that 'somebody made a mistake when he was still in the bottle; thought he was a gamma and put alcohol into his blood surrogate' – Bernard feels dissatisfied and out of place. But he lacks the inner self-assurance which would enable him to bear the solitude of the island where the outsiders are free to think as they like, and his names suggest that his defeat is also that of two ideologies. His first name evokes Saint Bernard of Clairvaux, the Cistercian monk whose 70 monasteries epitomised the Christian tradition of prayer and silent study. His second name, more obviously, embodies the socialism which was the major rival of Christianity in Huxley's lifetime. Neither ideology, Huxley suggests, can stand up against the power of applied science, and there is a sense in which this particular prediction is already proving accurate.

The second, more interesting rebel is a young man called John, born of a human mother, Linda, when she became separated from her lover – now Director of World Hatcheries – when on a trip to the Pueblo Indians, and discovered with horror that she was pregnant by him. John has been brought up by the Indians, but has also had access to one of the many forbidden books of A.F. 632, the complete works of Shakespeare. He finds, predictably, that the society of A.F. 632 does not fit in with the ideas which this unusual upbringing has given him, and his disillusion is expressed in a conversation with the World Controller, Mustapha Mond. 'So you claim', asks Mond,

the right to grow old and impotent; the right to have syphilis and cancer; the right to have too little to eat; the right to be lousy; the right to live in constant apprehension of what may happen tomorrow; the right to catch typhoid; the right to be tortured by unspeakable pains of every kind?

When the Savage takes a deep breath and replies 'I do', only to receive the World Controller's 'You're welcome to it',[7] the debate in *Brave New World* takes on the philosophical overtones which make Huxley's novel even more interesting than *A Clockwork Orange* as an experiment in science fiction. For the question that Huxley is asking is not just whether art can be produced and appreciated only when people are unhappy. It is also whether the biological accident which gave man his unique status as a suffering, thinking and imaginative being should in some way be rectified.

Huxley's ability to raise questions of this type makes him a more characteristically twentieth-century author than the strictly literary quality of his books might perhaps allow. Neither he nor Orwell enjoys as high a reputation as Conrad or E. M. Forster, and Huxley, in particular, is seen as belonging to an entirely different league from D. H. Lawrence. This is mainly because both Orwell and Huxley deal with ideas rather than with people. Neither is particularly interested in human relationships, and both tend to simplify issues to make them more immediately accessible to the reader. Perhaps this is why both of them did so well when they wrote novels which can be quite easily categorised as science fiction. This is a genre which, by definition, specialises in hypothetical situations rather than in real people. The ones evoked in Margaret Atwood's *The Handmaid's Tale* and P.D. James's *The Children of Men* are as frightening as anything in Orwell or Huxley, and raise questions which are just as interesting as the themes of *Brave New World* or *Nineteen Eighty-Four*.

II

The problem of fertility: Anthony Burgess, The Wanting Seed, *P. D. James,* The Children of Men, *Margaret Atwood,* The Handmaid's Tale.

While the authorities in Oceania do their best to limit the amount of sexual activity available to party members in order to make sure that their energy is left intact for Hate Week, the inhabitants of *Brave New World* are encouraged to have as much sex as possible with as many sexual partners as they can find. This will keep them from wanting to explore new ideas, as well as from developing an intense emotional attitude to one person which might disturb the balance of society. Children are essential in the world of *Nineteen Eighty-Four*, since otherwise the armies would run out of cannon fodder. Everybody must, as the saying is, do their duty for the Party. But the puritanism in sexual matters which characterised genuinely revolutionary leaders such as Cromwell and Robespierre is sufficiently present in the intellectual baggage of the members of the Inner Party who rule Oceania for them to discourage the idea that sex can be enjoyed. Winston Smith's rebellion is primarily an intellectual one. He wants to find a place in which he can be private, and think his own thoughts out of the range of the telescreen. But this rebellion also takes the form of a series of energetic encounters with Julia.

In Anthony Burgess's 1962 novel *The Wanting Seed*, as in P. D. James's *The Children of Men* and Margaret Atwood's *The Hand-maiden's Tale*, it is fertility rather than sex which provides the main theme. The problem is different in *The Wanting Seed*, where there are too many people, from what it is in P. D. James's 1992 novel. There, human beings have suddenly become incapable of having children, and there is a similar situation in *The Handmaiden's Tale*, where fertility has fallen to the point where women who are capable of bearing children have to become virtual slaves to the dominant males in the group. In each case, however, the situation has given rise to an increase in the power of the state. In Anthony Burgess's world, abortions are compulsory for women who have had one child, whether it has survived or not, and there are generous grants of food and money to women producing abortion certificates. Homosexuals and lesbians both benefit from positive discrimination in their careers because they do not produce children. There is, in this respect, an important difference between the

England of *The Wanting Seed*, where the action seems to be taking place at least a century after 1984, and the situation imagined by Orwell. When there are so many people that London extends in an urbanised mass from Brighton to Birmingham, and children have to be taught in shifts which go on day and night, there is a case for state intervention. In *Nineteen Eighty-Four*, in contrast, the point is specifically made that there is no need for the tyranny exercised by the state. Were it not for the lust for power of the members of the Inner Party, science could provide decent living standards for everybody. Both Orwell and Burgess, from this point of view, are writing very much with the immediate situation in mind, projecting the problems of the present into the future in order to warn people of what might happen. Just as *Nineteen Eighty-Four* is a very forties nightmare, based on the enormous increase in the power of the state in the dictatorships of Hitler and Stalin, so *The Wanting Seed* is very much a book of the 1960s, and of a period where people could still remember the food shortages of the war. Now, in the 1990s, farmers are being paid not to produce food. *The Wanting Seed* also has a feature which science fiction, as a genre, often shares with the detective story: the initial situation is well conceived and brilliantly presented; the solution to the problem – in Burgess's nightmare, through cannibalism and deliberately organised wars – is less convincing.

From a purely literary point of view, it is often a good idea to read a book which turns out to be disappointing. It makes you realise how good the recognised masterpieces of a particular genre are. There are also advantages in looking at a book which represents a new departure for a writer who has established a reputation in one genre and then turns to another, as when P. D. James temporarily forsook the detective story for a haunting experiment in science fiction in *The Children of Men*. From the publication of her first novel, *Cover Her Face* in 1962, she became the equal of the other women authors described in a slightly patronising manner as 'Queens of Crime' – Marjorie Allingham, Agatha Christie, Ngaio Marsh, Ruth Rendall, Dorothy Sayers – whose achievements in detective fiction are often better than those of their male counterparts. All writers reveal their value systems by the way they write, the good ones consciously, the less good without quite realising what they are doing, and there is little doubt, throughout *The Children of Men*, that it is the work of a traditionally minded Christian, the secretary of the Prayer Book Society, who showed

understandable disappointment that so few people could ident-
ify the source of the quotation which provided the title for her
1989 mystery thriller, *Devices and Desires*.[8]

This is not because she tugs at our sleeve, as William Golding
occasionally does, to remind us of her beliefs. Nor does she present
the catastrophe which begins to afflict mankind in the 1990s, the
sudden drying up of human fertility, as a punishment visited upon
us for our manifold sins and wickednesses. The drop in the birth
rate first becomes noticeable in the Roman Catholic countries. It
is not, therefore, the vengeance of a God whom we have so wearied
by our rejection of Natural Law that He has taken the gift of
procreation from us. It is indeed the fault of their upbringing
that the male Omegas, the children to be born in 1995, the last
year of recorded human births, are 'cruel, arrogant and violent'
as well as 'strong, individualistic and handsome as young gods'.
'If from infancy', the narrator tells us in the very first chapter of
The Children of Men, 'you treat children as gods they are liable in
adulthood to act as devils'.[9] But it is only by very distant implication that the phrase can be interpreted as a criticism of the
way people in England bring up their children nowadays, when
they have a reasonable hope that these children will grow up to
have children of their own.

What makes *The Children of Men* unmistakably the work of a
writer with strong religious beliefs is the conviction which runs
through the book that human beings are creatures of a very special
kind. The narrator, a 50-year-old Oxford historian, may well report the conversation of one of his colleagues who offers a scientific basis for Sartre's view of us as 'animals struck with disaster'
or Huxley's vision of the world as an accident in an evolutionary
process which might well have turned out quite differently. 'I
can't think', says David Hurstfield, a professor of statistical palae-
ontology whose views are probably meant to be recognised as
very similar to those of Stephen Jay Gould,

> why you all seem so surprised at Omega. After all, of the four
> billion life forms which have existed on this planet, three bil-
> lion, nine hundred and sixty million are now extinct. We don't
> know why ... In the light of these mass extinctions it really
> does seem unreasonable to suppose that *Homo sapiens* should
> be exempt. Our species will have been one of the shortest lived
> of all, a mere blink, you may say, in the eye of time.[10]

It is a remark which gives the book a philosophical dimension comparable to that of *Brave New World*. As in the conversation between the Savage and Mustapha Mond, we know that the latter is wrong but cannot quite explain why.

It is nevertheless not only the courage which P. D. James shows in thus confronting a central challenge to her faith which gives *The Children of Men* its excellence as a novel about the future. There is a nice balance in the depiction of the Warden of England, the narrator's cousin Xan. On the one hand, he is a man faced with the impossible situation of trying to make society work when it seems pointless to maintain roads in places where there soon won't be any people to drive along them, and in a country where the absence of young people deprives all activities of the long-term usefulness which gave them meaning. On the other, he becomes obsessed with the power at his disposal, as too does Harriet Marwood, the 'wise old woman of the tribe' whose authority so radiates from her presence on the television screen that she could 'make a law requiring universal suicide seem eminently reasonable'.[11]

By definition, the details in a novel about the future are what Barthes would describe as 'des effets du réel', rhetorical devices invented to make the story more convincing. It is therefore particularly appropriate to pay tribute to their persuasive power as illustrations of what might happen under these particular circumstances. It is quite probable that women grieving for their barren wombs might find solace in such mad devices as taking kittens to be baptised. It is equally understandable that the priest conducting the baptism service will weep at the sight of the animals calmly invading the sanctuary of his church, and ask with fury in his voice why they cannot just wait a few years until everything will be theirs.

In its story line, *The Children of Men* follows the convention whereby a dissident or group of dissidents has to survive in face of the persecution which the otherwise all-powerful state organises to crush them. The same situation occurs in Margaret Atwood's *The Handmaid's Tale*, which differs from *The Children of Men* as much by its setting as by the ideology inspiring it. P. D. James's novel ends with an event fully in the spirit of the Lord's promise in Genesis 8, 22: 'While the earth remaineth, seedtime and harvest, and cold and heat, and summer and winter, and day and night shall not cease.' The miracle that everyone has been praying for

happens. A child is born, a boy, whose sex 'seeming so dominant, so disproportionate to the plump, small body, was like a
proclamation'[12] and the novel ends with Julian, one of the dissidents, 'making on the child's forehead the sign of the cross'.

The future in *The Handmaid's Tale* is presented as being slightly
less distant from our own day than the events in *The Children of
Men*. The whole point about Ofred, the woman who tells her story,
is that she is still of child-bearing age, and she has memories of
a former life in which she was married, in which her husband's
name was Luke, and where she had an eight-year-old daughter. It
is not entirely clear what has happened to Ofred's husband and
daughter. Unlike most science fiction stories, in which there is an
omniscient narrator who explains how the new society came into
existence and what its main characteristics are, *The Handmaid's Tale*
is told by someone who, as the 'Historical Note' at the end points
out, could, by the very place assigned to her in society, have had
only a rudimentary grasp of what was happening. In the country
of Gilead, previously the United States of America, women oc-
cupy only the roles strictly assigned to them by men. That of the
Narrator in *The Handmaid's Tale* is to bear children who will bring
prestige upon the Commander to whom she has been allocated.

This role has been entrusted to her because of the fertility which
enabled her to have the child who may or may not have been
killed during the attempt which she and her husband made to
escape into Canada. The main problem in Gilead, as in the England of *The Children of Men*, is that of infertility, especially among
Caucasians. This has led to a society in which the dominant males
whose wives are not able to conceive are allocated a handmaid
who will act as the maid Billah did in Genesis 30:1–3 – the text is
quoted at the beginning of Margaret Atwood's novel – when she
bore Jacob the child which Rachel could not give him. Ofred derives her name from the fact that the Commander to whom she
has been allocated is called Fred, and she is in every sense his
property. The situation in Genesis 30:3 where Rachel asks that
Bilhah shall 'bear upon my knee' becomes one where Fred has
intercourse with Ofred while she is stretched out on the knees of
his wife, Serena Joy.

This is not an event which anyone enjoys, and the obsession
with fertility has led to a situation in which, as in *Nineteen Eighty-
Four*, nobody is expected to derive any pleasure from sex. When
Ofred does not immediately become pregnant by the Commander,

Serena Joy arranges for her to sleep with a younger man, Nick, a rather attractive lower-caste Guardian. Ofred is ashamed of the noise she makes in an experience which reminds her of what love used to be like, and the fact that she then finds herself pregnant leads to what the text presents as a possibly successful attempt to escape into one of the deviant communities known as Mayday which can sometimes be reached by the 'Underground Femaleroad'. She is helped in this by the Commander, who has grown quite fond of her as a person during the surreptitious games of Scrabble which he has played with her, and whose child she may, after all, be carrying.

It is fairly easy to agree on a basic criterion for judging a novel set in the future: is the situation it describes a convincing projection of what is happening now? *In vitro* fertilisation, already a theoretical possibility in 1932, the year of publication of *Brave New World*, is now actually practised. In 1948, the possibility of the world being divided up into three superpowers perpetually changing sides in their constant war with one another was a fairly convincing projection of what had happened between 1933 and 1945. In 1985, when *The Handmaid's Tale* was published, the situation it described seemed less likely than the setting in Orwell or Huxley, and events since 1989 have given a quaintly old-fashioned look to the reference in the 'Historical Notes' to the 'recognition of the superpower stalemate and the signing of the Spheres of Influence Accord'. Nor is the male Anglo-Saxon visitor to the United States in the 1990s particularly conscious of the build-up of forces which will lead to a take-over of the country by the fundamentalist 'Sons of Jacob' and the establishment of a military dictatorship. The idea of the imposition of a single state religion and the systematic persecution of Baptists and Quakers also seems fairly remote.

Other details in *The Handmaid's Tale* make the male reader even more vulnerable to the temptation of dismissing it as a nightmare constructed for the ideological purpose of advertising the women's movement. Like Margaret Atwood's earlier novel, *Bodily Harm* (1982) and the first novel by which she sprang into prominence in 1969, *The Edible Woman*, it is written from a fairly aggressively feminist standpoint. There is, it is true, less violence against women than in *Bodily Harm*, and less of a suggestion that all men tend to act badly towards women. The Commander, after all, behaves towards Ofred with as much generosity as the very repressive society in which he lives will allow. But the implication is there in *The Handmaid's Tale* that the desire to reduce women to a subordinate role plays an important part in the subconscious longings of Western society as a whole, and the fact that the book sold over a million copies is not just a tribute to a well-told tale. It suggests that the male reader who yields to the temptation of saying that Margaret Atwood is exaggerating may well be living in a fool's paradise. This, reluctant though he may be to acknowledge it, is how many women see the world.

When Henry Higgins asked plaintively in *My Fair Lady* 'Oh, why can't a woman,/be more like a man?' he was putting his finger on what has become a central issue in the women's movement. This issue did not loom large in the thinking of Simone de Beauvoir, whose remark 'You're not born a woman. You become one' is so gratifyingly pithy a rejection of any kind of physiological determinism. When told that she thought such and such a thing because she was a woman, she would reply that she thought it because it was true. Her claim was to a rational mode of thinking which she saw as equally available to men and women alike. Women had been excluded from it in the past, but a change in the way people thought, and in the way they organised society, could improve matters so as to bring about a genuine equality between the sexes. It is a point of view which makes her a very attractive thinker for the middle-class Caucasian male who tries to ensure that his treatment of women differs from his treatment of men only by being more courteous.

It is not, however, an attitude widely shared by feminists of the second and third generation. Their attitude consists of saying that there is something specifically female about women which makes it the worst of all possible insults to try to treat them as honorary men. Whatever the atmosphere of her novels, Margaret Atwood's definition of feminism as 'human equality and freedom of choice' nevertheless places her more in the Simone de Beauvoir camp than in that of a writer such as Toril Moi. Her statement that 'I don't think that all men are the same, any more than I think that all women are the same. And there is such a thing as an intelligent, cultivated, well-read and sensitive man' may contradict the impression given by some of her fiction. But it has the great advantage of making it clear that she is not one of those women writers who will produce the mirror image of Henry Higgins's complaint and declare that a man cannot understand her books precisely because he is a man.

10

Moral Dilemmas III: Ends, Means and Irony; the Examples of Shaw, Dürrenmatt, Steiner and Sartre

I

Arthur Miller and ethics, Bernard Shaw and Orwell on money; an illustration from Rupert Brook of the problem of irony; Shaw a writer whose political views expressed outside his plays make him benefit from Barthes's distinction between the author who writes and the man who lives.

The history of the theatre, especially in the nineteenth century, offers nothing comparable to the progression which leads in the novel from Fielding to Dickens, Thackeray and Trollope, and then through Conrad, E. M. Forster, D. H. Lawrence and Orwell to Salman Rushdie or Toni Morrison. The great innovation in the theatrical experience of the nineteenth century was in the operas of Richard Wagner, and one only has to look at the plot and dialogue in cold print to realise why they needed the music. The pastiche of Wagner's Rhine Maidens in Gilbert and Sullivan's *Iolanthe* is a reminder of the fact that the only English playwright of the nineteenth century whose words are still recognised by modern readers is W. S. Gilbert; a man who, by an odd quirk of fate, was tone deaf.

One reason why the playwrights of the twentieth century have been so much more successful than their nineteenth-century predecessors has been their readiness to deal with ideas that are essentially controversial. This does not always involve creating a climate of moral uncertainty. In two of Arthur Miller's best-known and most successful plays, *The Crucible* (1953) and *A View from the Bridge* (1956), the problem which the central character has to face is not that of being unable to choose one course of action out of a number of possibilities that present themselves to him. It is that of deciding whether or not to put this choice into action by performing one particular deed. In *The Crucible*, John Proctor knows perfectly well that it is wrong for him to sign a document confessing to involvement in witchcraft. The problem which obsesses him is the typically Protestant and Puritan one of being uncertain whether he is worthy to make the sacrifice which will bear witness to a truth of which he is fully convinced. Eddie Carbone, in *A View from the Bridge*, knows that he is wrong to denounce Mario, Tony and Rodolpho to the immigration authorities. The ethic of his social subgroup is, in this respect, as firmly based as that of the Puritan New England in which John Proctor has to decide what kind of a man he is. While Proctor's final upsurge of dignity stems from a rationally justifiable attachment to his own name, Eddie Carbone is driven to commit his act of betrayal by a set of complex sexual drives which he does not wholly understand.

It is, in contrast, hard to imagine any character in a play by Shaw, Sartre or Stoppard acting for motives of which she or he is not fully aware. There is certainly passion in Shaw's Saint Joan, and it loses nothing in intensity of dramatic form by being totally non-sexual. But what matters in the play are the ideas, whether they take the Humpty Dumpty form of defining a miracle as an event which creates faith, or the more serious contention that Joan represented the twin forces of nationalism and Protestantism which were destined, in the centuries immediately succeeding her martyrdom in 1431, to destroy the medieval synthesis of a Christendom in which a single religious faith transcended all national boundaries. The title of *Major Barbara*, first performed in 1905, has the same effect as *Saint Joan* of reminding the reader of how frequently Shaw's female characters are stronger and more interesting than his men. It is nevertheless different in other aspects apart from its modern setting from *Saint Joan*, the other play by Shaw which has best withstood the passage of time. It is about the difficulty of deciding between right and wrong, a problem which did not greatly trouble Joan. It is also a play in which, for once, the man is allowed to win the argument.

After a succession of scenes in which Barbara Undershaft, a Major in the Salvation Army, is made to carry all before her in her contest with various forms of male proletarian aggressiveness in the shelter which she runs in the East End of London, she is made to face the much more serious intellectual challenge presented by her father. As a highly successful armaments manufacturer, Undershaft represents all the forces of triumphant evil against which Barbara is struggling. He is also a realist, in the sense of a man totally free from humbug, who makes no secret of the injustice of the wars which his industry makes possible and even, on occasion, encourages. Think, he tells Mrs Baines, one of Barbara's supporters,

> Think of my business! think of the widows and orphans! the men and lads torn to pieces with shrapnel and poisoned with lydite! the oceans of blood, not one of which is shed in a just cause

and adds 'All this makes money for me. I am never richer, never busier, than when the papers are full of it.'[1]

Power, in modern society, depends on money, and money is morally neutral in that it can just as easily be a force for good as a source of evil. Undershaft wins the argument with Barbara because he can do two things which are impossible for her. He can provide the money without which the Salvation Army hostel which she runs in the East End of London cannot stay open; and he can offer the poor man for whose soul she is struggling something which all her Christian charity and moral courage cannot provide. He can give him a steady job, in good working conditions. It is this, he maintains, which will enable Nobby Clarke to win back his self-respect, and the fact that Nobby will be making guns which will be used to kill his fellow men will not prevent the work he does from enabling him to emerge from what Shaw defines in his preface as 'the greatest of our evils and the worst of our crimes': poverty.

Shaw was not the only twentieth-century writer attracted by socialism to express an enthusiasm for money which is not always entirely ironic. In 1936, Orwell prefaced his novel *Keep the Aspidistra Flying* with a rewriting of St Paul's words in I Corinthians 13, beginning with the opening verse:

> Though I speak with the tongues of men and of angels, and

have not money, I am become as a sounding brass and as a tinkling cymbal,

and going right through to the conclusion that 'now abideth faith, hope, money, these three; but the greatest of these is money'.

The fact of being clothed in the cadences of the New Testament makes Orwell's satire a more elegantly phrased version of the doctrine which Undershaft puts forward when he tells Barbara's fiancé, the Greek scholar Adolphus Cusins, that 'honour, justice, truth, love and mercy are the graces and luxuries of a rich, strong and safe life', and Undershaft's arguments are intellectually irrefutable. Men who work in armaments factories are well paid, and the money they earn gives them the opportunity to lead much healthier, happier and more interesting lives than if they were unemployed. The relative failure, in the 1990s, of the Western democracies to derive economic profit from the 'peace dividend' created by the end of the Cold War adds weight to Shaw's argument. Indeed, one almost forgets that he is not actually on Undershaft's side, just as one is tempted to applaud when Gordon Comstock, the main character in *Keep the Aspidistra Flying*, goes back to working in an advertising agency.

There is a poem by Rupert Brook (1887–1915) which shows him to have had more of a sense of humour than one might think when reading 'The Soldier' or hearing the query in 'Grantchester' as to whether there is honey still for tea. It is called 'Fish', and is clearly intended as a variation on Montesquieu's remark that if triangles had a God, He would certainly have three sides. 'For somewhere', dream the fish

> beyond space and time,
> Is wetter water, slimier slime.
> And there, they say, there swimmeth one
> Who swam 'ere rivers first began.
> Immense, of fishy form and mind
> Squamous, Omnipotent and kind.
> And underneath that mighty fin,
> The littlest fish may enter in.

Whenever I have asked students to talk to me about Rupert Brooke's 'Fish', roughly one in three has seen it as an endorsement of Christianity, arguing that if there is a God, and if Heaven therefore does exist, fish will be as much a part of it as their favourite dog. This is an understandable reaction, and the superiority of *Major Barbara* over most other Marxist literature lies precisely in the fact that it can be quite easily interpreted as a play which expresses a reluctant admiration for capitalism and an accept-ance of war as an inevitable part of the human condition. You need to know that Shaw was totally opposed to all forms of mili-tarism to interpret the mottoes of the first and of the sixth mem-bers of the Undershaft dynasty, 'If God gave the hand, let not man withhold the sword' and 'Nothing is ever done in this world until men are prepared to kill one another if it is not done' en-tirely as ironic. However, once you have digested all the impli-cations of the play, the case which Shaw makes against the institutionalisation of warfare, as well as against an economic system which depends on the manufacture of armaments, becomes irrefutable. Subjectively, Barbara Undershaft is a thoroughly vir-tuous person. She is brave, honest, charitable, self-sacrificing, and devotes her life to the service of others. But objectively, the only long-term effect of these virtues is to help people accept the in-justices of society. Just as her father is made to support Marx in the brazenness with which he defends the very men whose work is the living proof of the self-destructive nature of capitalism, she is unconsciously endorsing Marx's description of religion as the opium of the people. In a world in which evil is so consist-ently triumphant, the Devil is bound to have all the best tunes.

Like most authors, Shaw was more intelligent and impressive as a writer than he was in the solutions he proposed as a man. One can perhaps understand that he was unable, as an Irishman, to support Great Britain in the 1914–18 war, and even possibly see why he thought that it might be good for her pride if she almost lost. But at one stage, in the 1930s, he argued that both Hitler and Stalin deserved support because of their ability to pro-duce a more efficiently run society than the one to which parlia-mentary democracy had given rise. The remarks which he made about Stalin in 1937, after visiting the Soviet Union in company with Lady Astor, give him pride of place among the fellow-trav-ellers of the left in their mixture of naïvety and self-satisfaction. He clearly saw Stalin as a kind of Undershaft of the left, com-menting that the secret of his success lay in the fact that he was 'entirely indifferent to the *means*' whereby he was changing the nature of Russian society and adding:

I have been preaching socialism all my political life, and here at last is a country which has established socialism, made it the basis of its political system, and turned its back on capitalism.[2]

II

Full employment and the price to pay? the example of Dürrenmatt's
The Visit; *Kundera on anti-Americanism.*

Although Shaw can now be seen as obviously wrong, he was by no means alone in the admiration which he expressed for the Soviet Union. Not all writers had the prescience of Camus, Orwell and Koestler, and there is a case for saying that those who committed themselves to the Soviet Union deserved some credit by the mere fact of trying. The moral case for some kind of political commitment comes out if one compares the atmosphere of Shaw's or Sartre's work with that of the Swiss dramatist Friedrich Dürrenmatt, in the same way that the literary advantages of irony become even more apparent when Dürrenmatt's best-known play, his *Der Besuch der Alten Dame* (*The Visit*), first produced in 1956, is compared to *Major Barbara*.

Both plays depict the failure of capitalism, and the closing chorus of *The Visit* echoes the plight of the unemployed in terms very similar to those which Eliot had used in 1930 in *The Rock*, when he had them say:

No man has hired us
With pocketed hands
And lowered faces
We stand about in open places
And shiver in unlit rooms.
Only the wind moves
Over empty fields, untilled,
Where the plough rests, at an angle
To the furrow. In this land
There shall be one cigarette to two men,
To two women one half pint of bitter
Ale. In this land
No man has hired us.
Our life is unwelcome, our death

Unmentioned in 'The Times'.

In Dürrenmatt's play, the unemployed also express the collective nature of their misfortune by speaking in chorus:

Chorus Two:

These monstrous things
 do not exceed
The monstrous plight
 of poverty
Which excites
 no tragic deed
Is not heroic
 but condemns
Our human race
 to barren days
After hopeless
 yesterdays.

The Women:

The mothers are helpless, they watch
 Their loved ones pining away.

The Men:

But the rumour rebellion
 The men think treachery.

Man One:

In worn out shoes they pace the town.

Man Three:

A filthy fag-end in their mouths

Chorus One:

For the jobs, the jobs that earned the bread
 The jobs are gone.

The starkness of the chorus in *The Visit* is nevertheless nothing compared to the plot which they introduce. This describes how Claire Zachanassian, the richest woman in the world, returns to her native town of Guellen in search of vengeance. Forty-five years earlier, she had been seduced by Ill, who had abandoned her to marry Mathilda Blumhard, heiress to the town's little general store. Claire was pregnant, but her child died of meningitis, leaving her free to pursue her career as a high-class courtesan, eventually marrying an immensely rich old man. She has then gone from strength to strength, amassing a vast personal fortune which includes ownership of all the mills, factories and businesses in Guellen. These she has systematically deprived of business, so that when she arrives, it is to a town that is economically ruined. The price which she demands to restore it to prosperity by the gift of half a million to the town itself, together with half a million to be shared out equally among all its inhabitants, is the death of her former lover.

Initially, her demands are indignantly refused, with the mayor declaring that he would sooner endure absolute poverty than have blood on his hands. But the shape of things to come is visible in the refusal by the town policeman to arrest Claire for incitement to murder, his argument being that the size of the sum offered is so enormous as to place her promise in the world of fantasy. As the townsfolk begin to borrow money on the strength of their expectations, their resolution also weakens, with the schoolmaster producing a particularly telling argument for accepting Claire's suggestion. He is, as he says himself, 'a humanist, a lover of the ancient Greeks, an admirer of Plato', a man who speaks eloquently of Guellen as a 'city of Humanist tradition', where Goethe once spent a night and Brahms composed a quartet. And, he adds, it is the memory of these past glories which now makes him realise how guilty he was not to have spoken out earlier, at the time when Claire was first sent away in disgrace. But he is ready to make amends.

The mayor, while nevertheless insisting on the formality of a trial, says that it is Ill's duty to his fellow citizens to allow himself to be killed. The priest calls upon him to think of his soul's immortality and take the path of repentance. When the Police, the Medical Profession and the representatives of the Opposition party are asked for their opinion, they declare that they have nothing to say. Ill eventually dies, 'of joy' according the mayor and the radio reporter describing the scene, but in fact of a heart attack brought on by the terror of seeing the whole town willing him to die. The town itself, 'grown out of ashes anew' recovers its former prosperity. The old lady's visit has ended.

In a Postscript, Dürrenmatt insisted on two aspects of the play which he thought might perhaps have escaped some spectators: what he clearly regarded as its straightforward realism, and its mythological overtones. Claire Zachanassian, he wrote,

> doesn't represent justice, or the Marshall Plan, or even the Apocalypse. She is purely and simply what she is, namely, the richest woman in the world and, thanks to her finances, in a position to act as the Greek tragic heroines acted, absolutely, terribly, something like Medea.[3]

The evocation of Medea is not inappropriate. She avenges herself on her faithless lover, Jason, by sending his new bride a tunic of flame which she cannot shake off, and then punishes him further by killing the children she has had by him. Claire leaves the people who have betrayed her with what she hopes is a burden of guilt comparable to the one which Medea inflicts on Jason.

The mention of the Marshall Plan strikes an odder note and is another pointer as to the tendency of twentieth-century literary men to look at politics in a very odd way. In Hitler's Germany or Stalin's Russia the price for the prosperity constantly promised by totalitarianism was always made clear. It was the murder of the Jews or the elimination of the kulaks, just as the restoration of prosperity to Guellen depended on the murder of Ill. The $12 billion dollars provided for France, Italy, West Germany, Holland, Belgium and West Germany by the Marshall Plan between 1948 and 1952 were, in contrast, given entirely without strings. But as Milan Kundera was to observe as late as as 1984, in *The Unbearable Lightness of Being*, the great protest marches were 'always against the Americans';[4] and in 1956, Dürrenmatt clearly expected his audience to have the same hostility to the USA.

The comparison between *Major Barbara* and *The Visit* is instructive for historical as well as for literary reasons. In 1906, the debate about ends and means could be put forward in terms of a rational argument, conducted between civilised human beings, and with more than a touch of humour. While Claire Zachanassian is obviously mad, Undershaft is triumphantly sane. His arguments reflect, for all their irony, something of the optimism of the long

Edwardian afternoon. Just turn what I am saying around, Shaw suggests, and make sure that society is organised on a rational basis, and all will be well. But by 1956, the great disasters of the 1914–18 war, of the triumph of totalitarianism in Russia after 1917, in Italy after 1922, in Germany after 1933 and in Spain after 1936, accompanied by the discovery after 1945 of the extent of the Holocaust in which six million Jews were systematically murdered, made it impossible to discuss politics with the emotional detachment which characterises *Major Barbara*. Shaw sends the audience home smiling at the arguments. Dürrenmatt makes us wonder if we too would connive in murder if it promised to make us and our fellow citizens very rich.

III

Tragedy and irony in George Steiner: the example of The Portage to San Cristobal of A.H.; *the uniqueness of the Holocaust; a further comparison with* Major Barbara.

George Steiner's best-known book, *The Death of Tragedy* (1961) argues that there is something in modern society which prevents us from producing tragedy in the sense which the word has traditionally had when used in a literary context. He is not the only writer to put forward the thesis that the spirit of tragedy flies out through the window when the concept of bourgeois prudence and rationalism which governs Western society comes in at the door. The same theory runs through what used to be admired as a classic of Marxist literary criticism, the long analysis of the world of Pascal and Racine which Lucien Goldmann published in 1955 under the title *Le Dieu caché* (*The Hidden God*),[5] and can also be found in one of the few twentieth-century playwrights to confront the problem of tragedy in practice as well as in theory, Arthur Miller. He expressed the same idea as Steiner and Goldmann in more colloquial and practical terms when he made the chorus figure in *A View from the Bridge*, the lawyer Alfieri, describe the characteristic ethos of American civilisation as a readiness to 'settle for half'.

Steiner's argument is based on the idea that we lack the reverence for sacred and transcendent values which was an outstanding feature of the cultures which, like fifth-century Athens and

Renaissance Europe, originally gave birth to tragedy. When Arthur Miller's Alfieri contrasts this spirit of compromise with the passion for absolutes which the Sicilian immigrants into his part of New York have brought with them, he is also underlining the economic and social reasons which make the writing of tragedy so difficult in the twentieth century. An industrial economy like that of the United States can be kept going only by applied science and double entry book-keeping. These are not activities compatible with tragedy. A peasant economy, like that of Sicily, can afford to be less calculating. So, too, can the inhabitants of Provence who cause one another and themselves such pointless sufferings in Pagnol's *Jean de Florette* and *Manon des Sources*.

Like Arthur Miller, Steiner is a Jew and thus even more conscious than other people of the peculiar and extraordinary horror of Hitler's attempt to exterminate the whole Jewish race. Like Theodore Adorno, who said that there could be no poetry after Auschwitz, Steiner has also argued that the ultimate horror of the Final Solution meant that there could be no more tragedy either. However terrible the sufferings of an Oedipus or a Lear might be, they happened to an individual, and to an individual who could, in the final analysis, make sense of his suffering through words. The Holocaust happened to a whole people, and in the name of an ideology which defies rational comprehension. What is fascinating about Steiner's one play, *The Portage to San Cristobal of A.H.*, is that it is a work of art which tries to understand the Holocaust, and to do so in the only way in which, for post-modernist critics, such an understanding is possible: through derision, irony and paradox.

In *The Portage to San Cristobal of A.H.*, a group of Jewish Nazi hunters has succeeded in tracking down Hitler to his hideout in the depths of the Amazonian jungle. As they bring him to the port from which he can be taken to Israel for judgment, they relate some of the atrocities of the Holocaust while Hitler himself remains silent. Then, at the very end of the play, Hitler is given a long speech in which he justifies his behaviour on two main grounds. First of all, he argues, anti-semitism is understandable, and to some extent justified. It is, above all else, the reaction of the common run of humanity against the impossibly high moral requirements laid upon them by Jewish thinkers. Secondly, he maintains that the Holocaust accomplished something which all the efforts of the Zionist movement could never have achieved.

Thanks to the murder of six million Jews, the State of Israel was established as a homeland for those who survived.

There is also something oddly irrefutable about both arguments which Steiner makes Hitler put forward. Christ did demand that we should be perfect even as our Father in Heaven is perfect. Marx did look forward to the creation of the classless society, to the withering away of the state, to the ideal society in which each should give according to his ability and be rewarded according to his needs, to the replacement of the government of men by the administration of things. Freud did require of us that we be totally honest in our recognition of the unconscious desires which lie at the root of our sexual lives, and cease to be as hypocritical about our children's sexuality as we have traditionally been about our own. It is equally true that the State of Israel was more obviously born of the Holocaust than of any other single event. What is also true, and highly disturbing, is that these arguments are put forward by a man who is clearly insane.

There are, it is true, rational objections to these arguments. The moralists whom Steiner's Hitler presents as characteristically Jewish were not the only thinkers to proclaim moral absolutes. Kant required that every man should be treated as an end in himself and never as a means to an end, and laid upon us the duty to tell the complete truth at all times. Nobody, however, has ever suggested the wholescale elimination of German pietist philosophers. The State of Israel might have come into being in a different way, and six million lives is a price which no sane person would accept to pay for any objective. But the words that Steiner puts into Hitler's mouth send the audience away in a state of mind which is a good deal more perplexed than the one in which they emerge from *Major Barbara*; or even from Dürrenmatt's *The Visit*.

The Portage to San Cristobel of A.H. was clearly written against the grain in a way that nothing by Shaw or Dürrenmatt ever was. This, perhaps, is one of the reasons why it is so moving a play. Auden's remark that 'The truest poetry is the most feigning' can apply just as well to drama as to verse. But both Shaw and Steiner knew exactly what they were doing, and there is no chance of either of them ever being surprised by a reading of their work that they had not anticipated. What is odd about Sartre, the only professional philosopher ever to have become a best-selling novelist and a highly successful playwright, is that his best play, the 1948 political melodrama *Les Mains Sales*, is incapable of offering any support to the political causes to which he devoted so much of his life. Indeed, Sartre himself became so aware of its potentially anti-revolutionary message that from 1952 until 1970 he issued a ban on all new productions.

III

Sartre and politics: the dichotomy between his public statements and literary works illustrated by Les Mains Sales; *more thoughts on tragedy; further comparisons with Orwell, Arthur Miller and Shaw.*

Although Sartre was writing, as late as 1964, that 'whatever its crimes, the USSR has one extraordinary superiority over the Western democracies: it wants to bring about the revolution'[6] his work as an imaginative writer never gave anything like so un-ambiguous an endorsement of a particular course of political action. Between 1968 and 1973, he was unwavering in his opposition to the American involvement in Vietnam, just as he had opposed the attempt of the French government to hold on to Algeria by force of arms between 1954 and 1962. But the only work of imaginative literature inspired by his commitment to what he saw as the cause of all free peoples was an adaptation in 1965 of Euripides's *The Trojan Women*, a play directed against all wars, and far from being simply a denunciation of Western imperialism. And although the message which he wanted to come over from *Les Mains Sales* was that ends do justify the means, and that the good political leader is the one who accepts the need to get his hands dirty, the plot of the play by no means bears out this rather simplistic interpretation.

The action of the play takes place between 1942 and 1944 in the Eastern European country of Illyria and describes how a young bourgeois intellectual, Hugo Barine, accompanied by his wife, Jessica, accepts a mission to murder the current leader of the Pro-letarian Party, Hoederer, in order to prevent him from secretly changing the party line. He succeeds, but only through a fit of jealousy when the accident of finding Hoederer making love to Jessica gives him the ability to pull the trigger. What had been intended as political assassination becomes the 'crime passionnel' of the English title. Since the action of the play is taking place on the Continent, where the authorities traditionally take a fairly lenient attitude to such matters, Hugo is given only a two-year prison sentence. He also learns, on his release, that his mission to kill Hoederer had been based upon faulty information. Since Hoederer's death, orders have come through from Moscow instructing the Party to make exactly the change that Hoederer was recommending.

Hugo has thus, in political terms, killed for nothing. But although his intention, when he comes into Hoederer's study and finds him kissing Jessica, has been to tell him that he has changed his mind and is prepared to go along with the change of party line which Hoederer has been trying to bring about, such rapid changes of allegiance are not now something which he is prepared to accept. A man like Hoederer, he declares, lived and worked by political values, and deserves to die for them. If he, Hugo, refuses to go back into the Party, and insists that his action in killing Hoederer was a political act and not a crime passionnel, he will have shown by his own example that ends cannot be perpetually sacrificed to means. He will have proved that he was right in his earlier insistence that a party seeking to establish a just society cannot do so by lies. During the whole of the play, in which most of the action is told in flashback, Hugo and the audience know that the Party gunmen are waiting outside, ready to kill him if told to do so. If he refuses to accept that he killed Hoederer in a fit of sexual jealousy, and insists instead that it was to prevent him from putting into practice what is now official policy, he will be shot down as an inconvenient witness. The Party line, in the Illyria of 1944, as in the Oceania of George Orwell's *Nineteen Eighty-Four*, must always be shown to have been what it is now.

When the play was first produced, in Paris in April 1948, the audience's sympathy was almost entirely with Hugo, and especially in his final refusal to accept that he had committed only a 'crime passionnel'. His arguments might, on closer analysis, appear muddled, and his final action a gesture of romantic despair, and this, indeed, was what Sartre had intended the spectator to feel. What, after all, is the point of dying a martyr's death if nobody knows that you are doing it? When John Proctor, at the end of *The Crucible*, finally refuses to allow his name to appear on the list of those confessing to the use of witchcraft, he knows that he will be publicly hanged. His defiance of the witch-hunters will consequently become one of the actions whereby, as Miller himself puts it, the 'power of theocracy is eventually broken in Massachussetts'. In the immediate political context in which *The Crucible* was produced in 1952, the message of the play was quite clear: anyone required by the witch-hunt of Senator McCarthy to confess his membership of the Communist party, and to implicate others in his confession, should refuse. Tyrannies collapse when men of good will defy them publicly, and are prepared to pay the cost of this defiance. It is a message eminently suited to the Puritan ethic of early seventeenth-century America which provides the background for the play, as well as to the concept of personal responsibility which runs through all of Miller's work.

It is also an ethic which the political culture of the United States was mature enough at the time for people to put it meaningfully into practice. This was not the case in continental Europe in the middle of the twentieth century, and especially not in France. There, the political party which seemed most likely, not only to Sartre but to millions like him, to destroy capitalism and replace a decadent, unjust and inefficient system of parliamentary democracy by a more effective and egalitarian form of government made no secret of its loyalty to the Soviet Union. But the French Communist party had also been required, in the name of this loyalty, to subscribe to at least three changes in the party line which were as abrupt as those which provide the plot of *Les Mains Sales*, and to which Orwell was referring in *Nineteen Eighty-Four*.

Les Mains Sales, written and performed when events such as the Nazi-Soviet pact of 23 August 1939 were fresh in everybody's mind, is consequently, among other things, a play which explains why Orwell has never had the same importance for French readers as he has in England or America. They have their own version of the literature of the Cold War, even though its most effective work may have been written by a man who thought he was furthering the cause of the revolution. What Sartre's play also illustrated, with a vividness equal to that of Orwell's novel, was that the party line was at one and the same time sufficiently sacred to justify murder and yet sufficiently flexible to be changed at a moment's notice. This was almost certainly not what Sartre intended to say, but it was what the audience understood him to be saying. It was in this sense that he was more perceptive as a playwright than he ever was as a political philosopher or consciously committed writer, and that the way he highlighted the end/means dilemma took on tragic overtones. Hugo and Hoederer, like the real Communist leaders whom they resembled, had sought, as Oedipus had done in Sophocles's tragedy, to do good; and, like him, they had been brought to ruin by a false belief. In response to the truth told to him by the Oracle at Delphi, Oedipus had fled from Corinth in order to avoid killing Polybus, King of Corinth, who had adopted him as a child and whom he wrongly believed to be his biological father. His attempt to avoid committing the crime of patricide led him instead to the place near Thebes where three roads meet, and where he met and murdered Laios, the man who had engendered him, and whom he had been predestined to kill. Countless men and women refused to serve what they called bourgeois democracy, and sacrificed their lives in the service of the Marxist concept of the classless society. The illusion killed them. In so far as *Les Mains Sales* is an illustration of Napoleon's remark that tragedy, in the modern world, lies in the realm of politics, it is an unconscious tribute to their fate.

To the reader or spectator coming to it in the 1990s, the play is nevertheless like the song which Wordsworth's highland reaper sang

of old, forgotten, half dead things,
And battles long ago

with the only character with whom the spectator of 1994 can fully sympathise being that of Jessica. Throughout her life, she complains to Hugo, she has been told to mind her own business and let the men get on with the job of running the world. Now, she finds herself in the position where she has to keep quiet while her husband commits a totally pointless murder, and to the reader of the 1990s, her protest gives her an authenticity which was not there when the play was first performed. Then, she was seen as simply a device which Sartre introduced to give the play its plot. Now, and in spite of the fact that Sartre's long association with Simone de Beauvoir seems to have given him little enthusiasm for the women's movement, she becomes a highly persuasive spokesperson for it.

In *Les Mains Sales*, Hoederer is an Andrew Undershaft with even fewer illusions about the way in which power is obtained and exercised in the real world, and Hugo a Major Barbara who is presented as willing the end without accepting to endorse the means. He would like to see the advent of the classless society, but cannot accept the lies and ruthlessness which Hoederer tells him are essential to its realisation. He has, he tells Hugo, no objection to political assassinations. All parties use them as a means of obtaining and exercising power, and the impression which he gives of announcing a self-evident truth is another reminder of the unconscious realism of *Les Mains Sales*. In mid-twentieth-century Europe, it was only the English who had what Orwell described as 'the habit of *not killing one another*'[7] for political reasons. Undershaft, after all, killed only by proxy, and for money.

11

Politics, Commitment and the Responsibilities of the Scientist

I

Bertrand Russell and Solzhenitsyn: nuclear disarmament and the world of the Gulag.

The one political cause in the post-war world which attracted unambiguous support from writers outside what used to be the Soviet Union was that of nuclear disarmament. The opposition to nuclear weapons was most eloquently expressed by Bertrand Russell in a talk on the BBC on 23 December 1954, under the title *Man's Peril*:

> As geological time is reckoned, man has so far existed only for a very short period – 1,000,000 years at the most. What he has achieved, especially during the last 6,000 years, is something utterly new in the history of the cosmos, at least as far as we are acquainted with it. For countless ages the sun rose and set, the moon waxed and waned, the stars shone in the night, but it was only with the coming of man that these things were understood. In the great world of astronomy and the little world of the atom, man has unveiled secrets which might have been thought undiscoverable. In art and literature and religion, some men have shown a sublimity of feeling which makes the species worth preserving. Is all this going to end in trivial horror because so few are able to think of man rather than of this or that group of men? Is our race so destitute of wisdom, so incapable of impartial love, so blind even to the simplest dictates of blind preservation, that the last proof of our silly cleverness is to be the extermination of all life on our planet? – for it will be not only men who will perish, but also the animals, whom none can accuse of Communism or anti-Communism.[1]

202

The text was intensely moving at the time, and has remained so. It provided, should it have been needed, additional evidence of how fully Russell had deserved on the grounds of style alone the Nobel Prize for Literature given to him in 1950. But there is little evidence that the campaign he supported influenced the behaviour of any government. Like the novels of Solzhenitsyn, Russell's courage and eloquence profoundly influenced public opinion. But it would be hard to maintain that any philosopher, poet, playwright or novelist played a major role in either of the two crucial political events of the second half of the twentieth century: the avoidance of an atomic war between the United States and the Soviet Union, and the collapse of the Soviet regime in the early 1990s. Novels such as Alan Paton's 1948 novel *Cry the Beloved Country*, André Brink's 1988 *State of Emergency*, or the work of Doris Lessing may have helped to bring about the end of apartheit, and Norman Mailer's *Armies of the Night* may have hastened the end of the Vietnam war. No comparable claim can be made either for Solzhenitsyn or for writers who, like Bertolt Brecht or Friedrich Dürrenmatt, expressed views on nuclear weapons and the Cold War which were similar to those of Russell.

There is, from this point of view, an irony which matches the paradox whereby the rejection of Christianity by writers of the twentieth century should be so frequently based on the idea of the cruelty and injustice of God. Since at no point in human history do men seem to have behaved with more systematic cruelty towards one another, it is strange that they should not look more closely at the beam in their own eye. At no other time, except perhaps in the France of the eighteenth century, have so many writers seen literature as a privileged means for trying to improve the human condition. But at no other period do they seem to have had less influence on actual political decisions. Auden's remark that none of his poems saved a single Jew from the gas chamber expresses the irony of one of the greatest poets of the century coming to realise that there are times when the pen is not, after all, mightier than the sword.

By the time Solzhenitsyn's *A Day in the Life of Ivan Denisovitch* was published, in 1962, suspicion of the Soviet Union had already become sufficiently widespread in government circles in the West for resistance to its foreign policy not to need boosting by even the most brilliant and imaginative piece of reportage. The effect of Solzhenitsyn's *novella* might perhaps have been different if it had been published at the same time as Orwell's *Nineteen Eighty-Four*. It might, to change Frederic Warburg's phrase, have brought more than a cool two million votes for the Conservative party.[2] Indeed, the effect of so obviously accurate a personal account of what life was like in the Soviet forced labour camps might even have led the occasional Frenchman to think twice before voting for the Communist party. But in 1948, Solzhenitsyn was still in the middle of the eight-year sentence of hard labour in the Gulag imposed on him for the crime of having, in a private letter to a friend, expressed some doubt in 1945 about the political wisdom of 'the man with the moustache'.

Until the collapse of the Soviet regime in the early 1990s, *A Day in the Life of Ivan Denisovitch* remained the only book which Solzenitsyn had been allowed to publish in his home country. The reimposition in the Soviet Union of strict censorship in 1964, after the brief respite of the Khrushchev period, meant that Solzhenitsyn's other accounts of life under Communism, *The Cancer Ward* and *The First Circle* first appeared, translated, in the West. The overwhelming impact of these books is one of waste. Solzhenitsyn himself calculated the total number of Stalin's victims as 60,000,000 – not counting the 20,000,000 killed in the war which the attempt to appease Hitler by the pact of 23 August 1939 helped to bring about – and suggested that two-thirds of these died in the camps. This makes the case of Solzhenitsyn's first hero, Ivan Denisovitch Sukhov, an unusual one. The day in January 1951 which Ivan Denisovitch spends in the camp is essentially the story of his survival. In spite of the 20 degrees of frost in which he and his companions have to live, he has kept some shreds of human dignity and remained alive for another of the 3653 days of his sentence. He has even built a wall and has almost doubled his food ration. There is nevertheless immense and tragic irony in the concluding sentence: 'Nothing had spoilt his day and it had been almost happy'.

This is not how men were meant to live anywhere, least of all in the country of which Beatrice and Sidney Webb had written with such enthusiasm in 1935 in their *Soviet Communism. A New Civilisation*? or which Dr Hewlett Johnson, Dean of Westminster Cathedral, had praised in *The Socialist Sixth of the World*, in 1939, with none of the reservations which even the Webbs had expressed about its autocratic tendencies.

A Day in the Life of Ivan Denisovitch was published in the Soviet

Union in 1962, and praised in the official newspaper *Pravda*. The speech in the early summer of 1956 in which Nikita Khrushchev had denounced Stalin's crimes, and attributed them solely to the malign influence of the 'cult of the personality', seemed at the time to be leading to a thawing of attitudes in Soviet society. Solzhenitsyn himself benefited from this by not being required to serve the permanent exile in Siberia which had been supposed to follow his eight years in the Gulag. But in 1964, Khrushchev fell from power and a general clampdown followed. When Solzhenitsyn was awarded the Nobel Prize for Literature in 1970, he dared not leave Russia to attend the ceremony for fear of not being allowed back. In Stalin's day, the appearance in the West in 1974 of the first two volumes of *The Gulag Archipelago* would have led to Solzhenitsyn's rapid disappearance into what he described in that novel as the 'sewage disposal system', but he was by that time too well known, and in February 1974, he was bundled on to a plane and sent into exile. When he was allowed to return to Russia, in June 1994, he showed as little enthusiasm for the attempt to reintroduce capitalism as he had for the longer imposition of Communism.

Solzhenitsyn's novels about the forced labour camps in the Soviet Union make a very specific political point. Khrushchev's speech to the Twentieth Party Congress had argued that the horrors which afflicted the Soviet Union from the moment Stalin became General Secretary of the Central Committee of the Communist Party of the USSR in 1922 to his death in 1953 were the direct result of the way the cult of the personality had distorted 'Soviet legality'. On the contrary, argued Solzhenitsyn, these horrors were an integral part of the system established by the revolution of 1917. No reform would ever be possible, he insisted, unless this fact was acknowledged, and the leaders of the regime made to do penance for their sins. There is, in this aspect of his work, a strong similarity between Solzhenitsyn and Dostoievski, with Christian repentance seen as the only possible way forward, and the recognition of the diabolical nature of socialism an essential first step. This is very much what Dostoievski argued in *The Possessed* in 1871, and Camus's adaptation of this novel to the French stage in 1959 showed how far he had moved from his early sympathy with socialism.

Solzhenitsyn's analysis of the reasons lying behind what the British historian Robert Conquest called *The Great Terror* has other links with highly conservative modes of thought. Zbigniew

Brzezinski, whose Polish background and hawkish stance made him a surprising choice as President Carter's Assistant to the President for National Security Affairs between 1977 and 1982, began his career as a political analyst by arguing, in 1956, in a book called *The Permanent Purge. Politics in Soviet Totalitarianism*, that the main function of the show trials of the late 1930s was to reinforce Stalin's authority. So long as Stalin's colleagues and potential rivals were terrified that they might suddenly be subjected to torture, humiliation and death, there was no way in which they might challenge him as leader. Solzhenitsyn argues exactly the same case for the terror which, in the early 1950s, had created the world of the Gulag, where according to his calculations one in eight Soviet citizens was held prisoner, and whose total population exceeded that of countries such as Belgium, Denmark or Sweden. It was, in his view, the duty of everyone who had been a *zek* – a prisoner in the Gulag – to bear witness to what had happened, and one of the heroes of *The First* Circle, the mathematician Gleb Nerzhin, does precisely this when he gives up his original profession in order to become an historian.

The title of the book is from Dante, the 'first circle' in the *Inferno* being the one where the virtuous but pre-Christian philosophers work out their sentence, victims of the 'invincible ignorance' of not having had the opportunity to know the truth revealed by Christ's coming. In Solzhenitsyn, the term has an even more sinister ring. The inmates of this prison are not yet in the hell of the camps. Their task is to use their scientific knowledge to develop a scrambler telephone, a device which, as Solzhenitsyn points out, had been standard equipment in the West before the Second World War, but which the Soviet regime could not accept as coming from its chosen enemy. No progress is made towards its development, and the theme of the uselessness of the system of prison labour is as central as it is in *A Day in the Life of Ivan Denisovitch*. The same applies to the account in *The Gulag Archipelago* itself of the building of the White Sea Canal. In spite of the sacrifice of the 100,000 lives which it took to build it, this was too shallow to be used by any but the smallest ships.

Neither the concept of intertextuality nor the Barthesian notion of fiction as the exploitation of a set of codes could possibly be applied to the work of Solzhenitsyn. Even more than *In Cold Blood* or *Schindler's Ark*, they are examples of Truman Capote's ambition to write 'the Non-Fiction Novel'. The appearance of Solzhenitsyn's books had a greater impact in France than perhaps in any other country, since it was among French intellectuals that the myth of the Soviet Union had proved most resistant. Orwell's work had had little impact there, and a variant of the question asked by Squealer in *Animal Farm* whenever the animals complained – 'Surely no-one among you wants to see Jones come back?' – was addressed to anyone criticising the Soviet Union. It was an argument summed up in Sartre's phrase about the need to avoid doing anything which might 'désespérer Billancourt': cast the workers in the island in the Seine where the main Renault factory works were situated into despair.

II

The writer and politics. Brecht, Dürrenmatt and the responsibility of the scientist; some comparisons with John Osborne and Shaw.

When, in 1951, Lionel Trilling drew attention to the lack of enthusiasm which twentieth-century writers had for the ideals and practice of parliamentary democracy and the liberal society, he was concerned mainly with enumerating those writers who seemed most out of sympathy with the way their fellow citizens in the United States, the United Kingdom and Western Europe seemed to want to live. He was counting on his readers knowing enough about Yeats, Lawrence, Pound or Proust to recall the interest of the first in mythology and the occult, the hostility which he shared with Lawrence to all forms of industrialism, the sympathy which both he and Lawrence occasionally expressed for the Fascism so admired by Pound, as well as Proust's conviction that the religion of art was the only value worth pursuing. Perhaps rightly, he did not talk about the attitude which writers took on specific political issues. As I suggest in my references to Chesterton and Claudel, as in my discussion of Shaw and Sartre, writers who involve themselves in politics do not always do themselves much credit. It is nevertheless a curious feature of twentieth-century literature that the two events about whose beneficial effects there can be the least dispute, the victory of the Western democracies in the Cold War, following on their defeat of Hitler, should have been treated with such relative indifference both by imaginative writers and by their critics.

Yet while David Fraser's *August 1988* – mentioned above in Chapter 8 – sank without trace, it expressed a point of view which would probably have won enthusiastic support for Solzhenitsyn. He was hawkish enough, during his 20 years of exile, to accuse the West of systematic cowardice in what he regarded as its desire to appease the Soviet Union, and did not shrink from expressing admiration for the regime of General Franco. It is also a pity on purely literary grounds that *August 1988* did not go into paperback. It is as exciting a yarn as Eugene Burdicks's 1962 novel *Fail Safe*, a thriller in which a series of technical mishaps produces a situation in which the President of the United States finally has to drop an atomic bomb on New York in order to prove that a similar device dropped on Moscow was an accident and not a deliberate attempt to start a war.

The fact that David Fraser's novel is so little known to the reading public is nevertheless perfectly explicable. The presuppositions which governed the discussion of nuclear weapons among intellectuals and men of letters in Western Europe and North America throughout the Cold War were that such weapons served no useful political purpose. They were, on the contrary, nothing more than the manifestation of a peculiar kind of madness which was leading mankind to destroy itself.

Men of letters were not therefore particularly sympathetic to the argument put forward in *August 1988* that the point of having nuclear weapons was not to use them yourself but to deter your opponent from threatening to use them against you, and David Fraser's novel was prevented from reaching a wider public by not being given the reviews without which works of fiction fall dead from the press. The view of nuclear weapons as indefensible on any grounds governs the two best-known plays to deal with the issue, both of which support the total rejection of them expressed by Bertrand Russell in his 1954 broadcast: Bertold Brecht's *Galileo Galilei* and Friedrich Dürrenmatt's *The Physicists*. Both expressed a much more politically correct viewpoint.

The performance in America in 1947 of *The Life of Galileo* was nevertheless not an outstanding success. Although Brecht himself admired the size of Charles Laughton's belly, and regretted his own inability to eat as much, Laughton's performance in the title role did not show him at his best, and the production at the Coronet Theatre, Hollywood, on 31 July 1947 received few plaudits from the critics. Although the theatre was packed for the 30 performances scheduled, its transfer to the Maxine Elliot theatre, Broadway, ran for only a few weeks, and Brecht is unusual among modern playwrights, whether of the right or of the left, in having found his most enthusiastic audiences in state-supported theatres. From January 1949 onwards, the existence of the Berliner Ensemble made East Berlin into one of the great theatrical centres of the world. Seats were cheap, thanks to a generous state subsidy, thus enabling Brecht to fulfil the dream of all progressively minded twentieth-century dramatists and have members of the working class as well as of the bourgeoisie among the audience.

In the first version of *Galileo Galilei*, it is through a kind of peasant cunning that Galileo bows to the threats of the Inquisition and agrees not to persist with the heretical view that the earth goes round the sun. This subterfuge will enable him to stay alive and fight another day, confident in the knowledge that even the Papacy will one day have to acknowledge at least some of the truths discovered by science. In the second version, however, the one performed in the United States in 1947, Galileo's motivation changes, and the play has a less optimistic ending. It is also an ending which expresses a clearer and more intransigent attitude to what Brecht wanted his audience to see as the central dilemma of the twentieth-century scientist. Galileo is presented as wrong to have yielded to the Inquisition. He ought, Brecht implies, to have stood out for the integrity of the scientist. This would have enabled him, at the crucial moment when Western science was reaching take-off point, to have placed it on a firm moral footing. This foundation would, by implication, have been one in which scientists refused to collaborate with the state in the manufacture of weapons of mass destruction.

Brecht's attitude on the question of nuclear weapons is expressed in the final version of *Galileo* with a certainty about who is right and who is wrong in 'the perpetual struggle between good and evil' which would have delighted T. S. Eliot. Whatever objections Eliot might have had, as a Royalist and High Church Tory, to so obviously Marxist a play, it would have been illogical for him not to admire a fellow believer in ethical absolutes. The dramatic force of Tom Stoppard's plays stems from the fact that they deal with what Brice Gallie calls 'essentially contested concepts'.[3] Like Shaw and Sartre, he writes about issues on which there is no general agreement, and presents them in that light. Spectators of *The Life of Galileo*, in contrast, are left in as little doubt as to who was right and who was wrong as they are in a poem by Claudel or a short story by G. K. Chesterton.

The Galileo of the second version nevertheless remains, from a Marxist point of view, a scientist on the side of the angels. He is still the man whose scientific discoveries go against the interests of the aristocrats, the land-owners and the church. But he is also a hedonist, a man of the flesh. And since this has the effect of making his fear of pain as intense as his love of pleasure, the servants of the Holy Office need do no more, as the Cardinal observes, than to show him the instruments. The mere thought of the pain which he realises they can inflict makes him immediately retract. Instead of emerging as the incarnation of the sly wisdom which enables the peasant to survive in a harsh and cruel world, the Galileo of the second version ends the play as a broken man, his only consolation the thought of the succulent goose which will be served at the next meal.

In the fullness of time, the attitude which *The Life of Galileo* expresses on the question of nuclear weapons and on the social responsibility of the scientist helped Brecht's play to enjoy the success it deserved on purely theatrical grounds. The political objections to it which were valid in 1947, and which may have played their part in preventing it from being as immediately successful as Brecht's other plays, and especially his *Mother Courage*, have now disappeared. It no longer seems particularly important, as it did to some spectators in the West in 1947, that its plea for the scientist not to co-operate with the powers that be had very one-sided political implications. At the time, the Soviet Union had not yet developed its own nuclear weapons. It was therefore greatly to its advantage for scientists in America to agree with Brecht, opt out of nuclear research, and make sure that the United States of America did not improve on the strategic lead which it then enjoyed.

Technically, the Jimmy Porter of John Osborne's *Look Back in Anger* is sane, though it would not be difficult to imagine a production of *Look Back in Anger* in which he was depicted as being as mad as Hamlet seems in the eyes of Claudius. He nevertheless expressed a point of view which helps to explain the popularity of the opposition to nuclear weapons already voiced by Russsell when he proclaimed, in 1956,

I suppose people of our generation aren't able to die for good causes any longer. We had all that done for us in the thirties and forties, when we were still kids. . . . There aren't any good, brave causes left. If the big bang does come, and we all get killed off, it won't be in aid of the old-fashioned, grand design. It'll just be for the Brave New nothing-very-much-thank-you. About as pointless and inglorious as stepping in front of a bus.[4]

There were, naturally, other reasons for what now seems the surprising success of *Look Back in Anger* with English audiences in the 1950s. For the first time in the history of the English stage, a hero of working-class origins expressed his frustrations with the eloquence traditionally reserved for members of the intellectual middle-class. But when Jimmy Porter also spoke for the first generation to be aware that man himself might cause the disappearance from the planet of all forms of biological life, including his own, he touched the same chord which Dürrenmatt was to sound in *The Physicists* in 1963, just one year after Bertrand Russell, at the age of 90, had been sent to prison for causing an obstruction during a protest against nuclear weapons in Trafalgar Square.

The plot of *The Physicists* does not have the linear simplicity of *The Visit*. It is more reminiscent of the complex twists of fate whereby Pirandello's Henry IV is caught in his own simulacrum of madness, and leaves one with the impression that Dürrenmatt is trying to make the spectator's head spin as much by his theatrical technique as by his subject matter. What appears clearer on reading the text is that a physicist called Johan Wilhelm Möbius has unearthed what he calls the Principle of Universal Discovery. When he realises how valuable a commodity this is, he seeks protection against the evil forces of the outside world by having himself interned in Fräulein Doktor Mathilde von Zahnd's private nursing home. He then ensures that he will be incarcerated there for the rest of his life by strangling nurse Monika.

This does not, however, ensure that his discovery remains a private matter, unexploitable by the wicked world. His two fellow inmates, Herbert George Beutler, who pretends to be afflicted with the illusion that he is Sir Isaac Newton, and Ernest Heinrich Ernesti, who similarly pretends to be mad and to imagine himself to be Einstein, now reveal themselves in their true colours. They are not mad at all, but spies in the pay of the Intelligence Service, simulating insanity in order to keep an eye on Möbius and ensure that his discovery does not fall into the wrong hands. It is to strengthen their claim to be out of their minds as well that they too have strangled the nurses deputed to look after them, and thus brought about the visit of the inspector of police which provides the framework for the plot.

None of these plans, however, succeeds in protecting Möbius's discovery. The Fräulein Doktor has overheard the whole of the conversation between the supposedly mad physicists, and the knowledge that she has of their actual identity and real crimes enables her to hold them prisoner. She has, moreover, taken other precautions which will enable her to exploit Möbius's discovery for commercial ends. When he thought he had destroyed his manuscripts for ever, she had kept duplicates. While he was having his imaginary conversations with King Solomon, she had been bulding up a giant cartel which would enable her, like Claire Zachanassian, to control the world. Like Claire, and unlike the physicists who give the play its title, she really is mad, and the allegorical message of both plays is the same: the world is under the control of scheming, ruthless, and totally immoral old women, creatures whose biological sterility reflects the worthlessness of our whole civilisation.

It is a harsh verdict, reinforcing the temptation to look for the origins of the similarities betwen *The Visit* and *The Physicists* in some forgotten trauma in Dürrenmatt's childhood. But since there is no biographical evidence to back this up, it is more useful to see him as the son of his parents in a more ideological and less Oedipal way. It is, traditionally, the role of the Protestant minister to remind his congregation of their guilt. Dürrenmatt had all the disadvantages of social isolation produced by being the son of the Manse, coupled with the lessons inculcated by his formidable mamma. She, like Bertrand Russell's grandmother, laid great stress on Exodus 23: 2: 'Thou shalt not follow a multitude to do evil'. Whether the society he denounced deserved all the strictures which, like the Cousin Amos of *Cold Comfort Farm*, Dürrenmatt heaped upon it, remains an open question. These strictures nevertheless enabled him to remain one of the most widely studied of twentieth-century continental dramatatists.

The prophecies underlying *The Physicists* have not so far come true, and there are a number of replies to Kenneth Whitton's claim, in his discussion of the play in his 1990 book on Dürrenmatt, that 'Oppenheimer, Einstein *et al* were delivered up to the military and politicians to maim and kill'.[5] The first is that nuclear weapons were not used to maim and kill during the Cold War.

They had the opposite effect of preventing it from turning hot. The second is that it was Einstein himself who took the initiative, in 1939, of writing to President Roosevelt to set out his reasons for thinking that it was possible to make an atomic bomb, and that the Germans were carrying out research in that direction. One does not need to be a Jew and a refugee from the Nazis, as Einstein was, to be able to imagine what would have happened if Hitler's scientists had got there first. In one of the few books to be published in the late twentieth century and to give a positive account of soldiering, George MacDonald Fraser's autobiographical 1992 *Quartered Safe Out Here*, the question is raised as to how the men of the Border Regiment, who had just made a major contribution to the defeat of the Japanese in the Burma campaign, would have reacted if given the choice between taking part in an opposed landing on Japan itself and seeing the need for this landing removed by having the atomic bomb dropped on Hiroshima and Nagasaki. Since they are generous and humane men as well as courageous ones, he depicts them as shouldering their rifles with resignation but without either enthusiasm or resentment for a new campaign, and their decision is one which no man worthy of the name would refuse to take on his own behalf.[6] A politician faced with the same decision, and required to balance the number of people killed at Hiroshima and Nagasaki against what might have been an even greater toll in Japanese as well as in American, British and Australian lives required by a successful invasion of Japan, might well be forgiven for having acted differently.

The Physicists combines two kinds of theatre. There is the theatre of ideas, in the style of *Major Barbara*, which is exemplified in the debate at the beginning of Act II between Möbius and the secret policemen pretending to be Newton and Einstein; and there is, in contrast, the semi-surrealistic drama of defeat which makes up the body of the plot. The policeman playing Newton puts forward a view which has parallels with the motto devised by the first member of the Undershaft dynasty: 'If God made the hand, let not man withhold the sword'. It doesn't matter, he says, who guarantees the freedom of scientists to pursue knowledge in their own way, and continues:

I give my services to every system, providing that system leaves me alone. I know there's a lot of talk nowadays about the physicists' moral responsibilities. We suddenly find ourselves confronted with our own fears and we have a fit of morality. This is nonsense. We have far-reaching, pioneering work to do, and that is all that should concern us. Whether or not humanity has the wit to follow the new trails we are blazing is its own look-out, not ours.[7]

The same idea was more pithily expressed by the American satirist Tom Lehrer in his criticism of the German scientist whom the Americans were fortunate enough to capture at the end of the Second World War before the Russians could get hold of him, and whose engineering genius helped the United States to win the space race:

'Once the rockets go up, who cares where they come down?

'That's not my department', says Werner von Braun.

The secret agent playing Einstein has a different conception of the relationship which the scientist ought to have with the politician. Since, he argues, the physicists are providing humanity with such colossal sources of power, it is they who ought to dictate the conditions on which this power is used. 'If we are physicists' he says, 'then we must become power politicians, making the political system eat out of the scientist's hand'.[8] It is a dream which H. G. Wells expressed in 1938 in his novel *The Shape of Things to Come*, and which gave rise to a memorable movie in the following year. It is also, as Kingsley Amis points out in his *New Maps of Hell*, one which still inspires a certain amount of science fiction, a genre which 'may be a hilariously unreliable preview of science, but is apt to be much nearer the mark about scientists'.[9] For all its obvious drawbacks, the idea of the scientists taking power does propose a more definite plan of action than the proposal put forward by Möbius, the hero-victim of *The Physicists*, which is to abandon science and contract out of society completely. 'For us physicists', he states,

there is nothing left but to surrender to reality. It has not kept up with us. It distintegrates on touching us. We have to take back our knowledge, and I have taken it back. There is no other way out, and that goes for you as well.[10]

Although Dürrenmatt the thinker would clearly like to go back to a world in which physics had stopped short of splitting the atom, Dürrenmatt the playwright and imaginative writer sees matters differently. The external world, personified by Fräulein Doktor Mathilde von Zahnd, described in the stage directions as 'an insane female psychiatrist', has taken the decision out of the physicists' hands. Just as the humanist traditions of the town of Guellen cannot stand up to the power which Claire Zachanassian derives from her money, so the nuclear scientists whose skill has devised weapons capable of blowing up the world are powerless in what Dürrenmatt clearly intends his audience to see as another incarnation of the capitalist system. For Doktor von Zahnd, as she points out in Act I, is the daughter of an expert in economics, a man who saw 'revealed in human beings, abysses which are forever hidden from psychiatrists like myself. We alienists are still hopelessly romantic philanthropists.'[11]

It is a remark comparable in its humour and in its political implications to Evelyn Waugh's throw-away line, in *Put Out More Flags*, to the effect that 'If it were conceivable that one who had held the office of Chief Whip for a quarter of a century could be shocked by any spectacle of human depravity' it might have been Basil Seal's misdemeanours which had driven his father to an early death.[12] The similarities between Dürrenmatt and Waugh, perhaps surprising at first sight, will be discussed in the next chapter.

12

Madness, History and Sex

I

Madness in the theatre and the novel: Pirandello and Waugh.

The setting of Dürrenmatt's *The Physicists* in a lunatic asylum makes the play reminiscent of two other key works in twentieth-century literature, Pirandello's *Enrico IV* (*Henry IV*), and Evelyn Waugh's 1935 novel, *A Handful of Dust*. In the former, first performed in 1922, an aristocrat is condemned to continue with a pretence of madness which has already lasted for 20 years in order to avoid being put on trial for murder, and in the second, a comparable fate overtakes the wealthy British landowner, Tony Last. He ends his days as a prisoner of an illiterate lunatic in the depths of the Brazilian jungle, unable to escape because of his ignorance of the terrain, and compelled to satisfy the obsession of his captor by endlessly and repeatedly reading aloud to him from the works of Charles Dickens. The novel represented, Waugh was later to remark, 'all that he had to say about humanism',[1] by which he seems to have meant the belief that man could save himself by his own efforts, unaided by God.

Although Waugh volunteered immediately for military service in 1939, and bore, as he said himself, 'much discomfort and some danger', his published work shows no more sign than that of Dürrenmatt of any faith in the political system which he fought to defend. He was, he said, a conservative, who expressed the style of political thinking which underlay his novels when he wrote, in 1935:

> I believe in government; that men cannot live together without rules, but that these should be kept at the bare minimum of safety; that there is no form of government ordained by God as being better than any other; that the anarchic elements in society are so strong that it is a whole-time task to keep the peace[2]

216

but he did not support any political party. One of his most famous *boutades* was his reply, to a canvasser who asked him how he was going to vote in the General Election of 1964, that he 'would not presume to advise his sovereign as to her choice of ministers'. Although he regarded his conversion in 1930 as the most important event in his life, his Catholicism was no more able than the 'faith in the Kantian practice of pure reason' which Kenneth Whitton detects as Dürrenmatt's ethical ideal to suggest any way in which society could be improved.

When one considers how consistently other writers got it wrong when they involved themselves in politics, there is a good deal to be said for the Dürrenmatt–Waugh abstention. Both writers saw themselves primarily as artists, and Dürrenmatt's plays offer an interesting reply to the jibe which Graham Greene put into the mouth of Harry Lime in the film *The Third Man*:

> In Italy, for thirty years after the Borgias, they had warfare, terror, murder and bloodshed – they produced Michelangelo, Leonardo da Vinci and the Renaissance. In Switzerland, they had brotherly love, five hundred years of democracy and peace, and what did that produce? The cuckoo clock.[3]

For here is a writer from that very country, yet an author whose plays come perhaps closer than the work of any other author to expressing something of the central spirit of twentieth-century literature; so much so that one almost has the impression that he had been to see *The Third Man* and decided to refute Harry Lime's remark.

Waugh, in contrast, was more English and restrained than Dürrenmatt in depicting what he saw as the lunacy of modern society. There is nothing in his presentation of it which is in any way comparable to the way Dürrenmatt points out in his stage directions how the lunatic asylum in which the action of *The Physicists* takes place had previously housed 'not only decayed aristocrats, debilitated millionnaires, schizophrenic writers, manic-depressive industrial barons and so on' but also 'arterio-sclerotic politicians (unless still in office)'.[4] As befits a mature artist, Waugh refrains from direct comment of this kind, and lets the reader draw his own conclusions. His heroes undergo misfortunes which for the most part are essentially comic, as when Paul Pennyfeather is sent down from Oxford at the beginning of *Decline and Fall* for an offence he did not commit, finds himself unconsciously running the white slave business from which his elegant fiancée, Margot Beste-Chetwynd, derives her considerable fortune, behaves as a gentleman in taking the blame when the police find out what is happening, goes to prison in her place, and is finally released through the machinations of a corrupt society in which her fragrant beauty is absolutely at home. On other occasions, however, the misfortunes of Waugh's heroes take on the more tragic overtones of the early adventures of Basil Seal in *Black Mischief*. When the modernising programme in which Basil is involved in tribal Azania goes wrong, and the country reverts to barbarism, Basil manages to escape through putting on native dress and taking part in a banquet whose true nature he discovers too late. Its ingredients contain the flesh of his mistress, Prudence, who had failed to escape, and whom he had earlier told that he loved her so much that he could eat her.

Madness is as frequent a phenomenon in Waugh as it is in Dürrenmatt, and the Mr Todhunter who holds Tony Last captive at the end of *A Handful of Dust* differs from Waugh's other lunatics only in using his power particularly badly. Lord Copper is a complete megalomaniac, Brigadier-General Sir Ritchie-Hook, in the *Sword of Honour* trilogy, a fanatic who finally loses all touch with reality, and Colonel Blunt, the father of Adam Fenwick-Symes's fiancée in *Vile Bodies*, promises wealth to the young couple in cheques signed Charlie Chaplin. But although, at the end of *Vile Bodies*, Agatha Runcible goes mad after losing control of herself in a six-day motor race and dies, there are sometimes considerable advantages in the lack of conventional sanity which enables some of Waugh's characters to contract out of the modern world. At the end of *Scoop*, William Boot rejects the opportunity of becoming one of the highest paid journalists in a world where newspapers do more to create wars than to report them. Instead, he goes back to the cheerful disorder of the country house in the West Country where the only reliable source of money is provided by the ability of the aged Nanny Bloggs to bring off showy doubles in the flat-racing season.

When Waugh was asked why his Catholicism did not make him a nicer person, he made the rather convincing reply that without it he would be even more unbearable. His religious beliefs may have had a beneficial effect on his fiction, but it is hard to prove it. His best-known novel, *Brideshead Revisited*, is also his most obviously Catholic and his least satisfactory. Its defects were admirably summed up by Kingsley Amis in a review of the 1981 television adaptation entitled, 'How I Lived in a Big House and Found God'.[5] Waugh's fiction has the great advantage of not relying for its effects on the religious beliefs which help to underpin it. His belief in the absurdity and injustice of the world is just as intense as anything in Adamov, Artaud, Beckett, Camus, Dürrenmatt, Genet, Günter Grass, Ionesco, Sartre, Simpson or Peter Weiss, and nowhere is the starting point for Sartrian existentialism more pithily expressed than when Mr Prendergast, in *Decline and Fall*, summarises the Doubts which have led him to give up being a clergyman of the Church of England. 'You see' he tells Paul,

> 'it wasn't the ordinary sort of Doubts about Cain's wife or the Old Testament miracles or the consecration of Archbishop Parker. I'd been taught to explain all those while I was at college. No, it was something deeper than that. *I can't understand why God made the world at all*'.[6]

But while the writers of the absurdist school are content to mirror this absurdity in books and plays which are often as formless as the world they depict, Waugh goes beyond absurdity in bringing his world under complete artistic control.

Waugh's artistic practice is thus akin to what Matthew Arnold would have called an Apollonian concept of art, as distinct from the frenzy induced by the God Dionysus, and is open to the obvious objection, from the point of view of anyone who wishes to change society, of sending the audience home happy. Revolutionary art, in contrast, as Brecht argued, is one that should disturb human beings by reminding them of their alienation, and the presentation of the world as a madhouse, as in Peter Weiss's 1974 play, *The Persecution and Assassination of Jean-Paul Marat as performed by the inmates of the Charenton Lunatic Asylum under the direction of the Marquis de Sade*, certainly fulfils this criterion. Similarly, Claire Zachanassian's promise 'The world turned me into a whore. I shall turn the world into a brothel,[7] exactly announces the theme of Jean Genet's 1960 play *The Balcony*.

II

Peter Weiss and Jean Genet: the world as madhouse or brothel.

The most frequent and facile joke made when the *Marat–Sade* was performed at the English National Theatre in 1964 was that if you had read the title, you didn't really need to see the play. This was true in so far as the basic idea was concerned. The lunatics who performed the events leading up to 13 July 1793, the day on which Charlotte Corday, a fanatical royalist woman of 25 from Caen, stabbed the extreme revolutionary leader Marat in his bath, did more than bring out the emotional and physical atmosphere of the Terror of 1793. It also emphasised its political significance. A revolution begun with the noblest intentions had degenerated, in less than four years, to a situation where little children played with toy guillotines in the street, and where Yeats's lines

The best lack all conviction while the worst
Are full of passionate intensity

applied to every aspect of public life. The date at which de Sade's play was supposedly performed heightened the vision of history as a nightmare from which nobody could escape. The Marquis de Sade was interned at Charenton lunatic asylum from 1801 to his death in 1808, exactly the period during which the reign of Napoleon 1 was giving rise to the period of pointless slaughter which culminated in the final humiliation, for the French, of the battle of Waterloo.

Nothing could have been further from the revolutionary slogan of 1789, 'Liberté, Egalité, Fraternité', than the military dictatorship imposed on the French by Bonaparte. Even its most positive aspects, the creation of an efficient system of public administration and the establishment of a uniform legal code, brought obvious advantages only to the middle class. It also made the power which the rich had over the poor more tyrannical, because more systematic, than the arbitrary nature of the *ancien régime*. Officially, it is the spirit of liberalism which leads the governor of Charenton to allow the performance of plays in the hope that they will have a therapeutic effect on the inmates. In fact, the very nature of the institution over which he presides confirms Michel Foucault's thesis that the more rationally organised the care of the mentally ill becomes, the more it strengthens the ability of society to control anyone who steps out of line. It is a thesis which runs parallel to the anti-psychiatry movement in England and America, and which inspired Ken Kesey's novel and the 1975 film *One Flew Over the Cuckoo's Nest*, as well as Ken Roach's 1973 film, *Family Life*.

When one of his earliest twentieth-century admirers, Guillaume Apollinaire, claimed in 1913 that it would be the ideas of de Sade which dominated the twentieth century, he seemed at first sight to be like one of the Chorus of Women in Eliot's *Murder in the Cathedral* who, as Thomas à Becket tells them, 'speak better they they know, and beyond their understanding'. The twentieth century has witnessed scenes of unparalleled slaughter, and seen the total disappearance of the Rousseauist idea that human beings are naturally good. But in another, equally important sense, Apollinaire was wrong. Neither the Somme nor Auschwitz nor the Gulag was produced either by the passion for crime or by the conscious desire to do evil which de Sade celebrated in his books. There were sadists among the guards, and the account of life at the camp in *Schindler's Ark* emphasises the pleasure which some of the Nazis took in imposing even more suffering on their prisoners. But like the strategy inspiring the attack on the German lines on 1 July 1916, the origins of both the Nazi death camps and of the forced labour camps in which over ten million Soviet citizens met their deaths did not lie in a decision to choose evil rather than good. The British High Command thought they had found the secret of penetrating the German lines and putting an end to the war. The Nazis were obviously mad to think that the murder of six million Jews was necessary to improve European civilisation. This was nevertheless their belief, and they thought they were doing good. Stalin's crimes were similarly inspired by the desire to build a better civilisation, and might well have found historians to justify them if they had worked.

This is again totally different from the hells described with such loving detail in *Justine* or in the *Cent-Vingts Journées de Sodome*. There, power is exercised by a single nobleman, or by a small group of aristocrats, and the object of their cruelties is philosophical as well as sexual. They want to prove that the universe, and man himself, are totally evil. At the same time, they find that they can derive sexual pleasure from the torments which they inflict on their victims. They are mad, just as the Nazis were mad, but in a different way. Where twentieth-century history seems to show that de Sade was right is in the inescapable truth that the evil done by human beings, however inspired, far exceeds the good.

It is this awareness which runs through the whole of the *Marat–Sade*, and makes the contrast between Sade and Marat so crucial to its construction. Marat was a disciple of Rousseau, a fervent believer in the natural goodness of man. But since Robespierre, an even more murderous idealist than Marat, was also a pupil of Rousseau, the philosophy of the gentle Jean-Jacques is inevitably seen as causing, in the events of 1793 depicted in Weiss's play, far more suffering than de Sade ever dreamed of. Bertrand Russell argued that Rousseau was the father of two kinds of totalitarianism: the hard-hearted but weak-headed, which culminated in Hitler; and the hard-hearted and hard-headed, which reached its apotheosis in Stalin.[8] The effect of the *Marat–Sade* was to suggest how accurate history had shown this diagnosis to be. None of the people who went to see the *Marat–Sade* could forget that what lay waiting behind the horrors of the French revolution and Napoleon's military dictatorship were the even greater disasters engendered by the Bolshevik revolution of 1917 and the Nazi revolution of 1933. It has been calculated that for every five minutes Bonaparte lived, a human being died as a result of his actions. Hitler and Stalin had even more disastrous scores.

Even without the technique of production used by Peter Brook, the *Marat–Sade* would have brought home the madness of history. As it was, the application which Brooks made of the ideas of the French theoretician Antoine Artaud produced an even more perfect match between form and content than was already there in the text. Artaud himself was not quite sane, and spent a fair amount of his short life (1896–1946) in mental hospitals. His ideas on the theatre, set out in a book called *Le théâtre et son double* in 1938, were that it should totally destroy the spectator's belief in a rational universe, and produce the same terror as an outbreak of bubonic plague. While these ideas would be clearly of limited application in a production of *The Importance of Being Earnest*, and were never successfully applied in Artaud's lifetime, they exactly fitted the theme and atmosphere of the *Marat–Sade*. In 1966, some of them were also put into practice by Roger Blin in his production at the state-subsidised French National Theatre of Genet's *Les Paravents* (*The Screens*). But for all the controversy it caused at the time, this is not Genet's most interesting play. *The Balcony* – so called because 'un balcon' is a slang word for a brothel in French; as well as for a woman's breasts – which was also first produced by Peter Brook, though in London and not in Paris, is much more interesting, for a wide variety of reasons.

The theme of *The Balcony*, as with much of Genet's work, is that of illusion and pretence. When a revolution breaks out, in a country which the 1964 film presents as being somewhere in South America, the only official organisation to remain intact is the police force. But the Chief of Police, splendidly played in the film by Peter Falk, still suffers from what he sees as a serious social affront. The brothel run by Madame Irma – even more splendidly played by Shelley Winter – derives its success from the opportunity it offers men to live out their fantasies. While most of these take a conventionally sado-masochistic or infantile form, others offer a more interesting blend of sex with power or social prestige. A gasman suffering from acne plays a bishop, forgiving the sins of a pretty penitent. A certified public accountant plays a judge, interrogating even prettier offenders. While in a different room, a truckdriver plays a general, delightfully combining the imagined opportunity to mount a frisky mare in a military parade celebrating his victories with the more solid satisfactions offered by an accommodating whore. But nobody wants to be the Chief of Police.

It is all great fun, and makes a number of points about the nature of unorthodox sex. This is, to begin with, an activity that goes on rather more in the head than in the loins. The pursuit of it also tends to be a practice confined almost exclusively to men. It is impossible to imagine a woman asking for comparable services from Madame Irma's Balcony. In an age where easily available contraception has freed orthodox sex from the main problem which accompanied it in the past, the role of the prostitute consists of supplying the special services for which most men hesitate to ask their wives or girlfriends. *The Balcony* does, it is true, present one intriguing variation on what normally happens. While most men looking for something out of the ordinary have to go socially downmarket, Madame Irma's establishment offers a degree of comfort and sophistication which would not be out of place in Proust's Faubourg Saint-Germain. But the play is, for all its insistence on fantasies, a basically realistic one, especially in the way in which its plot highlights two important aspects of mid-twentieth-century history on the continent of Europe: the importance of money, and the growth in prestige as well as of power of the police.

What the Chief of Police wants to do is to pass from his physical ability to control the situation by the power of the forces under his command to the one where he enjoys the same prestige as judges, bishops or generals. He can do this only if the populace is made to see that the traditional power structure is still intact. Madame Irma creates this belief by persuading the gasman, the truckdriver and the chartered accountant to move their fantasies from the private to the public domain. The ruse succeeds, and the people fall back into line. They show themselves obedient worshippers of the monarchy – Madame Irma has no problems in playing the Queen – and remain faithful to the religious beliefs incarnated by the Church, as well as to a regime supported by the Army and seen to be exercising justice through the Law. The triumph of the Chief of Police is complete when the leader of the defeated rebellion arrives at the brothel asking if he personally can play out the fantasy of being the head of the police force. Although it is Madame Irma's money that has made it all possible, her triumph, like that of the Chief of Police, is not complete until the popular imagination has caught up with the realities of the social situation.

The social realism of *The Balcony* is clearly less applicable to English-speaking societies than to those on the continent of Europe. When, like Germany or Russia, you have had a full-blown dose of totalitarianism, or suffered the milder attack which afflicted Italy, Spain, Portugal, or the France of Marshal Pétain, it is easier to see what Genet is talking about. In Germany and in Russia, as in the Oceania of *Nineteen Eighty-Four*, it was the police who exercised a power unrivalled by any influence still possessed by the Church or the Law, and which surpassed even that of the Army. One of the minor criteria by which a society can be judged to be satisfactorily democratic is the absence of a personage such as the Chief of Police. In Stalin's Russia, in contrast, Beria's name was as known and feared as that of Himmler was in the Germany of the Third Reich. What might perhaps be called the magic realism of Genet's theatre expressed a truth about social relationships which was mainly a characteristic of totalitarian societies, and which therefore seems at the moment to be a thing of the past.

13
Magic Realism,
Post-modernism and
Toni Morrison

I

Magic realism and the South American experience: the example of García Márquez.

The term 'magic realism' first came to be widely used in English-speaking culture after the translation, in 1970, of the Colombian writer Gabriel García Márquez's 1967 novel, *Cien años de soledad*, *One Hundred Years of Solitude*. South American critics themselves are not fond of the term, and Norman Thomas de Giovanni, who has translated much of the work of Borges, describes it as a 'pernicious phrase', rejected by every South American writer of his acquaintance, and over whose meaning there is no agreement whatsoever.

It is argued by its opponents that the term has the major disadvantage of failing to recognise that some of the incidents related in South American fiction are based not on the totally free workings of the author's imagination but on the social and political realities of countries such as Argentina, Bolivia or Colombia itself. In *One Hundred Years of Solitude*, for example, a banana company sets itself up in the town of Macondo, the setting for all the action in the novel, and treats its workers so badly that they all go on strike. This leads them to assemble in the main square of the town, where the government has them surrounded by soldiers armed with machine guns. When the crowd refuses to disperse, the order is given to open fire, and 3000 people are killed. Their corpses are then put on trains and sent off to the sea, and the whole incident officially denied to the point where José Arcadio Segundo, one of the large family whose adventures provide the central theme of the novel, finds it impossible to persuade anyone that it has taken place even when, later in the novel, the child Aureliano 'speaking with such good sense' that to his grandmother, Fernanda, he seems like a new version of Jesus among the wise men,

> described with precise and convincing details how the army had machine gunned more than three thousand workers penned up in the station and how they had loaded the bodies onto a two-hundred-car train and thrown them into the sea.[1]

Nobody will believe him, and his grandmother accuses him of having inherited the anarchist ideas of his famous ancestor, Colonel Aureliano Buendia.

To the European observer, the ability of a government to hide such incidents is indeed unbelievable. Neither the government of the Second Republic in France, which shot down 10,000 workers in Paris during the 'June Days' of 1848, nor the administration of Adolphe Thiers, which killed 20,000 Parisians during the repression of the Commune in May 1871, managed to hide the violence inflicted on their citizens, and in most Western countries the omnipresence of the press and television nowadays exercises a salutary check on the abuse of power. But in the Argentina of the 1970s, relatives of the *desaparecidos*, the 'dead without corpses', who were numbered in thousands as victims of the brutal military regime, were actually reassured when they discovered that their loved ones were still being tortured. This, at least, was proof that they were still alive.

There is also the argument that the apparently incredible details which García Márquez provides in *One Hundred Years of Solitude* have the more obviously mundane purpose of enabling him to avoid censorship. To the eye of European or North American common sense, the career of one of the central characters in the novel, Colonel Aureliano Bueno, clearly belongs to the realm of magic and not of reality. For in the course of his career he

> organised thirty-two armed uprisings and lost them all . . . had seventeen male children by seventeen different women and they were exterminated in a single night before the oldest one had reached the age of thirty-five . . . survived fourteen attempts on his life, seventy-three ambushes, and a firing squad . . . lived through a dose of strychnine in his coffee that was enough to kill a horse, and shot himself in the chest with a pistol and the

bullet came out through his back without damaging any vital organ.[2]

But although, even to the South American eye, such descriptions might seem more like an allegorical account of one of their many leaders of revolt, and thus belong to the real world in a way that an outside observer could not appreciate, this is not always the case. Isabel Allende, talking about writing in Chile during the Allende dictatorship, points out that a censorship-induced symbolism

> happens in all dictatorships. New keys and symbols are invented to make points, to get round the censors. But sometimes when a writer manages to elude the censor, he does so at the expense of changing the language to the point that it becomes laby-rinthine. In eluding the censor, he may elude the reader too.[3]

These are not, however, the only aspects of life in South America which parallel the other apparently magical details and events provided by the text of *One Hundred Years of Solitude*. Albert Camus noted in the journal which he kept during his visit to Mexico in 1950 how the children in the street ate sugar figurines in the shape of skeletons on the Day of the Dead, and there is a museum in Guanajuato where those who cannot keep up the payments on the plot of land in the cemetery where their relatives have been buried can go and gaze at the mummified corpses which have been dug up to make place for the bodies of those whose relatives have more money. Nowhere do tourists – and relatives – have to wait longer in a queue. André Breton, the self-appointed head of French surrealism, said that there was really no point in trying to spread his movement to South America. Life there already possessed a surreal quality which Europeans could only dream of.

If what Breton saw was anything like life in García Márquez's Macondo, he was obviously telling the truth. Although nobody knows the exact age of Ursula Buendia, the wife of the José Arcadio who founds the town of Macondo, it is calculated that she was already between 115 and 122 at the time of the banana plantation. José Arcadio, her eldest son, goes round the world 65 times, and returns with so elaborately tattooed a penis that he can rent it out for 8 pesos a night. When he marries, he and his wife Rebecca make love eight times a night and three times during each siesta, praying as they do so that the noise of their passion will not disturb the dead. Fernanda, who marries Aureliano Secundo, is from so aristocratic a lineage that ever since she has had the use of reason, she has 'done her duty in a gold pot with the family crest on it'.

It is consequently perhaps not surprising that when, after the massacre of the 3000, the officer in charge comes to search the house of Aureliano Secundo, he finds 72 chamber pots piled up in the cupboards. After she is married, her father sends them a box of gifts every Christmas which is so enormous that it can scarcely be carried through the door. On the tenth Christmas, after he has died, it is discovered that he has arranged to have a similarly shaped box sent with his own corpse in it, accompanied by a letter 'addressed in the usual Gothic letters to the Very Distinguished Lady Dona Fernanda de Carpio de Bundia'. Aided as usual by their father, the children open the box and see Don Fernando 'dressed in black and with a crucifix on his chest, his skin broken out in pestilential sores and cooking slowly in a frothy stew with bubbles like live pearls'.[4] Yet there were, though not always in so extreme a form, writers in Europe who can be seen as precursors of the movement whose name South American critics seem so anxious to reject.

II

Kafka as the first magic realist; some political readings and a comparison with Carroll; a quotation from Eliot and the alternative attitude of Shaw and Camus.

One obvious European precedent is in the novels of the Czech writer Franz Kafka. The posthumous publication of *Der Prozess* (*The Trial*) in 1925, and of *Das Schloss* (*The Castle*) ran parallel to the Impressionist painting fashionable at the time in Germany, and there is a strangeness about both the fiction and the painting which seems to prefigure the events which came close to destroying European civilisation completely between 1933 and 1945. It was natural for Kafka, born a citizen of the Austro-Hungarian Empire in 1883, to write in German, and he benefited as much as the Koestler of *Darkness at Noon* did from the excellence of the translations made available in English. What also happened in the case of Kafka is that the dream world which he created came to be seen as so curious an anticipation of what happened to millions of people.

This is not because he deliberately set out to anticipate the arrival in Europe of the phenomenon of totalitarianism and of the power which this placed in the hands of the bureaucrats called upon to impose its decrees. As Lawrence Langer points out in *The Holocaust and the Literary Imagination*,

> an intricate maze leads from the claustrophobic law offices (of Kafka's world) to the gas chambers, and indeed winding corridors may connect the two, but neither Joseph K. nor his creator ever trod them.[5]

The 1919 short story 'In The Penal Colony' may indeed be seen as a prefiguration of what happened to ordinary people in the totalitarian Europe of the dictators which Kafka did not live to see. It is nevertheless a strange one in a number of ways. At first sight, the 'remarkable piece of apparatus' which the officer describes to the explorer with such enthusiasm, and which has the ability to inscribe on the skin of the offender the name of the commandment which he has disobeyed, would certainly not have been out of place at Auschwitz. But as the story proceeds, and the apparatus fails to work properly, the similarity becomes less obvious. What characterised the organisation of the Holocaust was precisely its extreme efficiency. The trains arrived on time and the gas chambers worked. Nothing comparable occurs in *In The Penal Colony*, in which the machine goes berserk and drives a great iron spike through the head of the officer demonstrating it. Without the victories of the Red Army and the liberation of Europe from the West, the camps would have continued to function until the Final Solution had been carried out with the Teutonic efficiency which had characterised it throughout.

But although Kafka's view of the world was a poetic and semi-magical one, the personal obsession with guilt, judgement and the mysteries of power which seems to have led him to write as he did, gave his novels a curious applicability to the experience of people totally unlike himself. When Mr Norris is summoned to see the police in Berlin, for example, just as the Nazis are coming to power, William Bradshaw accompanies him to the Headquarters and describes how

increasingly apprehensive and depressed, we wandered along
vistas of stone passages, with numbered doors, were misdirected
up and down flights of stairs, collided with hurrying officials
who carried bulging dossiers of crimes

until they eventually come into a courtyard 'overlooked with
windows with heavy iron bars'.[6] It is exactly the world of
continental bureaucracy as seen by one of its victims, and the
world of Kafka when transformed from a dream into reality.

The plot of Kafka's other major novel, *The Castle*, describes how
a land surveyor, K., arrives in a village with the order to make
himself available to the authorities who live in the castle of Count
West-West situated high above it. But every time he tries to get
there, or to find out what he has to do, a bramble of bureaucratic
obstacles rises before him. He finds himself accompanied by two
mysterious helpers, whose presence is in fact a considerable hin-
drance, and is frustrated at every move by the discovery of new
requirements which he must fulfil. Two remarks in *The Trial*,
however, suggest that the resemblances which struck readers in
the 1930s and 1940s between his world and that of Hitler's Europe
or Stalin's Russia were nevertheless so far from being deliberate
as to be based on a serious misreading of the text. After beginning
the book with one of the most famous opening lines in the history
of the novel – 'Somebody must have been telling lies about Joseph
K., for without having done anything wrong he was arrested one
fine morning' – Kafka makes a very specific point. Since, as he
says, his hero 'lived in a country with a legal constitution', where
there was 'universal peace' and 'all the laws were in force', it
was incredible that he could be arrested as he is in his own home.
In the last chapter, as K. is being taken off to be executed by two
men in frock coats, 'pallid and plump, with top hats that were
apparently irremovable', he deliberately pulls his captors forward
so that they will not be stopped if they arouse the suspicion of
the solid-looking policemen on patrol in the street. The situation
of anyone arrested either in Hitler's Germany or Stalin's Russia,
or in any of the countries occupied by their armies, was totally
different. It was a defining characteristic of totalitarianism that
the state was not there to protect its citizens against arbitrary
arrest. Its function was to lend its support to the police terror on
which its power relied.

Whatever Kafka's intentions might have been, however, a number

of features in Joseph K.'s experience in *The Trial* awoke v
political echoes among European readers, especially du
triumphs of totalitarianism in the period between 1917 and the
ending of the Cold War in the late 1980s. However hard he tries,
Joseph K. can never find out what he is supposed to have done
wrong. The Law – always capitalised – is totally different from
the law in a democratic society, where it is a fundamental principle
that the offences it punishes and the penalties it lays down are
defined in advance and are publicly accessible to everyone. In a
totalitarian society, in contrast, the law is arbitrary, unknown,
and perpetually changing. One of the features of Orwell's *Nineteen
Eighty-Four* which most struck the inhabitants of countries such
as Poland or Hungary as being an accurate transcription of their
own experience when they read it in *samizdat* during the Soviet
occupation, was the frequency with which members of the Party
who thought they were totally loyal to it were suddenly thrown
into prison. This is even more clearly visible in Solzhenitsyn's
description at first hand of the world of the Gulag, where the
political prisoners, men and women who have frequently been
arrested without having consciously done anything against the
state, are treated very much worse than the ordinary criminals,
who have knowingly broken the law. The adjective 'Kafkaesque',
often used in a sense similar to that of a 'Catch 22 situation',
expresses precisely the impression which the citizens of totalitarian
states have of being required to follow a set of rules which they
not only cannot know in advance, but which are also so absurd
that there is no possibility of their being understood anyway. As
the wife of one of the Court Ushers explains to K., 'it is an essential
part of the justice dispensed here that you should be condemned
not only in innocence but also in ignorance'.[7]

It is unusual for the text of *The Trial* to provide such clear support
for a reading of the novel as an allegory of totalitarianism which
is comparable to Camus's treatment of the same subject in *The
Plague*, or which can be found in the plays of Vaclav Havel. The
atmosphere which Joseph K. finds when he sets out for the Court
where he will have to answer the mysterious charges made against
him is more frequently similar to the dream sequences in *Alice in
Wonderland* or *Alice Through the Looking-Glass*. It is a similarity
which is there in *The Castle* as well, since at one point in the
novel K. has the very looking-glass experience of finding that
the more he walks towards the castle, the further away it seems.

When Joseph K. discovers that one of the anterooms in the ramshackle building where he goes in search of the Examining Magistrate 'which had contained nothing but a washtub last Sunday, was now a fully furnished living room'[8] we are very much in a nightmare version of Carroll's dream world. Similarly, the scene in which Alice finds herself suddenly transported from the train in which she cannot find her ticket to a shop where an old sheep sits knitting, and discovers that

> whenever she looked hard at any shelf, to make out exactly what it had on it, that particular shelf was always quite empty, though the others round it were crowded as full as they could hold[9]

is one that could go perfectly into a Kafka novel.

The same is true of a number of incidents in *One Hundred Years of Solitude*, and the claim made by the French surrealists that Dodgson was one of their number without realising it could also be argued of the general movement known as magic realism. Early in García Márquez's novel, a mysterious girl arrives who either cannot or will not speak and whom they decide to call Rebecca. She brings with her the 'sickness of insomnia', of which the most fearsome part, as an Indian woman explains,

> was not the impossibility of sleeping, for the body did not feel any fatigue at all, but its inexorable evolution towards a more critical manifestation: a loss of memory.

This leads to the very Carrollian situation – in Chapter IV of *Through the Looking Glass*, Alice also forgets what things are called – in which the inhabitants of Macombo have to write down the names of all the objects in common use for fear of forgetting what they are called, and there is a comment about José Arcadio Buendia which reads like an absurd opposite of the stylised aggressiveness of Tweedledum and Tweedledee. He could never, writes García Márquez, 'understand the sense of a contest in which the two adversaries had agreed upon the rules'.[11]

There are naturally differences between Carroll's world and that of Kafka or García Márquez. When the Alice books were dramatised on BBC television in 1967, they were accompanied by the triumphant strains of the hymn

Immortal, invisible, God only wise,
In light inaccessible hid from our eyes

in which the High Victorian self-confidence of the music totally
contradicts the positively existentialist vision of a totally unknowable God expressed in the words. There is no place in the
world of the twentieth-century magic realists for the certainty
running through the hymns of the Victorians that the rule of British
imperialism is ultimately good, any more than there is for the
cool common sense which enables Alice to remain pert and
unperturbed by the absurdity of the events into which she is
plunged. For when Joseph K. enters a lumber room in the bank
where he works as Chief Clerk, which is full of useless old papers
and empty earthenware ink bottles, he finds a terrifying and totally
unCarrollian spectacle, that of the Whipper who proceeds to inflict
punishment on the two men who had originally come to arrest
him for not having complied exactly with their duties. Nothing
in the novel happens in the way that Joseph K. and the reader
think that it should, and the only time he comes near to getting
some kind of explanation, it turns out to be one which insists on
the impossibility of anyone ever receiving an answer to a rationally
formulated question.

The scene takes place in the Cathedral, where Joseph K. is
supposed to meet an Italian who is one of the bank's most
important customers. The Italian does not turn up, and Joseph
K. wanders around in the gradually darkening Cathedral until
he comes across a priest who explains to him, through a long
and mysterious story, just how mistaken he is to think that the
Court before which he is on trial will ever provide him with an
explanation of what he is supposed to have done. This story
describes a man from the country who begs for admittance to
the Law. But the doorkeeper refuses him admission, so that he
waits for days, months and finally years, constantly asking for
admission and constantly being refused. Then, when his life is
about to draw to its close, he asks how it can be that in all the
years he has been waiting, nobody else has come, like him, to
ask for admission to the Law. Since by now the man has become
almost deaf, the doorkeeper bellows in his ear: 'No one but you
could gain admittance through this door, since this door was
intended for you. I am now going to shut it.'[12]

Joseph K. and the priest then have a long discussion about the

rights and wrongs of the doorkeeper's behaviour, but the religious
message of *The Trial*, for those who think it should be interpreted
in spiritual terms, has by now been made clear. Thomas Mann
described Kafka as a religious humourist, and there is a legend
that when Kafka read the first chapter of *The Trial* aloud to his
friends, they all burst out laughing. It is nevertheless a purely
black humour, darker even than the passage in the second of T.
S. Eliot's *The Four Quartets*, 'East Coker', which reads

> Our only health is the disease
> If we obey the dying nurse
> Whose constant aim is not to please
> But to remind of our, and Adam's curse,
> And that, to be restored, our sickness must grow worse.
> The whole earth is our hospital
> Endowed by a ruined millionaire,
> Wherein, if we do well, we shall
> Die of the absolute paternal care
> That will not leave us but prevents us
>   everywhere.

A man may receive the call, as Christian does at the beginning
of *The Pilgrim's Progress*, and he will set off alone as Christian
does. There is no question, in Kafka's world any more than there
is in that of Bunyan, of a woman receiving the call. Nor is there
any notion of people working or travelling together, or of a man
finding helpers upon his path in the way that Christian does.
Everyone whom K. meets explains to him that he is not needed
in the castle, and neither the women nor the men in the village
are of any use to him in the attempt to get up the hill and find
out whether the summons which brought him there was an illusion
or not. In both *The Trial* and *The Castle*, the women who offer
themselves to the hero do so in order to distract him from what
he sees as his mission, and if the novels are looked at as a kind
of fictional black mass, inverting all the traditional Christian
symbols, then both the Leni of *The Trial*, who has the curious
deformity of having a web of skin connecting the two middle
fingers of her right hand, and Klamm's former mistress in *The
Castle*, play a diametrically opposed role to that of the Virgin
Mary with her power to intercede with God on behalf of mankind.
There is no support in Kafka's life for Nathan A. Scott's

contention that *The Trial* and *The Castle* should be seen as expressing the same message as Kierkegaard's Christian existentialism, any more than there is for an interpretation of the books as an allegory of the Jew in Christian culture. Kafka was Jewish by birth – a fact that required the chapter on him to be omitted from Camus's *Le Mythe de Sisyphe* (*The Myth of Sisyphus*) when it was published in German-occupied France in 1943 – and was brought up as a non-orthodox Jew in the fairly tolerant Austro-Hungarian empire. Although one of the recurring themes in *The Adventures of the Good Soldier Sjevk and his Fortunes in the World War* by Kakfa's near-contemporary and fellow countryman Hasek is that 'an empire as absurd as ours ought not to exist', it was a regime which seems, in retrospect, to have a good deal more to be said in its favour than in that of the regimes which followed it after 1918. As John Osborne pointed out in his 1966 play *A Patriot for Me*, it was remarkably tolerant in its treatment of the different linguistic and racial groups which came under its authority, and there is another parallel here with Solzhenitysn. One of the dominant themes in the opening chapters of Part I of *The Gulag Archipelago* is the contrast between the leniency shown by the Empire of the Tsar to its political opponents and the ferocity with which the Bolshevik regime which replaced it in 1917 treated all its citizens.

If there is a Jewish aspect to Kafka's work, it is in the vision of God given in the Book of Job. For the only answer which God makes when Job asks for an explanation for all the sufferings inflicted upon him is another question: 'what right has he, a mere man, to understand?' says God, as 'by his mighty works', as the summary of Chapter 38 puts it, he 'convinceth Job of his weakness and imbecility'. It is a very different attitude from the spirit of Protestant independence evoked by Shaw's Saint Joan in her question: 'By what judgement can I judge by but mine own?' Any attempt at a Christian reading of Kafka is open to the same criticism of Kierkegaard's religious views which Camus makes in the second sermon which Father Paneloux delivers in *The Plague*. After Judge Othon's son has died of the terrible sufferings inflicted by the disease, Paneloux is forced to abandon his original view that the plague had been sent by God to punish the inhabitants of Oran for their wickedness. Instead, he calls upon his congregation to make a clear choice: either they must deny God completely, and accept that they live in a world which is totally devoid of transcendent purpose; or they must recognise that God's ways are not our ways, that He is not required to act in conformity with human notions of right and wrong, and that we must worship Him precisely because His actions are not explicable in human terms. It is not a view which Camus accepts. He is, from this point of view, in exactly the same tradition of rational enquiry evoked in the question which Joan asks her Inquisitors; which Kafka decidedly is not.

If God's behaviour does not come up to human notions of justice, suggests Camus, so much the worse for God. If there is a religious dimension to *The Castle* and *The Trial*, it does not lie in a comparable invitation to agnosticism. It is more in the area of psychology, or even that of anthropology. Although there is no God, in the sense of one who, as Luke 23: 41 puts it, deals justly with men, the desire to find such a God still continues to exist in certain human beings. Not everyone receives the summons which brings K. to *The Castle*; and not many people are arrested like Joseph K. Those whom God leaves alone are in this respect very fortunate, since they do not then waste their life or meet their death in an attempt to find out what He wants of them or why He has suddenly decided that they are guilty. The final impression left by *The Trial* and *The Castle* is that the religious instinct has survived the death of God, and remains among human beings in order to torment them.

This reading of his work makes Kafka into a kind of metaphysical rebel in spite of himself, and a representative of the kind of disbelief which I mentioned at the very beginning of this book. It is far from being the only reading of his work, and there is no means of telling whether he would have agreed with it or not. It could even be argued that his world, like that of the magic realists which it so strangely anticipates, is one which we should not try to understand in rational terms. It is not always easy to do this. When Oliver Edwards remarked that he had often tried to be a philosopher, but that cheerfulness kept breaking in, he also anticipated the reaction of the reader brought up in the essentially rational tradition which characterises the thought of Western Europe and North America when faced with novels in which, as Rosencrantz observes to Guildernstern after one of their meetings with Hamlet, 'Half of what he said meant something else, and the other half didn't mean anything at all'.

III

Kafka's 'The Metamorphosis' *and Salman Rushdie's* The Satanic
Verses: *two experiences of oppression; Rushdie's novel as magic realism,
as criticism of England; a comparison with E. M. Forster;* The Satanic
Verses *as a Voltairean denunciation of all religions.*

At the beginning of Kafka's most famous short story, 'Die Ver-
wandlung' ('The Metamorphosis'), Gregor Samsa wakes up one
morning to find himself 'transformed in his bed into a gigantic
insect'. He survives for some time, looked after mainly by his
sister, but is eventually quite happy to die and release the family
from the terrible burden which he realises he has become to them.
After his death, his mother, father and sister go out into the country,
where Mr and Mrs Samsa become aware of their daughter's 'in-
creasing vivacity' and realise that she has 'bloomed into a pretty
girl with a good figure'. The story ends with what Maurice Blanchot
has argued is its most terrible sentence, as Kafka describes how
Gregor's parents

> grew quieter and half unconsciously exchanged glances of
> complete agreement, having come to the conclusion that it would
> soon be time to find a good husband for her. And it was like a
> confirmation of their new dreams and excellent intentions that
> at the end of their journey their daughter sprang to her feet
> first and stretched her young body.

The fact that Kafka had three sisters, the eldest of them six years
younger than himself, offers a strong temptation to read 'The
Metamorphosis' in autobiographical terms. In it, he is expressing
what he half consciously thinks his parents think of him, and
how they prefer his younger and more attractive sisters. Such an
interpretation is nevertheless very difficult to sustain from what
we know of Kafka's life. He got on very well with his youngest
sister, Ottilie, with whom he stayed very happily when he went
to Zurau in an attempt to cure his tuberculosis, and looked to
her for comfort and protection against his tyrannical father. Both
the atmosphere and the ending of 'The Metamorphosis' nevertheless make it understandable why his parents were not keen
on his becoming a writer.

Although there is a parallel to the central incident in 'The

Metamorphosis' in what happens to the Bombay-born Saladin Chamcha in Salman Rushdie's *The Satanic Verses*, it is one which underlines the principal difference between Kafka and the magic realists whose work his fiction so often seems to anticipate. For when, shortly after his arrival in England, Saladin finds himself transformed into a goat, this is a very obvious allegory of how the racialist-minded English think of immigrants from the Third World, and in that respect far more comprehensible in rational terms than any of the allegories or symbols in Kafka. The remark made to Saladin by one of the other animals in the hospital from which he eventually escapes – who include

> businessmen from Nigeria who have grown sturdy tails ... a group of holidaymakers from Senegal who were doing no more than changing planes when they were turned into slippery snakes[13]

– merely underlines a point already implicit in the narrative. There is nothing in Kafka to match the clarity of the statement that 'they have the power of description and we succumb to the pictures they construct'.

The fact that *The Satanic Verses* is occasionally rather crude in its symbolism does not prevent it from being, in the remark attributed to the Ayatolla Khomeini in a *Guardian* competition in 1989 for the most improbable quotation of the year, 'a thundering good read'. It was clear, from the $850,000 advance paid to Salman Rushdie by the publishing house of Viking Penguin that they expected it to be a bestseller on literary grounds alone, even without the predictable boost to sales provided by the *fatwa* of 13 February 1989, and in 1991, the authorities responsible for the award of the Booker Prize for fiction marked the tenth anniversary of the award by signalling out Rushdie's earlier novel, *Midnight's Children*, as the best book to be honoured by it. It is, for this and other reasons, a great pity that discussions of the book's literary value have been overshadowed by arguments about whether or not the offence it apparently caused to large numbers of devout Muslims should take second place to the principle enshrined in the First Amendment to the Constitution of the United States: 'Congress shall make no law abridging the freedom of speech or expression'.

Although it would be naïve for Salman Rushdie to claim that

he was surprised by the furore created in Muslim circles by *The Satanic Verses*, it is clear from the text of the novel that any desire which he may have had to shock believers in Islam was a very minor element in the book. In a conference held in London in March 1985, when the book was still only a project in his mind, he explained how, in his native India, the storyteller would arrive at a village, sit under a tree, and start to tell his tales. Like Chinese boxes, these stories would all fit into one another, but with each retaining its own autonomy. The villagers would come and go, staying either for a complete story or for a self-contained episode in a longer yarn, returning from time to time to catch up with the main narrative. Although much of *The Satanic Voices* is written in what a Barthesian would call the accepted codes of realistic fiction, its originality for the Western reader lies just as much in the link between its form and the Indian storyteller's art as in the elements of magic realism contained in its plot.

Its main story line describes the adventures of two male characters of roughly the same age and of comparable professions. Gibreel Farishta, an Indian movie star, and Saladin Chamcha, an actor whose skill in imitating a wide variety of voices has earned him a fortune as the voice-over in a multitude of radio and television commercials, were both born in the same year as Rushdie himself, 1947. It is the year in which, on 1 January India became an independent country, and *Midnight's Children* describes what happened to a number of children born at midnight of the last year in which India was part of the Raj. The main action in *The Satanic Verses* takes place in the early part of the 1980s, not long after the election of Margaret Thatcher as Prime Minister in May 1979. This has enabled her to begin the process described with some enthusiasm in the novel by the film producer, Hal Valance, after a 'predictably jingoistic' lunch of '*rosbif, boudin Yorkshire, choux de Bruxelles*' washed down by a 'thunderous Burgundy' and followed by Armagnac and cigars, and much of the pleasure which *The Satanic Verses* gives to the English reader lies in the forthright comments it contains about life in Great Britain. 'What she wants', Hal explains,

> what she actually thinks she can fucking *achieve*, is literally to invent a whole new middle class in this country. Get rid of the old woolly incompetent buggers from fucking Surrey and Hampshire, and bring in the new. People who really *want*, and who

know that with her they can bloody well *get*. Nobody's ever tried to replace a whole fucking class before, and the amazing thing is she might just do it if they don't get her first.[14]

There is clearly some irony in this, and the portrait of England in *The Satanic Verses* is not a favourable one. As far as Chamcha himself is concerned, the novel is a kind of *bildungsroman*, in which he grows out of an idealised vision of England and comes to be reconciled with India itself as well as with his father. The irony of the treatment he receives at the hands of the immigration authorities, and of his transformation in their eyes into a stinking goat, stems from the fact that he had always been a lover of the England of myth and tradition, a country which he had learned to idolise as well as to idealise in his boyhood in Bombay. There, when India played the MCC, he had prayed for an England victory, 'for the game's creators to defeat the local upstarts, for the proper order of things to be maintained' only to be continually frustrated when

the games were invariably drawn, owing to the featherbed somnolence of the Brabourne stadium; the great issue, creator versus imitators, colonizer against colonized, had perforce to remain unresolved.[15]

Chamcha had thought he had found the ideal England in the person of his wife, Pamela Lovelace, someone whose 'aristocratic bellow of a voice marked her out as a golden girl', and who later remarks to her lover, Jumpy Josh, how she was, in her husband's eyes, 'bloody Britannia. Warm beer, mince pies, common-sense and me'.[16]

The Satanic Verses makes conscious and ample use of intertextuality, and the second sentence of Pamela's account of how her husband saw her inevitably evokes the opening sentence of Eric Heller's best-selling novel of the 1970s, *Love Story*, 'She loved Bach, Beethoven, the Beatles and me', just as the wish expressed before by Gabriel Farishta's mistress, Alleluia Cone – 'let the best minds of my generation soliloquize over power over some other poor woman's body, I'm off' – also inevitably echoes, in calmer and ironic tones, the opening of Allan Ginsberg's *Howl*:

I have seen the best minds of my generation destroyed by

madness, starving hysterical naked, expelled from college for printing obscene odes in the desert of sexless windows of men's dormitories and burned alive in bloody flannel suits of innocence amid the cannonblast bestsellers and shrapnel of leaden verse and nitroglycerine shrieks of fairies and mustard gas of sinister intelligent editors.

Similarly, the longer description of Pamela Lovelace recalls the girl in Evelyn Waugh's short story 'On Guard', whose most outstanding feature was a nose which

pierced the thin surface crust of the English heart in its. warm and puppy cast; a nose to take the thought of English manhood back to its schooldays, to the doughy-faced urchins on whom it had squandered its first affection, to memories of changing rooms and chapel and battered straw boaters.[17]

But although Pamela's voice is similar, in that it is 'composed of tweeds, headscarves, summer pudding, hockey-sticks, thatched houses, saddle-soap, house-parties, nuns, family pews, large dogs and philistinism'[18] it belies her true nature. She has nothing but contempt for the 'gentlemen farmers and debs' delights and somethings in the city' who pursue her with such relentless enthusiasm, and wants above all to be accepted by the 'greenies and peacemarchers and world-changers' who will never trust her because of the way she speaks. Her character had, in fact, been formed by tragedy, her father and mother had 'committed suicide together when she had just begun to menstruate'[19] and the hatred which this had given her for all things English – her father had been a Classicist and pathfinder pilot who had never adjusted to civilian life – makes her more sorry than sad at the news that Chamcha had died when the 747 in which he was travelling, the Bostan, flight 420, blew up in mid-air after being hijacked and held 'marooned on a shimmering runway' for 111 days by a group of Canadian-Sikh terrorists.

It is this explosion which provides the starting point for the main story in the novel. In accordance with what had, by 1988, become the conventions of magic realism, Saladin Chamcha and Gibreel Farishta survive their 30,000 foot fall into the 'slow congealed currents of the English sleeve', and it is the account of the different adventures which they then have which provides the framework for Rushdie's exploration of what he sees as the state of England in the 1980s. He said in his essay 'Outside the Whale', in 1990 that 'There is a genuine need for political fiction, for books that draw new and better maps of reality, and make new languages with which we understand the world' and *The Satanic Verses* is, for an English reader, precisely such a book. It shows him his society as seen from outside but by an author sufficiently from the inside – Rushdie was educated at Rugby, which he disliked, and at Cambridge, which in the best Public School tradition he found more enjoyable – to understand how it works, and to write its language with a different perfection to that of Tom Stoppard but with comparable effect.

It is also a book whose title has another and more interesting meaning than the one which led to the protests against it, and caused it to be banned not only in Islamic countries but also in Japan, South Africa and Venezuela. While Saladin Chamcha's arrival in the London whose initials, phonetically spelt out as Ellowen Deeowen, give its name to Part III of the novel, is disastrous, that of Gibreel Farishta is, at least initially, more fortunate. He finds that he has lost the halitosis which made his breath smell like sulphur – for movie buffs, perhaps another example of intertextuality, since Clark Gable had something of the same problem – and which he has passed on to the unfortunate Chamcha. The resentment which Chamcha feels at having been abandoned by Gibreel the moment the pair landed in England is exacerbated by Chamcha's discovery that Pamela, who had consistently failed to conceive with him, is pregnant by his former friend Jamshez Josh, appropriately known as Jumpy because of a nervous disposition which Chamcha's return does nothing to assuage. When Gibreel embarks on a love affair with Alleluia Cone, the first woman to climb Everest without oxygen, but who unfortunately suffers from flat feet, Chamcha uses his capacity to imitate voices to destroy the relationship between the two.

This sparks off a series of events which Rushdie describes as 'tragedy', 'or, at least, the echo of tragedy, the full-blooded original being unavailable to modern men and women, so it's said',[20] a clear reference to George Steiner's 1961 essay, *The Death of Tragedy*. The lewd suggestions which Chamcha makes over the telephone exacerbate the paranoiac illusion which Gibreel has that he has become the Archangel Gabriel, and in a moment of fury he shoots the film producer, S. S. Sisodia, before turning the gun on himself. What is satanic, from the humanist perspective within which Rushdie is working, and in which he was clearly expecting to be read, is the use that Chamcha's jealousy leads him to make of the ability which originally enabled him to rise above other men. He has the gift of tongues, but he uses it to destroy a relationship in which he had no reason to feel that he could be included, and thus to cause the deaths of two people who have not done him any harm. But perhaps out of recognition of the fact that, especially in tragedy, evildoers do sometimes escape the consequences of their misdeeds, and also because he is interested in another aspect of Chamcha's personality, Rushdie makes his story end on a note of reconciliation and even of happiness.

Understandably disillusioned by his discovery of the unpleasant underside of the London he had idealised as a boy, Chamcha goes back to Bombay to look after his father, who is dying of cancer. This puts an end to the long period of estrangement provoked by his father's second marriage, and leads to Chamcha's recognition of how mistaken he had been in his quest to become English. He changes his name from Saladin to Salahuddin, and realises, as the last page of the book puts it, that 'in spite of all his wrong-doing, weakness and guilt – in spite of his humanity – he was getting another chance'.[21]

The Satanic Verses is a long book, of 547 pages, and any summary is bound to do injustice to its complexity as well as to its humour. But although the implied perspective is that of the humanism which sees that the harm which people do to one another is infinitely worse than anything which their words may do to the gods, it is also a book about religion. This is especially so in the long passages about an extremely beautiful girl called Ayesha, who persuades the whole village of Titlipur to walk to the sea in the expectation that the waters will open and all its inhabitants will be able to walk to Mecca on dry land. The expected miracle does not happen, and the cancer of Misal, wife of the Zamindar Mirza Saeed, is not cured. The seas do not open, and almost the whole village is drowned.

The fate of the villagers of Titlipur is a reminder of Aldous Huxley's remark, in *Do What You Will* in 1929, that 'one is all for religion until one goes to a really religious country. Then, one is all for drains, machinery and the minimum wage.'

The comparison with the agnostic humanism which informs E.M. Forster's *A Passage to India* is, from this point of view, also an inevitable one, and both books are equally critical of English racialism. Because his skin is the wrong colour, Dr Aziz is excluded from the club to which his intelligence and skill give him every right to belong, and the moment an accusation is made against him, the Europeans immediately believe it on the slenderest of evidence. There is nothing in this to surprise the reader of *The Satanic Verses*, and the metaphysical pessimism is also the same. When the only reply which the echo in the Marabar caves sends back to Mrs Moore is 'ou-boum', this indicates the ultimate lack of meaning in the universe just as graphically as the more colloquially expressed message which Alleluia Cone's father gives her when he says

> Anyone ever tries to tell you how this most beautiful and most evil of planets is somehow homogeneous, composed only of reconcilable elements, that it all *adds up*, you get on the phone to the straightjacket tailor.[22]

His message, that of 'a survivor of a wartime prison camp whose name was never mentioned throughout Allie's childhood', is in this respect remarkably similar to what the echo from the Marabar caves tells Mrs Moore: 'Pathos, piety, courage – they exist but they are identical, and so is filth. Everything exists, nothing has value.' And Forster adds that

> If one had spoken with the tongues of angels and pleaded for all the unhappiness and misunderstanding in the world, past, present and to come; for all the misery men must undergo whatever their opinion or position, and however much they might dodge or bluff, it would amount to the same.[23]

Alleluia Cone's father, who after his release from the camp became an art historian and biographer of Picabia, would conclude his advice, somehow managing as he did so to 'give the impression of having visited more planets than one before coming to his conclusion', with a final observation:

> The world is incompatible, just never forget it: gaga. Ghosts, Nazis, saints, all alive at the same time; in one spot, blissful happiness, while down the road, the inferno. You can't ask for a wilder place[24]

and makes this aspect of *The Satanic Verses* into a rationally formulated version of the absurdist universe of Beckett or Ionesco.

It was not, however, this fundamentally irreligious vision of
experience which led to the campaign against Salman Rushdie,
and which led him to being the first author to go in fear of his
life in Western Europe on a charge of blasphemy since before the
first French revolution. Indeed, it is as difficult for the average
Westerner to see precisely where the blasphemy lies in *The Satanic Verses* as it would have been for an agnostic Muslim to
understand why the Europeans of the sixteenth and seventeenth
centuries killed one another with such enthusiasm because of the
differences separating Catholics and Protestants over the doctrines
of transubstantiation and consubstantianism. Daniel Pipes's *The
Rushdie Affair*, a study which Basic Books commissioned but then
declined to publish, talks of 'a terrible misunderstanding about
the book's title' which led a number of devout Muslims to believe that it alleged that the whole of the Koran had been written
by the Devil. Since Islam, like Christianity, is a religion based on
the belief that a particular book is divinely inspired, it would
indeed have been a serious blasphemy on Rushdie's part to argue that the whole of the Koran was of Satanic origin. It was,
apparently, this misunderstanding which led to the many protests against its publication which pre-dated the *fatwa* of 13 February 1989, and to the sending of some 100,000 letters of disapproval
to Rushdie's publisher. 'The case against Rushdie' writes Daniel
Pipes in the book which the Carol Publishing Group, New York,
did have the courage to publish in 1990, 'was a populist one,
with the leaders only joining in afterwards'[25] and there is a parallel here both with the Inquisition in Spain and with European
anti-semitism. Neither the institution nor the attitude were ever
rejected by the mass of the population, and the portrait in Jerzy
Kosinski's *The Painted Bird* of the peasants in Europe jeering at
the trains carrying the Jews to the gas chambers was based upon
fact.

The two main passages in *The Satanic Verses* judged blasphemous by theologians, and which eventually attracted the ire of the
Ayotallah Khomeini, concerned two matters: the suggestion that
a number of verses intercalated in the Koran were subsequently
revealed as diabolically inspired; and the allegation that the twelve
wives of Mohammed were in fact prostitutes. The first issue is
clearly the more complicated, since it is also accompanied by the

allegation that it was Archangel Gabriel who told Mohammed that the verses which said of the goddesses Lat, Uzza and Manet that 'they are the enchanted birds and their intercession is well founded' had in fact been dictated by the Devil and therefore included in the Koran by error. This allegation leads to the heretical claim that Gabriel simply made up ideas which he then dictated to the Prophet, a claim which, if true, would prove that the book was not of divine origin.

It is clearly not a compliment to suggest that any man's wife is a prostitute, and it is hard to explain why Rushdie included either this obvious heresy, or the more obscure passage about the 'enchanted birds', in a novel where they add little to the plot and nothing to the interest. The adventures of Gibreel and Chamcha, like the imagined lives and entertaining exploits of Rosa Diamond, Alleluia Cone, the expert conman Billy Battuta, the jealous threesome from the London Underground – Orphia Phillips, Uriah Moseley and Rochelle Moseley – the black leader Dr Uhuru Simba, whom others could remember when he was plain Sylvester Roberts from down New Cross way, are sufficiently entertaining in their own right to give the book its fascination and intense readability. So, too, are the views of Inspector Stephen Kinch, who thinks that if the coloured inhabitants of London think they are badly treated in British society:

> They should consult their own kith and kin. Africa, Asia, the Caribbean: now those are places with real problems. Those are places where people might have grievances worth respecting. Things aren't so bad here, not by a long chalk; no slaughters here, no torture, no military coups.[26]

Had the protests against *The Satanic Verses* focused on the portrait of the Imam, whose 'great gnarled hands, granite grey, rest heavily on the wings of his high-backed chair', and who teaches that History is

> the blood-wine that must no longer be drunk. History is the intoxicant, the creation and possession of the devil, of the great Shaitan, the greatest of the lies – progress, science, rights, – against which the Imam has set his face. History is a deviation from the Path, knowledge is a delusion, because knowledge was complete on the day Allah finished his revelation to Mahound[27]

it would have been easier for Americans and Europeans to understand, on rational grounds, why the book was as unpopular with fundamentalist Muslims in Bradford as it was in Rushdie's native Bombay. Rushdie's attack on theocracy is as well founded as Orwell's indictment in *Nineteen Eighty-Four* of the tyranny of Big Brother, and focuses on a very similar aspect of totalitarian society:

> After the revolution, there will be no more clocks; we'll smash the lot. The word *clock* will be expunged from the dictionaries. After the revolution there will be no more birthdays. We shall be born again, all of us the same unchanging age in the eye of Almighty God.[28]

Rushdie's case against religion is in the tradition of European thinkers who, like Voltaire, Feuerbach and Bertrand Russell, see it as the most poisonous gift that humanity has invented to torment itself. It is for this reason that, in a dream sequence, Gibreel 'sees the Imam grown monstrous, lying in the palace forecourt with his mouth yawning open at the gates', so that as the people march through, he 'swallows them whole'.

IV

Modernism and post-modernism: an attempt at definition; illustrations from Margaret Atwood, John Updike and David Lodge; a plea for directness.

There are other, more strictly literary, reasons to regret that the arguments about *The Satanic Verses* should have concentrated on the question of whether it ought or ought not to have been banned on the charge that it was blasphemous. While there is a reasonable measure of agreement among literary historians about what modernism is, and an excellent anthology by Malcolm Bradbury and James McFarlane illustrating their views, it is much harder to find a satisfactory definition of the phenomenon known as Post-modernism. Modernism is Proust, Joyce, Eliot, and Lawrence and Pound, the breaking up of the narrative tradition embodied in Dickens, Thackeray, Tolstoy, Balzac and Zola, the realisation that experience was too complicated to be depicted in conventional narratives or analysed through recognisable characters. In poetry, it is experimentation with new forms, and the transfer of the burden of understanding from the writer to the reader. Post-modernism, in contrast, not only seems a chronological contradiction, in that it is hard to see how anything can be meaningfully described in that way when the very term used to evoke it implies that it is not due to come into existence until tomorrow. It is also very difficult, especially when presented by the critics, to understand.

It is not, however, as obscure a notion as Baudrillard and others have made out. It also has the great advantage of having been put forward in its most interesting and challenging form by the creative writers themselves. For when Margaret Atwood makes the narrator of *The Handmaid's Tale* write

> By telling you anything at all I'm at least believing in you, I believe you're there, I believe you into being. Because I'm telling you this story, I will your existence. I tell, therefore you are[29]

she is saying something quite different about the relationship between the writer and the reader than anything in Proust or Joyce. They presupposed, for all their experimentation, a reader of basically the same cast of mind as themselves. Proust knew his reader to be a cultivated member of the French middle or upper-middle class, probably unhappy in love, certainly in the habit of keeping a mistress, well acquainted with the structure of his own society, and more particularly of the many differences between Paris and the Provinces. Joyce presupposed a knowledge of the classics, an interest in Dublin, a distaste for Catholicism, and a good deal of spare time. The post-modern writer, as Margaret Atwood points out, can count on nothing. If she or he is going to be read, it is by someone whom they, in a sense, create. It is more than Wordsworth's remark that: 'Every author as far as he is *great* and at the same time *original*, has had the task of *creating* the taste by which he is to be enjoyed'. It is the person, almost the existence, of the reader that Salman Rushie, for example, has to create. Many of the problems of *The Satanic Verses* stem from the fact that Rushdie does not really know who is he writing for. In that, he represents an important aspect of the post-modernist temper.

Rushdie is also, like Milly Battuta's girl friend, Mimi, 'conversant with post-modernist critiques of the West, e.g. that we have a society capable only of pastiche: a "flattened" world'.[30] *The Satanic*

Verses can be read as one long pastiche, its rejection of traditional concepts of realism – even in Joyce, people don't fall 30,000 feet out of an aeroplane and survive – running parallel with a constant quest for some kind of stable identity. It is not an accident that the two main characters are both actors, men whose reality is constantly called into question by the different roles they play. As John Updike observed in *Memories of the Ford Administration*,

> Modern fiction ... thrives only in showing what is *not* there: God is not there, nor damnation, nor redemption, nor solemn vows and the sense of one's life as a matter to be judged and refigured in a later accounting, in a trial held on the furthest, brightest quasar.[31]

Once one takes away the questions it raises in the reader it creates, nothing in *The Satanic Verses* is ultimately real, and there is not even any certainty about these. There is no way in which my reading of the novel could be the same even as that of a fellow Englishman, and even less of a Muslim living down the road from me in Leeds.

There is, of course, a sense in which this has always been the case. But while no two people have ever read the same book in exactly the same way, the awareness of how differently we react to the same linguistic symbols is another aspect of post-modernism which, for all its association with the ideas of Jacques Derrida, can be expressed quite clearly in English. Maurice Zapp does it with great elegance in his lecture in David Lodge's *Small World*,[32] and it is even easier to do the same with phrases about the 'end of the grand narratives' and the 'disappearance of the subject'. All that the first means is that we no longer believe that history can be written in terms of Christianity, Marxism, Islam, or even of the gradual and irresistible rise to power of the sceptically-minded, English-speaking middle class. History is, as Alleluia Cone's father would readily have agreed, just one damn thing after another. What the second phrase means is that there is no central core to our existence. We are like the onion peeled by Ibsen's Peer Gynt, organisms whose identity consists solely of the interrelation of the otherwise discrete elements composing us.

V

Toni Morrison and the problems of a deliberately limited readership;
some comparisons with Faulkner; the problem of interpreting Tar Baby;
ghosts and magic realism in Beloved; *final thoughts on commitment*
and the concept of literature as catalyst.

Inspector Kinch's views on race and immigration are not entirely
unknown in North America, where conservatively minded politicians in the Southern States are wont to observe that nowhere in
the world do people with black skins enjoy a higher standard of
living than in the USA. Stanley Crouch, reviewing Toni Morrison's
Beloved in the *New Republic* for 19 October 1987 under the ironic
title 'Aunt Medea' noted the omission in the account it gave of
the sufferings endured by Negro slaves in America of any mention of the way in which the blacks in Africa had collaborated in
the slave trade by 'raiding the village of their enemies to sell
them for guns'. Commenting on Toni Morrison's remark to the
PEN Congress of 1986 that she has 'never considered herself
American', he concluded his review with the claim that 'with *Be-*
loved, she proves that she is as American as P. T. Barnum'.[33] The
suggestion that it was all a great circus act was an unkind comment to make about the author of a book which is also as, Mr
Crouch had earlier remarked, 'a blackface holocaust novel', but it
did highlight the extent to which literary reviews can reflect political attitudes, and cause considerable controversy by doing so.
Since the 1960s, it has been one of the claims of the right, in England as well as in America, that its attachment to the freedom of
expression is stronger than that of the left, and the conservatively
minded *New Republic* was very forthright in bringing out what it
saw as the political implications of the Salman Rushdie case:

> If you are for the banning and burning of books, if you deny
> the right of a writer to write and a publisher to publish, if you
> believe that an opinion may be refuted by a bullet, you are
> anti-American. The militant mullahs are right. Philosophically
> and historically, the United States is the enemy. The defender
> of *The Satanic Verses* is the Great Satan. For this we may be
> proud.[34]

Salman Rushdie may well have seen things differently. His own political attitude is described by Daniel Pipes as the 'classical anti-Americanism of the third-worldists'[35] and the political cause for which he has expressed most support is that of the Sandanista rebels in Nicaragua. Although it would be hard to imagine Toni Morrison as a subscriber to the *New Republic*, she has not so far adopted such a clearcut attitude on any specifically political issue. Her commitment, as she made clear in her Nobel Prize acceptance speech in December 1993, is primarily to language, and there is a strong similarity in this respect between her and William Faulkner, on whom she wrote a Master's thesis when at Howard University in the 1950s. It is words, she argued in her acceptance speech, which protect us from 'the scariness of things with no names', and she expressed a humanist attitude very close to that of Camus or E. M. Forster when she said:

> We die. That may be the meaning of our lives. But we do language. That may be the measure of our lives.

In 1950, when the award of the Nobel Prize for Literature enabled William Faulkner to achieve something of the recognition in the United States that he had enjoyed since the 1930s in Europe, he put the same idea more dramatically in his acceptance speech when he said of man that:

> When the last dingdong of doom has clanged and faded from the last worthless rock hanging tideless in the last red and dying evening, even then there will still be one more sound: that of his puny, inexhaustible voice still talking.

There are other similarities between Faulkner and Toni Morrison, especially on the level of technique. Both write a prose which is different in every respect from the sparse narrative style of Ernest Hemingway, and both require a more sustained effort from the reader. One sentence in Faulkner's *Sartoris* goes on for five pages, an achievement which exceeds anything in Proust, and much of the story in one of his most famous early novels, *The Sound and the Fury* (1929), is quite literally told by an idiot, Benjamin Compson, whose obsession with his sister Candace makes him haunt the fields around the golf club in the hope of hearing what he thinks is her name when the players call 'Caddy'. Faulkner also perfected an elliptical technique whereby the rape of Temple Drake by the gangster Popeye in *Sanctuary* is alluded to without ever being described. Since Popeye's impotence meant that this rape was carried out by a corn cob, this may have been a concession to the censor, though Faulkner had a highly successful imitator in this aspect of his presentation of the criminal world in James Hadley Chase's best-selling 1939 novel, *No Orchids for Miss Blandish*. It may even have been *Sanctuary* which launched the fashion for sexually inept and even impotent gangsters, to which twentieth-century fiction owes the characters of Pinkie in *Brighton Rock* and Scaramanga in Ian Fleming's *The Man With the Golden Gun*, and to which the cinema has a comparable debt in *The Maltese Falcon* and the male tearaway in *Bonnie and Clyde*.

The literary similarities between Toni Morrison and Faulkner also recur, albeit in a rather unexpected and somewhat disturbing form, in her attitude on a number of social and political issues. She does not, of course, underwrite the slightly paternalistic and protective attitude towards the Negro expressed in Faulkner's novels. Although there are occasional incidents in her fiction in which white people do behave with a semblance of humanity towards the blacks, nothing in the historical experience which she describes gives any grounds for believing that any organisation in which blacks find themselves side by side with whites will do anything but give preferential treatment to the latter. Apart from the portrait of the Bodwins, in the 1986 novel *Beloved*, who help slaves to escape across the Ohio river, or of Lady Jones, who is described in the same novel as providing education for the black children in mid-nineteenth-century Cincinatti, the dominant mood in Toni Morrison's fiction is one of despair at the possibility of members of the white population in the United States ever managing to do anything meaningful to help the blacks, even if they were to try. Where she does see eye to eye with Faulkner is on the issue of integration which she rejects for different reasons. For it would imply, as she said in an interview in 1986, that we 'would not have a fine black college or fine black education'[36] and she seems to have as little sympathy as Faulkner did with the view that it is the right as well as the duty of the Federal government to intervene in the Southern States in order to bring about a more rapid improvement in the living conditions of the blacks by legal means.

Another remark which she made in an interview in 1986, this time with Sandi Russell in *Women's Review* for 5 March, is also difficult to reconcile with the essentially humanistic approach expressed in her Nobel Prize acceptance speech. For when she said 'I write for black women', adding on behalf of other black women writers apart from herself that

> We are not addressing the men, as some white female writers do. We are not attacking each other, as both black and white men do. Black women writers look at things in an unforgiving/ loving way. They are writing to re-possess, re-name, re-own[37]

it is hard not to see her attitude as embodying a kind of sexual and social apartheit in reverse. Indeed, her attitude in this respect represents a major development not only in the imaginative literature of the late twentieth century but also in the thought and social attitudes of certain sections of the intellectual middle class.

Thus for writers in the humanist tradition represented by writers such as Camus, E. M. Forster, André Gide, Thomas Mann, Santayana or Bertrand Russell, there was no serious doubt as to the way society ought to be going. The traditional liberal values which encouraged people to eschew violence, to be intellectually tolerant, permanently curious about their own nature, and sensitive to the cultural achievements of all societies, offered a model to which it was reasonable to assume that everybody wished to aspire. Beyond what were regarded as the superficial differences of race, colour, gender and nationality, there lay a universal ideal of mankind. Actions and attitudes which encouraged the development of such a society were good, and its advent was regarded as desirable precisely because it would bring about the recognition of a humanity which was common to everyone. One of the most valuable qualities of such a society was the guarantee it provided that human beings would, in spite of the very real and passionately held differences separating them, understand one another both as individuals and as members of different ethnic and religious groups. The words of Schiller's *An die Freude* (*Ode to Joy*), set to music by Beethoven in the Choral Symphony, date from the late eighteenth century. They nevertheless represent the universal ideal to such perfection that the *Ode* was adopted in 1973 as the anthem of what is now known as the European Union.[38]

One of the major differences between Sartre and Camus is that while the Camus of *The Rebel* accepted this ideal, the whole of

Sartre's political thinking was directed against it. This was partly because of his sympathy for Marxism, but more particularly because of his awareness of the injustice meted out to the Third World by the inhabitants of Western Europe and North America. For him, traditional humanism of the type embodied in Schiller's ode could never have come into being without the wealth created first, by the exploitation of the proletariat and, second, by the plundering by the West of the resources of the colonised Third World. So long as human beings with white skins battened off the labour of those with brown or black ones, all talk of human brotherhood was a snare and a delusion. Similarly, and here his views were taken up in a slightly different form by Jacques Derrida and the deconstructionists, the idea of language as communication was based on the totally false premise that the words used by the oppressor had the same meaning as they had for the oppressed.

For the more radical members of the women's movement, the same argument applies to the relationship between men and women. Not only had men deliberately refused to accept the rewriting of the *Déclaration des Droits de l'Homme* by the eighteenth-century feminist Olympe de Gouges, and thus tacitly acknowledged that they had implicitly excluded over half the human race. They had also developed a particular mode of speech which may have been adequate to describe their experience of the world, but which had no applicability whatsoever to that of women. For writers such as Julia Kristeva and the women grouped in the Paris-based *Psych et Po* movement, the prime need was to develop a new kind of speech which did away with the presuppositions of what they called patriarchal discourse.

Part of the interest of Toni Morrison lies in the fact that the expression which her novels give to the experience of one of the most oppressed groups in history, black American female slaves, coincides with the growth in the United States of a very comparable set of attitudes. What she seems to be recommending is the conscious exclusion of white males from any kind of intellectual contact with black females. The experience of oppression, she suggests, has been such as to make it impossible for the two races ever to come together in harmony. The blacks can understand the whites. The sufferings which they have experienced at their hands have taught them all they need to know. But the whites, in contrast, will never be able to understand the blacks. Their past behaviour, coupled with the unconscious attitudes which they will never be able to shake off, means that no solution to the problem of race relations in the United States can be found in the liberal attitudes of the Northern whites.

One of the more direct ways in which Toni Morrison's fiction brings out a central aspect of black experience in the United States in the nineteenth century is the uncertainty about what some of her characters are really called. This is a reflection of the habit of the plantation owners in the eighteenth and nineteenth centuries of simply bestowing a name of their own choosing on their slaves, just as Lillian Garner, in *Beloved*, decides to call one of her slaves Jenny because she thought it went well with the name of Whitlow which was on the bill of sale. It is only quite late on in the novel that the reader discovers that this is the grandmother always referred to as Baby Suggs, so called because her husband, Paul Suggs, liked the name Baby. When Baby talks to her daughter Sethe and her grand-daughter Denver about 'the lesson that she has learned from sixty years a slave and ten years free: that there was no bad luck in the world but whitepeople'[39] she sounds like a spokesperson not only for Toni Morrison herself but for the whole movement which she represents.

One of the problems which Toni Morrison's fiction sets the white, male, middle-class reader is that of the opprobrium he risks bringing down upon himself by criticising the social and intellectual attitudes which she seems to endorse. If he says that these attitudes are a kind of mirror image of the 'segregation imposed on the blacks in the past, and are therefore likely to prove just as self-defeating, he immediately labels himself as one of the oppressors who require the oppressed to adopt a set of humanistic values which have never brought them anything but a sense of exclusion. These values have, it could well be argued, totally discredited themselves by the oppression which they have done so little to prevent. It is consequently unfair as well as presumptuous to expect the oppressed suddenly to start accepting them. On the other hand, the idea that black women are so totally different from white males that no rational communication is possible between them is a highly reactionary one. It goes against the drive towards universal values which the white, middle-class male reader has been taught to see as the sole justification for human existence.

It is in this respect that Toni Morrison's most recent novel, *Jazz*, and an earlier book, the 1973 *Sula*, are accounts of black experience which make white readers feel that they are peeping over a hedge to look at events on which they have no right to express an opinion. The first of her novels to become a bestseller, the 1981 *Tar Baby*, is nevertheless different from her other books in that it gives literary expression to the problem which I have just tried to outline. It offers a different type of challenge to the one presented by *Beloved* or *Sula*, and one which offers at least the possibility of rational discussion. It is a characteristic of all fiction that it should read its readers at the same time as its readers read it, bringing out their attitudes, preferences and values in the way they react to the words on the printed page. What is, one asks oneself after finishing *Tar Baby*, the right way for black women to live? Is it in the kind of self-imposed intellectual ghetto implied by Toni Mor-rison's claim to be writing only for black women? Or is it in a way which recognises that white society, for all its faults, can nowadays offer black women the same opportunities for self-realisation which it has traditionally made available principally to Caucasian males who have chosen their parents with unusual care?

There is, naturally, no way in which any reader can approve of the principal white male character in *Tar Baby*, Valerian Street. He makes a habit of publicly humiliating his wife, and chooses Christmas dinner as the moment at which to dismiss his two most loyal servants, Ondine and Sydney Childs, allegedly for stealing apples. This provokes Ondine to reveal how cruelly Valerian's wife Margaret used to behave towards their son Michael when he was a small child, making small but painful cuts on his body, and burning him with cigarette ends. Valerian, a rich but now retired manufacturer of confectionery, had originally married Margaret, a much younger woman than himself, for her extraordinary beauty. He had then, however, effectively prevented her from growing up, and the disastrous marriage which ensued is the only relationship between white people studied in Toni Morrison's novels. Its devastating excellence as a portrait of selfishness and failure creates a certain regret that she did not give freer rein to this aspect of her talent. The world of Ivy Compton-Burnett is idyllic in comparison. But the way the book ends seems to go so much against Toni Morrison's remarks to Sandi Russell, and the ideas it suggests are so different from the ones which her admirers would like her readers to hold, that questions of literary interpretation become inseparable from issues of social, sexual and even political preference.

The one generous action which Valerian Street has performed in his whole life has been to ensure that a young black girl, Jadine Childs, the niece of his black servants Sydney and Ondine, received a good education. He has sent her to art school, enabled her to obtain a doctorate in art history from the Sorbonne, and put her into a position where she can profit from her outstanding beauty to enjoy a successful career in Europe as a top model. The plot of *Tar Baby* describes how William Green, otherwise known simply as Son, dishonourably discharged from the United States Army and guilty of having killed his wife's lover by driving a car through the house in which she was being unfaithful to him, arrives on the Caribbean island where most of the action takes place. To the horror of his wife, Street makes him very welcome, and Son becomes Jadine's lover. They go off to New York together, where he has difficulty in finding a job, and where she therefore provides most of the income. Then, at Son's insistence, they visit the small town of Eloe, in Florida, where he grew up and where he 'has roots'.

The visit is a disaster from Jadine's point of view. She dislikes Eloe intensely, seeing it as 'a burnt-out-place', a 'medieval slave basket', a town which may have had a past, but which certainly has no future, and which can hold no interest for her. Where she is at home is in New York, a 'blackwoman's town', where women with the same colour skin as hers are 'snapping whips behind the tellers' windows, kicking ass at Con Eddisons offices, barking orders in the record companies'. It is there that black women can be seen as enjoying their power as they

> refused loans at Household Finance, withheld unemployment checks and drivers' licences, issued parking tickets and summonses. Gave enemas, blood transfusions and please lady don't make me mad.[40]

It is a passage whose accuracy and humour reinforce what is considered to be a very reactionary point of view. This is that any member of an oppressed minority who wants to improve not only her or his personal condition but that of everybody like them should not take courses in black studies, female consciousness-raising or Chicano self-awareness. The way to do it is to become an accountant, a dentist, a plumber, a policeman, a specialist in immediate household repairs, an expert in Word Perfect 5.1,

one of those people whom society can't do without, and there
are moments in *Tar Baby* when it almost seems that this is a view
which Toni Morrison shares. The visit to Eloe leads to a blazing
row between Jadine and Son, in which she talks to him about the
importance of education. When he tells her that all she has learned
is 'bullshit', she replies with some conviction:

> The truth is that when you were playing the piano in the Night
> Movies café, I was in school. The truth is that while you were
> driving your car into your wife's bed I was being educated.
> While you were hiding from a small-town sheriff or some in-
> surance company, hiding from a rap a two-bit lawyer could
> have gotten you out of, I was being educated. I was working,
> I was making something out of my life, I was learning to make
> it in *this* world, the one we live in, not the one in your head.
> Not that dump Eloe; *this* world.[41]

Son's only reply to this is to say that all this education doesn't
enable her to understand *him*, and to terrify her by holding her
out of the window, so much so that she wets her pants. After
this, their relationship understandably breaks down. She takes
the plane back to Paris, where she will join up again with an
earlier, European, lover, go back to her job as a model, and presumably continue the process of integration into white society
begun by the education provided for her by Valerian Street. Son,
as penniless as he was at the beginning of the novel, goes back
to the Isle des Chevaliers, and to what may well be a less friendly
welcome than he enjoyed on his first visit. Sydney, who has never
liked him, has threatened to shoot him if he finds him maraud-
ing about the grounds again.

There is an ambiguity in the title of the novel which is echoed
in the different interpretations which can be placed on the plot.
In the original Uncle Remus story, Brer Rabbit becomes stuck on
the tar baby which Farmer Brown has hung out to catch any animal trying to steal any of his crops. He is then himself hung out
at the gate post to serve as a warning. With characteristic cunning, Brer Rabbit tells the farmer that he does not mind what is
done to him so long as he is not thrown into the briar bush. This,
naturally, is precisely what the farmer does, thus enabling Brer
Rabbit to get the tar off himself by rubbing against the brambles
and thus to effect his escape. For Eileen W. Taylor, this makes

Toni Morrison's novel into a kind of allegory of black–white relations from which the superior cunning which black people have
been forced to develop by centuries of oppression enables them
to emerge triumphant from any attempt which the whites make
to trap them into accepting the culture and values of white society.
In this reading of the novel, Son has managed to escape from the
corrupting culture of the whites, while Jadine, described by Eileen
Taylor as 'the tar baby who ensnares son' has remained its
prisoner.[42]

It is quite possible that this is how Toni Morrison wanted the
book to be read. If the names of the people to whom *Tar Baby* is
dedicated are, as Eileen Taylor claims, those of 'the grandmother,
mother, aunts and sisters of the writer ... the guides to whom
the narrative voice of the writer is accountable' then the women
at Eloe whose presence Jadine finds so oppressive could well be,
as Eileen Taylor also says,

> the progenitors of and the heirs to the fundamental ethos of
> African American sensibility untainted by pretension, unpol-
> luted by the storm of bilious thought that pummels the world
> in which they live.[43]

It may well be, in this reading of the text, that Jadine's protest
against the world of Eloe has nothing admirable about it. It may
indicate what is wrong with the European education she has received, whose only real effect has been to teach her to despise
her own race and the authentic, independent values it has developed. The text of the novel does indeed make it clear that in
order to remain successful in the world of fashion, 'she needed
only to be stunning, and to convince them she was not as smart
as they were'[44] and there are other remarks which suggests that
her career as a model may not last long. Although she is not
quite 25, she is already having to pretend that she is much younger
than she is. She has not, in this respect, acquired the kind of
skills which offer their owner a way to genuine self-respect by
the need which society has of them.

But however meretricious the world to which Jadine is going
back to may be, it cannot be worse than the life which she would
have to lead if she stayed with Son. He is a marvellous lover,
who 'fucks like a star', but he is also – like Walter Morel in *Sons
and Lovers* – very violent. As he and Jadine grow older, the

discrepancy between their tastes and characters can only get worse, and there is nothing in his tastes or behaviour which might help her to make the transition from modelling into the world of art history where her success would not be dependent on her staying young and beautiful. One may well feel some sympathy for Son's interior monologue at the disastrous Christmas dinner, in which he says to himself, thinking of the whites, that

> This was the sole lesson of their world: how to make waste, how to make machines that make more waste, how to make wasteful products, how to talk waste, how to design waste, how to cure people who were sickened by waste so they could be well enough to endure it, how to mobilize waste, legalize waste and how to despise the culture that lived in cloth houses and shit on the ground far from where they ate.[45]

On the other hand, it is another black man, Jadine's uncle, Sydney, who says to Son

> I am a Phil-a-delphia Negro mentioned in a book of the same name. My people owned drug stores and taught school when yours were still cutting their faces open so as to tell one from the other,[46]

and unfortunate as well as perhaps irrelevant that his views coincide so closely with those of Inspector Kinch.

Tar Baby is the first novel which Toni Morrison has so far published to raise the question of the relationship between white and black culture in such starkly intellectual terms. In the others, the alienation and oppression which the blacks suffer at the hands of the whites are so great as to exclude the possibility of any debate as to the relative merits of their respective cultures. The blacks see white culture from below, and their view of its alleged superiority is rather like the image which the victims in Kafka's *In The Penal Colony* must have had of the machine which inscribed their offence in their living flesh. In Toni Morrison's first novel, *The Bluest Eye*, her young heroine Pecola Breedlove is obsessed by the idea that only people with blue eyes can ever be truly beautiful, and is so misled by the 'true Spiritualist and Psychic Reader', Micah Elihue Whitcomb, alias Soaphead Church, that she blinds herself in an attempt to conform to this idea. In her best-known novel, *Beloved*, this inner alienation takes an outward form when the character simply referred to as 'Schoolteacher' tells a group of white children to study a black girl and write her animal characteristics in one column and her human ones in another.

It is Schoolteacher – 'a little man. Short. Always wore a collar, even in the fields'[47] – who also plays a central role in the events around which the plot of *Beloved* is constructed. The main incident takes place when Sethe Halle cuts the throat of her two-year-old daughter and tries to kill her other children rather than let them be recaptured and taken back into slavery. Sethe has managed, sometime in the mid 1850s, to escape from the slave state of Kentucky by crossing the Ohio river, and has given birth on the way to another daughter to whom she gives the name Denver in memory of the girl from Boston, Amy Denver, who helped her with the delivery. She was, before her escape, so savagely whipped by Schoolmaster's nephews that she has a scar the shape of a chokecherry tree on her back, so that it is fully understandable that the arrival of a posse of four men, Schoolteacher, one nephew, one slave catcher, and a sheriff, should drive her to such despair. But although she carves the name 'Beloved' on to the headstone of the grave in which her two-year-old daughter is buried, the ghost of this daughter remains to haunt her.

It is the need which the reader has to believe in ghosts which links *Beloved* to the magic realism of *One Hundred Years of Solitude* or *The Satanic Verses*. In García Márquez's novel, the gypsy magician Melquíades returns from the dead after many years and is immediately recognised by Aureliano Secundo, who had never seen him, because of 'a hereditary memory transmitted from generation to generation and which has come to him through his grandfather'[48] while in *The Satanic Verses*, Gibreel Farishta sees the ghost of his former mistress Rekha Merchant flying alongside the train carrying him to London. There are nevertheless a number of differences, of which the first and most important is that while the ghosts in Márquez and Rushdie are only incidental to the main action, the whole of the second part of the plot of *Beloved* depends for its ultimate credibility on a belief in ghosts as something real.

The story line of *Beloved*, like that of Faulkner's *The Sound and the Fury*, moves rapidly between past, present and future, so that it is only gradually that the meaning of the different events becomes clear. There are comparable time shifts in *One Hundred*

Years of Solitude, where the text begins by evoking the day on which Colonel Aureliano Bueno stood facing the firing squad, but where the reader is subsequently told that he is never executed and spends the closing years of his life quite peacefully making silver fishes. American critics are sometimes no kinder about the writers they discuss than the F. R. Leavis who could find no time for the novels of J. B. Priestley, and it has been argued that the shift of style which separates *The Bluest Eye* from Toni Morrison's other fiction was adopted for mainly tactical reasons. Martha Bayles, in an article called 'Special Effects, Special Pleading' in *The New Criterion* for June 1988, claimed that *The Bluest Eye* had been 'blown to obscurity by the firestorm of Márquez', and pointed out that by 1974 it was out of print. It was this, in her view, which made Toni Morrison deliberately latch on to the phenomenon of magic realism in order to make her novels more fashionable. This, for Martha Bayles, was a mistake, since it led Toni Morrison to 'neglect her strengths and indulge her weaknesses',[49] and may well explain why a prosaically minded reader like myself prefers the more conventional style of story-telling which makes earlier novels such as *The Bluest Eye* (1970) as well as *Tar Baby* (1981) so readable.

The suspension of disbelief required by the ghost theme in *Beloved* is made more difficult by the fact that so much of the rest of the novel is told in the traditional code of realistic narrative which has always characterised the novel of social protest. It is, in contrast, pretty clear from the beginning of *The Satanic Verses* that we are on a wild carpet ride under the guidance of 'some sort of bum from Persia by the outlandish name of Salman'[50] and Rushdie makes another appearance as the novelist-in-the-novel when he writes of Gibreel that

> I am giving him no instructions. I, too, am interested in his choices – in the result of his wrestling match. Character *vs* destiny: a free-style bout. Two falls, two submissions or knockout will decide.[51]

One of the first of the South American writers who can be categorised as a magic realist, Jorge-Louis Borges, entitled one of his collections of short stories *Ficciones*, a conscious wink to let the reader know that he was as far removed as possible from Balzac's claim in *Le Père Goriot* that 'All is True', and it is obvious from the very beginning that García Márquez is no Isherwood gazing passively with his shutters open. The dedication of *Beloved* to 'Sixty Million and more' is a reference to the number of Africans brought over as slaves, and there is no doubt about the reality of the oppression it describes. Paul D., Sethe's lover, spends part of his life linked to 46 other black men by 'a thousand feet of the best hand-forged chain in Georgia'. He is also described, in a phrase which further emphasises the alienation of the slave, as being 'astonished by the beauty of the land which is not his' and the cruelty of white slaveowners comes out in his memory of how he once saw 'a witless coloured woman jailed and hanged for stealing ducks she believed were her own babies'.[52]

There is another equally realistic detail in the description of the newspaper cutting from which Paul D. (short for Paul D. Garner; like a number of slaves, he was made to take the surname of his owner) learned of Sethe's action in killing her own daughter. For when Toni Morrison writes that 'there was no way in hell a black face could appear in a newspaper if the story was about something anybody wanted to hear' and that a picture of a black person would not appear in a newspaper 'because that person had been killed, or maimed or caught or burned or jailed or whipped or evicted or stomped or raped or cheated, since that could hardly qualify as news in a newspaper'[53] she is underlining not only how natural the ill-treatment of blacks was in nineteenth-century America but how the silent the white-controlled media then were. She is also, however, setting the mind of her reader on to a track in which ghosts, real or imaginary, play little part. The horror of the events related elsewhere in *Beloved* is of strictly human origin.

Were the readers of *Beloved* not expected to believe in ghosts in order to accept the plot, the role which they play in Toni Morrison's novel might be seen as merely another realistic detail, a sign of how a people torn from its roots tries to make sense of its experience through a reversion to primitive superstitions. Another black writer, Maya Angelou, depicts her ancestors as doing this in what strikes the European reader as a more satisfactory manner by their recourse to the myths of Judeo-Christianity. As she points out in the second volume of her autobiography, *Singin' and Swingin' and Gettin' Merry like Christmas*:

for hundreds of years, the Black American slaves had seen the parallel between their oppression and that of the Jews in Biblical times,

'Go down Moses
Way down into Egypt land
Tell old Pharaoh
To let my people go'.[54]

It is a remark which underlines an aspect of North American slavery which is only implicit in Toni Morrison's novels. There, Christianity is barely mentioned, whether as a justification for the oppressors or as a consolation for the oppressed. The one undisputable social achievement of Christianity lay in its replacement of the slavery which was an integral part of Graeco-Roman culture by the universalist message of Galatians 3: 28: 'For there is neither Jew nor Greek, there is neither bond nor free, there is neither male nor female: for ye are all one in Christ Jesus.' The reinstitution of slavery in Christian culture through the slave trade of the seventeenth and eighteenth centuries, like the use of slaves in the sugar and cotton plantations of the West Indies and North America, was a step backwards comparable to the revival of torture in twentieth-century Europe after its abolition in the eighteenth and nineteenth centuries.

The absence of even the most rudimentary religious practices from *Beloved* comes out in one of the main incidents in the novel: that it is Paul D., on his arrival at 124 Bluestone Road, where Sethe is living with her surviving children, who first casts out the ghost of the two-year-old baby whose throat Sethe had cut. The Christian sects which believe in evil spirits generally entrust the task of casting them out to one of their priests, and the fact that nobody is available to do this underlines how rare even the most primitive Christian presence was in the Ohio of the 1850s. The exorcism carried out by Paul D. is nevertheless not permanent, since after he has lived quite happily for some years with Sethe, they return from a carnival one evening to find a young woman waiting for them on the steps of their house. She has 'new skin, lineless and smooth, including the knuckles of her hands', and starts off by refusing to say anything other than her name, which she gives as Beloved. The fascination which she comes to exercise over Sethe leads to a complete breakdown in the arrangements whereby Sethe, Paul D., and Sethe's other daughter, Denver, have managed to live together, and the impression which the reader has is of an evil creature seeking vengeance.

This is one of the functions traditionally attributed to ghosts, and the sceptically minded reader is offered only a small sop of comfort in the remarks made by another former slave, Stamp Paid, who talks about

> a girl locked up in the house with a whiteman over by Deer Creek. Found him dead last summer and the girl gone. Maybe that's her. Folks say he had her in there since she was a pup.[55]

There is not, however, much encouragement elsewhere in the novel for a rational interpretation of events, according to which this girl has heard about Sethe's story, and decided to profit from the situation by moving into her home under the pretence of being the ghost of her murdered daughter. It is a group of singing black women who eventually come to drive out the ghost, and it is difficult to fit the obvious symbolism of the action into an interpretation of the story which sees Sethe as merely the victim of a confidence trickster. What Toni Morrison is suggesting is a view which runs parallel to the interpretation of *Tar Baby* which sees Jadine as the alienated victim of white society. For what the reader of *Beloved* is asked to believe is that only the solidarity of her black sisters can rescue a black woman from the ghost of her dead past. Only a singing sorority can cleanse her of the guilt for the crimes which a white, patriarchal society has forced her to commit.

The disadvantage of this very ideological interpretation of *Beloved* is that it makes the book more of a *roman-à-thèse* than any of Toni Morrison's other novels. This is, however, not an entirely justified criticism, since *Beloved* is also an experiment in narrative technique as well as what Toni Morrison described as the account of 'five years of terror in a pathological society, living in a bedlam where nothing makes sense'.[56] For the European reader, who knows about slavery in America only by hearsay, and is not directly concerned by the tensions created in its long aftermath, the novels of Toni Morrison raise particularly interesting questions about the role of commitment in literature as well as about the culture of the United States. The essential evil denounced in *Beloved* has disappeared. It is well over a century since Lincoln's signing of the Emancipation Proclamation on 22 September 1862, and the gradual ratification by the defeated Southern States of the Thirteenth Amendment of December 1865, officially abolishing

slavery. Although it was some time before its abolition became a
reality below the Mason–Dixon line – the text of *Beloved* talks of
how, after the war between the states, the 'Yankees in control
left the Rebels out of control', and describes, how, as late as 1874,
there were 'whitefolks still on the loose. Whole towns wiped clean
of Negroes; eighty-seven lynchings in one year alone in Kentucky'[57]
– the specific and officially tolerated abuses she denounces have
disappeared. One no longer sees, as Denver does in *Beloved*,

> a blackboy's mouth full of money. His head was thrown back
> farther than a head could go, his hands were shoved in his
> pockets. Bulging like moons, two eyes were all the face he had
> above the gaping red mouth. His hair was a cluster of raised
> widely spaced dots made of nail heads. And he was on his
> knees. His mouth, wide as a cup, held the coins needed to pay
> for a delivery or some other small service, but could just as
> well have held buttons, pins or crab-apple jelly. Painted across
> the pedestal he knelt on were the words 'At Yo Service'.[58]

There is no need, as there had been in 1851, when *Uncle Tom's
Cabin* was published, for literature which so changes people's minds
that they decide to bring about a change in the laws and formal
organisation of society.

VI

*The problem of commitment; more on the possible effectiveness of liter-
ature; literature as a catalyst.*

There is, in this respect, an important difference between the view
taken of literature in the twentieth century and the reputation it
enjoyed in the nineteenth. The impact on America of *Uncle Tom's
Cabin*, like that of *Oliver Twist* in England, strengthened the view
that imaginative literature could have a beneficial effect on society, and quite often did so. Just as the writings of Voltaire,
Rousseau and Beaumarchais had, it was argued, helped to bring
about the French revolution, so Harriet Beecher Stowe's novel
had created a climate of opinion which made the emancipation
of the slaves virtually inevitable. If Abraham Lincoln did indeed
say to her, on their meeting in 1862, 'So. You're the little woman

who wrote the book that made this great war' he was saying something which seemed as obviously true at the time as the idea that the abolition of the workhouse was due at least in part to the novels of Dickens. In 1874, Arthur O'Shaughnessy repeated Shelley's idea that 'poets are the unacknowledged legislators of mankind' when he claimed that

> We are the music makers, we are the dreamers of dreams
> Wandering by lone sea breakers, or sitting by desolate
>   streams
> But we are the makers and shakers
> Of the world for ever it seems

and it was not, at the time, a view from which writers of a more prosaic caste of mind would have dissented. In Russia, the decision of Tsar Alexander II to emancipate the serfs in 1861 was said to be the almost direct consequence of the impact which Turgeniev's *A Sportsman's Sketches* had on his own as well as his father's sensitivity. In both cases, as Michael Hanne points out in his *The Power of the Story* (1994), there had been roughly the same time lag. Like most nineteenth-century novels, *Uncle Tom's Cabin, or Life Among the Lowly* was first published in serial form, appearing in an abolitionist journal, the *National Era*, in 1851. It came out in book form in 1852, selling 300,000 copies within the year, an extraordinary achievement at a time when there were no paperbacks, no book clubs and no national book chains, and it is very tempting to link the passion it aroused in the Northern States with Lincoln's signature of the Emancipation Proclamation. Turgeniev's novel appeared in 1852 and although it took some time for the Tsar to persuade his bureaucrats and landlords that serfdom had to be abolished, the decree allowing the serfs to buy their freedom was finally published by Alexander II in 1861. While nineteenth-century critics recognised that books could often take some time to exercise their influence, it was equally axiomatic that they could help to change society and that they would do so for the good. Another example was conveniently to hand in England in the relationship between the publications of the Fabian Society and the reforms of the 1906 Liberal government. It was also obvious that it was the personal intervention of writers such as Zola and Anatole France which eventually led the French government to rehabilitate Alfred Dreyfus.

A number of events in the twentieth century have called both these beliefs into doubt. The awareness of how fully the ideas of Rousseau had helped to inspire the tyranny of Robespierre was a major factor in leading the celebrations of the bicentenary of the French revolution in 1989 to being a good deal more muted than those which had taken place in 1889. Nietzsche was a master of German prose, and it may well be that it was only by a misunderstanding of his writings that he came to be regarded as one of the inspirers of the Nazi movement. But Hitler put two quotations from his writings on his door – 'Do not drive the hero from your heart' and 'The shame is not to fall but to stay down' – and when one looks at the attacks against the Jews which run throughout Nietzsche's work, it is hard to avoid seeing links between what he wrote and what happened in Germany between 1933 and 1945. There is no need to speculate about the support provided by Count de Gobineau's claim, quoted by Toni Morrison in *The Bluest Eye*, that

> all civilisations derive from the white race ... none can exist without its help, and a society is great and brilliant only in so far as it preserves the blood of the noble group that created it[59]

for the theories of white racism which have played so important a role in the history of the United States as well as in that of South Africa.

When Auden wrote in his poem on the death of Yeats that 'Poetry makes nothing happen' he was expressing a view which was already widely held by formalist literary critics such as I. A. Richards, and which went back to the Symbolist movement of the late nineteenth century. There is no case, in the symbolist aesthetic, for claiming that literature plays any more of a part in influencing political events than music or painting, and the experience of the twentieth century may well show that this is the right way to look at it. Philosophy may play a major part in politics, but its more disastrous effects have had to be overcome, in the twentieth century at any rate, essentially by military means. Hitler's Fascism was defeated by the armies of the United States, the Soviet Union and the United Kingdom. Soviet Communism collapsed at least partly because the United States made clear that it would stick by its allies. It was Karl Popper who put the case against Hegel and Marx better than any imaginative writer has

ever done, both in the arguments of *The Open Society and its Enemies*, in 1946, and in those of *The Poverty of Historicism*, in 1957,
a work appropriately dedicated to the

> memory of the countless men and women of all creeds or nation
> or races who fell victim to the fascist and communist belief in
> the Inexorable Laws of Historical Destiny.

Readers who admire imaginative literature for the impact which
it has on human behaviour may be on safer ground if they point
to the way it has affected the way human beings spend their
leisure time. In the seventeenth century, travellers required to
undergo a journey through the Alps or Pyrenees drew the curtains
of their coaches in order not to see the horror of wild mountains
and rushing torrents. The writings of Jean-Jacques Rousseau taught
people to look on nature differently, and the difficulty one now
has of ever being alone on the fells in the Lake District owes a
good deal to the influence of Wordsworth. Until the Romantic
revolution, the adjective 'gothic' meant barbaric or primitive. It
was only after Chateaubriand had tried to prove the superiority
of Christianity by the beauty of the architecture and poetry it
had inspired that it became normal practice in the tourist season
for non-believers to outnumber practising Catholics in Chartres
Cathedral or in Notre Dame.

In 1970, John Weightman argued in an article entitled 'The so-
lar revolution' that the popularity of holidays in the sun also owed
a good deal to the influence of imaginative writers. The success
of the 'Club Méditerranée', he suggested could be traced back to
the way three authors, André Gide, D. H. Lawrence and Albert
Camus, wrote about the sun, and presented exposure to it as not
only physically beneficial but spiritually meritorious. To swim in
the sea and come out to let the sun dry its salt water on your
skin, as Meursault and his girlfriend Marie do in *The Outsider*,
was to take part in what was almost a religious ceremony. It put
you in harmony with nature, and was idolatrous only in so far
as it led to a worship of the source of all life. But while writers
can obviously influence attitudes in this way, there are other ex-
planations for a practice which is now seen as just as likely to
cause skin cancer as it was to help to cure the tuberculosis from
which Gide, D. H. Lawrence and Camus all suffered. Once holidays
with pay became virtually universal, people had to go somewhere;

and it is generally more agreeable to spend your leisure time where it is not raining.

A more convincing way of looking at the relationship between literature and society is to see novels, poems and plays as catalysts. What they do is enable attitudes which are diffusely distributed in society to come together in a more coherent form. The novels of Toni Morrison may not have the same direct impact on American society as *Uncle Tom's Cabin*, or even as the work of the black writers who came before her such as Richard Wright or James Baldwin. White middle-class Americans already feel sufficiently guilty about the injustice from which blacks have suffered in the past and still suffer from to-day not to need to be told about it again. They are unlikely to be moved to action by any increase in this guilt which a novel such as *Beloved* may produce, especially as it is difficult to know what more can be done by legal or political means to bring about racial equality in America. But the themes which she treats enable a set of attitudes to crystallise in society. What she does is to make the awareness which this society has of itself and of its history become widespread and more acute.

This is not so much because the novels of Toni Morrison encourage the attitude which Maya Angelou criticised when she wrote: 'Oh the holiness of always being the injured party. The historically oppressed can find not only sanctity but safety in the state of victimisation'.[60] One can well imagine Toni Morrison's novels doing this, but here again one comes up against the problem of any reader not belonging to the group for which she says she is writing ever being able to judge what effect her novels are likely to have. To the outsider, one of the most striking themes in Toni Morrison's fiction is the frequency with which she describes black people being violent to other blacks. This happens when Sethe kills her daughter, when Violet Trace, in *Jazz*, the 1992 novel, slashes the face of her husband's young mistress, Dorcas, whom he has just killed, as she lies in her open coffin, and when Eva Peace, in *Sula* (1973), kills her last child, Plum, to whom she had 'hoped to bequeath everything' by setting light to the bed in which he is lying in a drunken stupor. There is no way in which Toni Morrison could be seen, in this aspect of her work, either as playing on the feeling of guilt to which white Americans are so vulnerable, or as encouraging people who have the same colour skin as hers to wallow in misfortune. Her books are very different, in this respect as in many others, from *The Catcher in the Rye*, which still sells a quarter of a million copies a year. The danger of Salinger's novel is that it is rather too easy to read in such a way as to 'lay a flattering unction' on the soul of inadequate adolescents, whose wounds are so often intensely painful mainly because they are self-inflicted. This is far from being the case with the novels of Toni Morrison. The violence which her characters inflict on one another, as in the rape of Pecola Breedlove by her father Cholly in *The Bluest Eye*, is the product of two things: the conditions in which the race to which they belong has for so long had to live; and the psychological law which says that what you have never had as a child, you can never give as an adult. For the two crucial events in Cholly's life had been, as the conclusion to one of the most dramatic and moving scenes in the novel observes, when he was 'abandoned in a junk heap by his mother and rejected for a crap game by his father'.[61] In a notation such as this, Toni Morrison becomes like the other writers whom it is best to read in the light of D. H. Lawrence's injunction to 'trust the tale not the teller'. If one takes this approach to her work, she becomes a good deal better and more interesting a writer than her theory of literature would ever allow. For if she does indeed see her books as exclusively a means whereby black women can communicate with one another, she is failing quite dramatically to recognise what she can bring to a completely different type of reader.

There are a number of advantages to comparing the relationship of literature to society with that of the catalyst which causes the solids held invisibly in suspension in a liquid suddenly to solidify and make themselves visible. The first is that it applies just as well to a work of psychological analysis such as *Remembrance of Things Past* as to a social satire like *Major Barbara*. There is no way of knowing whether our vision of childhood would be all that different from what it now is if Proust had never written his novel. What is nevertheless fairly certain is that this vision would not be so intense. The idea that money makes the world go round is fairly banal, though given vivid expression in the song sung by Joel Gray in the film *Cabaret* which Rolf Zehtbauer derived in 1972 from Christopher Isherwood's *Berlin Stories*. *Major Barbara* makes us more conscious of how the same tediously familiar idea can alter our concept of religion and of what constitutes virtuous action. There is nothing new about the notion of the incompatibility between an all-powerful and all-merciful God and the physical suffering of the innocent. What is new is the frequency with which this idea is articulated nowadays in discussions about religion in terms of Camus's treatment of it in *The Plague*.

The second advantage of looking at literature in this way is that it does not lead to exaggerated claims as to its importance. There is no need for the defender of committed literature to defend Sartre's view that it is 'the self-consciousness of society in permanent revolution', or to claim that literature gives an account of an independent reality which exists outside the book or play depicting it. Even something which is patently untrue, such as the events in *The Satanic Verses* or *Angels in America*, can make you see an experience in a different and often very revealing light. When Jean Cocteau said that 'il faut mentir pour être vrai' (you must lie to tell the truth), he was underlining how differently language is used in literature than in history or sociology. It is almost a defining characteristic of literature that it should have a different impact from that of the disciplines which, like history, present material that can be empirically verified by using independent and even rival sources.

The third advantage of seeing literature as a catalyst is that such a definition corresponds so closely to what so often happens. It is more than the experience which Browning put into the mouth of Fra Lippo Lippi and which is mentioned in Chapter 1. It is not so much that we have passed before things and not bothered to look at them. It is more that we have had an experience in a diffuse form but not been able to define it to our own satisfaction until the happy accident of reading a book or poem or seeing a play, has given us an intellectual awareness which we would have otherwise never obtained.

Suggestions for Further Reading

In addition to the major encyclopaedias, all of which provide basic facts about leading writers, there are a number of more specialised publications. The St James Press, in London, like the St. Martin's Press in New York, publishes volumes entitled *Contemporary Dramatists*, *Contemporary Literary Critics*, *Contemporary Novelists*, and *Contemporary Poets*. These are regularly updated, and can be found in most public reference libraries as well as in all good university libraries. In 1984, the St James Press also published *Great Foreign Language Writers*, edited by James Vinson and Daniel Kirkpatrick. *The Cambridge Guide to World Theatre*, edited by Martin Banham and published by the Cambridge University Press in 1988, enables twentieth-century dramatists to be seen against a broad geographical background as well as in their historical context.

There is also a *New Pelican Guide to English Literature*, edited by Boris Ford, and a *History of Literature in the English Language*, edited by Bernard Bergonzi and published by Sphere Books. The *Oxford Companion to Literature in French* has recently been re-edited by Peter France, and there are parallel volumes published by the Oxford University Press on other major literatures. Critical studies of most leading twentieth-century authors have been published in the *Macmillan Modern Dramatists* and *Macmillan Modern Novelists* series. Like the guides published by the St James Press, these studies all contain extensive bibliographies.

Students wishing to see how the novels and plays discussed in *Twentieth-Century Literature: Critical Issues and Themes* were greeted by the critics on first publication will find an invaluable guide in *Contemporary Literary Criticism*, a yearbook published annually by Gale Research, Detroit and New York. These volumes also contain extracts from more extensive, book-length studies published by critics and scholars who had longer to think about the issues raised, and are thus an excellent introduction to the debates sparked off by the works under discussion.

Students interested in a different and more challenging approach to literature than the one I have adopted will find it in A. Alvarez, *Beyond All This Fiddle. Essays, 1957–1967* (Allen Lane, The Penguin Press, London, 1967); in Harold Bloom, *The Western Canon. The books and school of the ages* (Harcourt Brace, New York, 1994); in Catherine Belsey and Jane Moore, *The Feminist Reader: Essays in Gender and the Politics of Literary Criticism* (Macmillan, 1989); in Malcolm Bradbury, *The Social Context of Modern English Literature* (Blackwell, 1971), as well as in the very substantial anthology entitled *Modernism. A Guide to European Literature, 1890–1930* (Penguin, 1976, revised edition, 1991), which Bradbury published in collaboration with James McFarlane; in Frank Kermode, *A Sense of Ending* (OUP, 1967); in R. A. Brower, *Twentieth Century Literature in Retrospect* (Harvard and Cambridge University Press, 1971); in the three volumes of *No Man's Land. The Place of the Woman Writer in the Twentieth Century*, by Sandra Gilbert and Susan Gubar (*The War of the Words* [Yale University Press, 1988]; *Sexchanges* [YUP, 1989] and *Letters from the Front* [YUP, 1994]); in Terry Eagleton, *Criticism and Ideology. A Study in Marxist Literary Theory* (Verso, London, 1978); David Lodge, *The Novelist at the Crossroads and other Essays in Fiction and Criticism* (Routledge & Kegan Paul, 1971) and *Modern Criticism and Theory* (Longman, 1988), and especially in *The Art of Fiction, Illustrated by Classic and Modern Texts* (Secker & Warburg and Penguin, 1992); in Blake Morrison, *The Movement. English Poetry and Fiction of the 1960s* (Faber and Faber, 1963); in Edward Said, *The World, The Text and the Critic* (Faber and Faber, London, 1984), and *Orientalism* (Penguin, 1994); in Eileen Showalter's anthology *The New Feminist Criticism* (Virago, 1986); in Gayatri Chakravorty Spivak, *In Other Words. Essays in Cultural Politics* (Routledge & Kegan Paul, 1988); and in Raymond Williams, *Keywords* (Fontana, 1976), *Marxism and Literature* (Fontana, 1977) and *Culture* (Fontana, 1981).

Paul Fussell's *The Great War and Modern Memory* (OUP, 1975) is usefully complemented by John Cruickshank's *Variations on Catastrophe: Some French Responses to the Great War* (Clarendon, Oxford, 1982) as well as by Samuel Hynes, *A War Imagined. The First World War and English Culture* (Bodley Head, London, 1990).

Another contrast to my approach, this time in the form of the texts which might be studied as a starting point for an introduction to twentieth-century literature, can be found in Cyril Connolly's *The Modern Movement: One Hundred Key Books from England, France and America, 1890–1950* (André Deutsch, London, 1965). There is a similar list by John Braine, not restricted to works of imaginative literature, entitled *Great Books of Our Time*, published by *The Sunday Times* in 1961. A different set of themes and variations in twentieth-century literature would emerge from a study which concentrated not on the authors whom I have chosen to discuss but on writers such as Isaac Babel, Heinrich Boll, Jean Cocteau, Osamu Dazai, Witold Gombrowitz, Seamus Heaney, Ted Hughes, Doris Lessing, García Lorca, Edna O'Brien, Osip Mandelstam, Carson McCullers, Octavio Paz, Harold Pinter, Sylvia Plath, Barbara Pym, Rainer Maria Rilke, George Seferis, C. P. Snow, Paul Valéry and Thomas Clayton Wolfe.

It has also been suggested to me that my own interest in politics, history and ideas is more appropriately satisfied less by works of imaginative literature than by books such as Hannah Arendt's *Origins of Totalitarianism* (1951), Isaiah Berlin's *Two Concepts of Liberty* (1959) and *The Crooked Timber of Humanity* (1990), Robert Conquest's *The Great Terror*, John Kenneth Galbraith's *The Affluent Society* (1958) or *The Age of Uncertainty* (1977), Paul Kennedy's *The Rise and the Fall of the Great Powers* (1990), A. J. P. Taylor's books on the First and Second World Wars, or Martin Walker's admirable *The Cold War and the Making of the Modern World* (1993).

Preface

1. See *The Function of Criticism*, 1935, in *Selected Essays* (Faber and Faber, London, 1951), p. 25.

Chapter 1   Themes, Variations and Constants

1. *The Satanic Verses* (Viking, Penguin Group, London, 1987), p. 232.
2. See *Racing Demon* (Faber and Faber, London, 1990), p. 38.
3. *Moon Tiger* (André Deutsch, London, 1987; Penguin Books, 1988), p. 55. *Moon Tiger* won the Booker Prize for fiction in 1987. One of the incidental criteria which has guided my selection of which books and authors to discuss has been whether or not they have won one of the better-known literary prizes. Another criterion for the inclusion of authors has been whether or not they have been awarded the Nobel Prize for Literature.
4. See p. 221 of the collection *'What became of Jane Austen?' and other essays* (Jonathan Cape, London, 1970).
5. *The Collected Essays, Journalism and Letters of George Orwell*, vol. IV (Secker & Warburg, London, 1968) p. 228.
6. See p. 454 of vol. I of the *Pléiade* edition (Paris, 1958).
7. For 'Why I am not a Christian', see *The Basic Writings of Bertrand Russell* (Allen & Unwin, London, 196), p. 590.
8. Penguin edition (1963), p. 118. In Chapter 7, I suggest a number of reasons why Somerset Maugham received neither the official honours nor the recognition in literary society which he himself, like his admirers, thought were his due. Like Aldous Huxley, whose reputation I discuss later in this chapter, he gave a great deal of pleasure to a large number of readers, but was never admitted to the acknowledged canon of twentieth-century English literature.
9. Ibid., p. 117.
10. *Point Counter Point* (Chatto & Windus, 1928, collected edition, London, 1947), p. 2 and p. 205.
11. See the *Pléiade* edition of Sartre's *Oeuvres romanesques* (Paris, 1982), p. 438.
12. See his interview with Jacqueline Piatier in *Le Monde*, 18 April 1964. For a discussion of the similarity between Sartre and the palaeontologist Stephen Jay Gould, see my 1992 study of Sartre in the Macmillan Modern Novelists series.
13. *Catch 22* (New York, 1961; Black Swann Paper, London, 1985), p. 567.
14. See the 1946 essay 'The Prevention of Literature' in vol. IV, p. 69, of *The Collected Essays, Journalism and Letters of George Orwell* (Secker & Warburg, London), 1968.
15. The poem, which had never been out of print, was republished in

1994 in *Tell Me The Truth about Love: Ten Poems* (Faber and Faber, London).

16. For a longer discussion of this tendency, see Anthony Quinton's *Thoughts and Thinkers* (Duckworth, London, 1982), p. 55. For a *caveat* as to the dangers of too prosaic an approach to poetry, see A. Alvarez's *Introduction* to *The New Poetry* (Penguin, London, 1962), and its advice to 'drop the pretence that life, give or take a few social distinctions, is the same as ever, that gentility, decency, and all the other social totems, will eventually muddle through'.

17. It is also possible to read *Who's Afraid of Virginia Woolf?* in a very different way. It is not because he wishes to win the final battle in their war that George finally compels Martha to acknowledge that the son they mention so frequently never existed. It is to enable her to live a more authentic life by freeing her from an illusion. Like Hemingway's *The Short Happy Life of Francis Macomber*, analysed in Chapter 7, Albee's play can be interpreted in a number of different ways.

Another minor but immediately noticeable difference between twentieth-century literature and that of the nineteenth lies in the use made in fiction of a university setting. Until the publication in 1912 of Max Beerbohm's *Zuleika Dobson* – which ends with all the undergraduates in Oxford committing suicide in a fit of unrequited love, while the heroine asks her maid for the timetable of trains to Cambridge – novels about university life were marked by a certain earnestness. The publication in 1955 of Kingsley Amis's *Lucky Jim* introduced a welcome change. The novels of David Lodge, Malcolm Bradbury and Tom Sharpe – like the appearance of Alison Lurie's novels in the United States – showed that this change was not a false dawn.

18. See pp. 97–8 of the 1938 Penguin edition of *Cold Comfort Farm*, first published in 1932. Among its many qualities, this novel has the ability to create the object of its satire at the same time that it makes fun of it. There is no need to have read the novels of Mary Webb, or even of Thomas Hardy, to see why the Starkadders are funny. Stella Gibbons also based her novel on the manuscripts submitted for publication to the women's magazine of which she was fiction editor in the 1920s. Aunt Ada Doom's claim to have 'seen something nasty in the woodshed' figures in *The Concise Oxford Dictionary of Quotations*. The book from which the heroine of the novel, Flora Poste, draws her inspiration to tidy up the Starkadder family – the Abbé Fausse-Maigre's *The Higher Common Sense* – is one of the unwritten masterpieces of twentieth-century literature.

19. See his Minute of 2 February 1835 on *Education in India*, The World's Classics, CDXXXIII, *Macaulay's Speeches*, A Selection (OUP), p. 349.

20. Under its French title, *Le Zéro et l'Infini*, this became a best-seller in France in 1945. This may have been because the French Communist party, having failed to have the book banned, told its members to buy as many copies as possible so that it could burn them. It was also praised by F. R. Leavis on p. 22 of *The Great Tradition*

(Secker & Warburg, London, 1955) as a 'very distinguished novel' which showed that Koestler, like Joseph Conrad an author 'not born to the language', could nevertheless write admirable English. The compliment, albeit sincere, was nevertheless based on a misunderstanding. *Darkness at Noon* had originally been written in German, and translated into English by Koestler's mistress, Daphne Hardy.

Koestler explains the readiness of the old Bolsheviks who confessed to crimes they had never committed by the desire which they had to continue to be useful to the revolution. If its failings could be attributed to treason and sabotage, and not to an inherent weakness in Marxism itself, there might be still some hope that it could recover from the temporary aberration of Stalin's dictatorship. It is a tribute to Koestler's imaginative grasp of the revolutionary temperament that *Darkness at Noon* is still in print, and is still highly readable, even though the problem it analyses belongs so completely to the past. Even before the collapse of the Soviet Union in the early 1990s, all the victims of the Moscow trials had been rehabilitated.

21. *The Invisible Writing* (Hamish Hamilton, London, 1954), pp. 403–4.
22. For Steinbeck, see Chapter 18 of his 1939 novel, *The Grapes of Wrath*, analysed in more detail in Chapter 6. For Huxley, see Part III, chapter ii of *After Many a Summer*.

   Like a number of other English writers working in Hollywood and living in Southern California, including P. G. Wodehouse, Huxley had been a guest at Hearst Castle, also known as Saint Simeon and 'La Cuesta Encantada' (The enchanted hill) in the late 1930s. Like Xanadu in Orsen Welles's 1939 film, *Citizen Kane*, Jo Stoyte's castle is clearly based upon San Simeon, though the similarities between Stoyte and Hearst – as between Hearst and Charles Foster Kane – are not very close. As Welles observed in his Foreword to Marion Davies's *The Times We Had* (Ballantine Books, New York, 1975) 'William Randolph Hearst was born rich. He was the pampered son of an adoring mother. That is the decisive fact about him. Charles Foster Kane was born poor and raised by a bank.' Welles also points out that there were no similarities between the Susan Alexander of *Citizen Kane*, who was an unsuccessful singer, and Hearst's mistress, Marion Davies, who was a successful and quite accomplished *comédienne*. Hearst was married, had five sons, and was over six foot tall. Jo Stoyte is short, fat and unmarried. The origin for the idea of Hearst as a man terrified of dying appears to be an incident in which he grew tired of hearing a group of young people playing the same record of 'I wish you was dead, you rascal, you' again and again, took it from them and broke it.
23. In his review in the *Nouvelle Revue Française* in June 1939 of the French translation of Dos Passos's *1919*. It was not only Dos Passos's technique of narration which aroused the admiration of Sartre and of other French writers. It was also his politics. Like the Steinbeck of *The Grapes of Wrath* and *Of Dubious Battle*, the Dos Passos of the

1930s wrote from a very left-wing, Marxist point of view. Later in his career, however, especially with *Adventures of a Young Man* in 1939, and more especially *The Theme is Freedom* in 1956, he became much more conservative.

24. In *The New Statesman and Nation*, 8 August 1945. Although C. E. M. Joad held the title of Reader in Philosophy at Birkbeck College, University of London, he was always referred to as Professor, especially when, from 1941 onwards, he became part of the extremely popular programme on BBC radio, *The Brains Trust*. He invariably prefaced his replies with the remark 'It all depends what you mean by', and was widely in demand as a public lecturer. Unfortunately, in 1946, he lost some of his claim to speak with authority on ethical questions by being caught travelling first class on the railway with only a second-class ticket.

25. In *Horizon*, August 1946, 'Novelist-Philosophers'.

26. The essay was published by the Editions du Seuil, in Paris, in a volume entitled *Mythologies*, in 1957, and published by Jonathan Cape in England in 1972 in a translation by Annette Lavers. Since 1973, it has been available in a Paladin paperback.

27. *Moon Tiger*, p. 67.

28. Barthes made no secret of his debt to the Swiss linguistician Ferdinand de Saussure (1857–1913) and to his posthumously published *Cours de Linguistique générale* (translated by Baskin, *Course in General Linguistics*, 1959). For Saussure, it was important to distinguish between 'le signifié', the thing signified, and the signifier, or the sign, as well as to recognise that the relationship between the two was arbitrary: 'cow' and 'vache' are both linguistic signs, but it is only through the conventions governing the linguistic codes of English and French that they both mean the same thing. For Barthes, literary language differs from other types of discourse by having no 'signifié', nothing to which it refers. There are a number of books on Barthes, of which the most widely admired are Jonathan Culler's 1983 *Roland Barthes* (OUP) and Michel Moriarty's *Roland Barthes* (Polity Press, Cambridge 1991). Readers consulting these books, or reading Barthes's own *S/Z* (Paris, 1970), translated by Richard Miller, and published by Jonathan Cape in 1975, will find that I have somewhat simplified the issues involved.

29. First published in 1967; translated by Gregory Rabassa (Jonathan Cape, 1970; Picador, London), p. 185.

30. *The Great Tradition* (Chatto & Windus, London, 1955), p. 3. The Leavises were unenthusiastic about a number of other authors who have given pleasure to many readers. Q. D. Leavis did not mean it as a compliment when she remarked of Dorothy Sayers, in *Scrutiny* 1937, that she had 'stepped out of the ranks of detective writers into that of best-selling novelists', and her husband commented in 1955 in *D.H. Lawrence, Novelist* on 'how promptly the tiny talent of Katherine Mansfield was acclaimed, and to what an inflationary tone'. Mrs Leavis nevertheless kept her severest strictures for P. G. Wodehouse. When the creator of Jeeves, Bertie Wooster, Lord

Emsworth, Psmith, the Oldest Member and Mr Mulliner was awarded a D. Litt., *Honoris Causa* by Oxford in 1939, she commented in the Cambridge based *Scrutiny* that 'His humour is a cross of prep-school and *Punch*, his invention puerile, the brightness of his style the inane, mechanical and monotonous brightness of the worst schoolboy slang'. A more sympathetic view of Leavis can be found in William Walsh's essay 'A Sharp, Unaccommodating Voice: the Criticism of F. R. Leavis' in his *The Human Idiom* (Chatto & Windus, London, 1966).

31. J. D. Salinger, *The Catcher in the Rye* (1945, LB Books paperback edition, 1991), p. 18.
32. *Collected Essays . . . Orwell*, vol. II, p. 190. The lines are from Kipling's 1895 poem *In the Neolithic Age*.
33. First published in 1946. See Penguin edition, 1951, p. 197.
34. *Heart of Darkness*, pp. 151–2.
35. *Heart of Darkness* was first serialised in *Blackwood's Magazine* in 1899. See The World's Classics (OUP, 1990), p. 140.
36. The first reference is to the second stanza of Henry Newbolt's poem *Vitae Lampada*, with its message that courage and skill on the sports field will lead to courage and skill on the battle field:

'There's a breathless hush in the close to-night –
Ten to make and the match to win.
A bumping pitch and a blinding light
An hour to play, and the last man in.
And it's not for the sake of a ribboned coat
Or the selfish hope of a season's fame.
But his Captain's hand on his shoulder smote
"Play up! Play up! and Play the Game!"'

The sand of the desert is sodden red, –
Red with the wreck of the square that broke; –
And the Gatling's jammed, and the Colonel dead,
And the regiment blind with the dust and smoke.
The river of death has brimmed his banks,
And England's far, and Honour a name.
But the voice of a schoolboy rallies the ranks,
"Play Up! Play Up! And Play the game!"'

The second is a reference to a poem by W. E. Henley:

'What have I done for you,
    England, my England?
What is there that I would not do,
    England, my own?
With your glorious eyes austere,
As the Lord were walking near,
Whispering terrible things
    and dear

As the song on your bugles blown,
England –
Round the world on your bugles blown!'

It would be an interesting experience to see whether the inclusion of either of these two poems in a film would have the same effect on the audience as Auden's *Funeral Blues* (see note 15 above). It has been known for Englishmen to begin to recite *Vitae Lampada* as a joke, only to notice a suspicious dampness around the eyes in some of their audience, as well as a lump in their own throats, as they come to the third and final stanza:

'These are the words that year by year,
As in her place the School is set
Every one of her sons shall hear,
And none that hears it dares forget.
This they all with a joyful mind,
Bear through life like a torch in flame.
And falling, fling to the host behind,
"Play up! Play up! And Play the game!"'

37. See *The History Plays* (Faber and Faber, London, 1984), p. 36.
38. *Collected Essays ... Orwell*, vol. II, p. 190.
39. Published by Hodder & Stoughton in 1928. *Bulldog Drummond's Four Rounds with Carl Petersen* (*Bulldog Drummond*, 1920; *The Black Gang*, 1923; *The Third Round*, 1924 and *The Final Count*, 1926; all by 'Sapper' = H. C. MacNeile) are very well analysed by Richard Usborne in his 1953 essay, *Clubland Heroes* (Constable, London). The extent to which novels of this type helped to shape the political attitudes and expectations of a whole generation is visible in John Weightman's only half-ironic remark in his review of Usborne's essay that he was surprised when the Communist double agents Burgess and MacLean escaped to the Soviet Union in 1955 since this went against all his expectations that Bulldog Drummond would always catch such villains in time.
        Richard Usborne's essay is one of the best examples of a genre first practised by Q. D. Leavis in 1932 in her *Fiction and the Reading Public* and by George Orwell in essays such as 'Raffles and Miss Blandish', 'The Art of Donald Magill' and 'Boys' Weeklies'. The object of books and essays of this kind, of which another well known example is Richard Hoggart's *The Uses of Literacy* (Chatto & Windus, London, 1957), is to analyse popular culture with a view to what it can tell us about modern society. Some of the conclusions reached are more convincing than others, and Orwell was famously taken to task by Frank Richards for a number of mistakes in 'Boys' Weeklies' (cf. *Collected Essays, Journalism and Letters*, vol. I, pp. 485–93). It could also be argued that the traditional description of Sapper's novels as 'the literature of British Fascism' neglects the fact that the historical discoveries of the 1970s, like

the changes brought about by the collapse of Communism in the 1990s, made some of the political attitudes inspiring the activities of Drummond and his friends less outlandish than they seemed to critical observers at the time. The German historian Fritz Fischer's long and detailed *German War Aims in in the First World War* (London/New York, 1967) suggests, for example, that Drummond's antipathy to 'the Huns' was fully justified in the light of what they were trying to do: annex Belgium and Luxembourg; reduce France to a satellite state from which all British goods were excluded, and which had no army to defend itself; transfer control of France's and Belgium's African colonies to Germany. Like the James Bond novels of Ian Fleming, Sapper's work also had a hostility towards the Bolshevik Revolution which seems less unreasonable now that the study of Soviet archives has shown what the KGB was up to.

The long essays putting the case for the women's movement are less vulnerable to criticism. After Simone de Beauvoir had shown the way in *Le Deuxième Sexe* (1949; *The Second Sex*, Gallimard, Paris, 1949; translated by H.M. Parshley, Cape, London, 1953; Four Square Paperback, 1960), Bettie Friedan applied the same technique of analysis to English-speaking society in *The Feminine Mystique* (W. H. Norton, New York, 1963). The publication of Germaine Greer's *The Female Eunuch* (MacGibbon & Kee, London, 1970) coincided with the general rebellion against established society which characterised the 1960s, as did Kate Millett's *Sexual Politics* (Rupert Hart-Davies, London, 1971). By including extracts from the work of such forerunners as Mary Wollstonecraft and Harriet Martineau, Leslie B. Tanner's *Voices from Women's Liberation* (Signet Classics, New York, 1971) showed how continuous the struggle had been against male dominance in Western society, and what obstacles it had encountered. In a more strictly literary context, Patricia Beer's *Reader, I married Him* (Macmillan, 1974), Sandra Gilbert and Susan Gubar's *The Madwoman in the Attic. The Woman Writer and the Nineteenth Century Literary Imagination* (YUP, 1979) and Phyllis Rose's *Parallel Lives* (Penguin, 1986) showed how the insights of the women's movement could be used to provide illuminating and totally new ways of looking at traditional literature. So, too, did Naomi Segal's 1986 essay, *The Unintended Reader. Feminism and Manon Lescaut* (CUP, 1986).

*Chapter 2   Visions of Childhood I: The Child Unhappy on its own
               Account*

1. Yerofeev (1938–90) was a Russian dissident who spent much of his life in the labour camps of the former Soviet Union. His novel was originally circulated in *samidzat* before being published after the collapse of the Soviet regime in 1989. Stephen Mulrine's adaptation was performed as a one-man-show at the Garrick Theatre, London, by Tom Courtenay in 1994.
2. See *The Catcher in the Rye* (1945), Chapters 13 and 3.

3. *Six Degrees of Separation* was produced at the Lincoln Center in 1990, and published by Random House in the same year. The claim of the title is that there are never more than six degrees of blood relationship between any two living human beings.

4. Published by Secker & Warburg, London, 1993; and in 1994 by Minerva paperbacks. Roddy Doyle is also the author of *The Barrytown Trilogy*, of which the second play, *The Snapper*, was made into a very successful film in 1990.

5. Thus Dodgson was a bachelor with an interest in photographing pre-pubescent girls in the nude which would have attracted the interest of the police in present-day England. Kenneth Grahame had great difficulty consummating his marriage, and it is almost certain that his only son, Kenneth, for whom *The Wind in the Willows* was written, and who died at the age of eighteen, committed suicide. In *The Enchanted Places* (Eyre & Methuen, London, 1974), Christopher Milne makes every effort to be fair to the creator of Winnie the Pooh. His narrative nevertheless makes it easy for the reader to agree with the passage in the Epilogue in which the boy who had good reason to wish at school that he was called Charles Roberts wrote that it seemed to him, in his twenties, that his father had 'got to where he was by climbing on my infant shoulders, that he had filched from me my good name and had left me with nothing but the empty fame of being his son'.

Jeremy Treglow's biography of Roald Dahl (Faber and Faber, London, 1993), emphasises his opportunism, his anti-semitism, the rudeness with which he treated his publishers and his tendency to behave 'less as a writer than as a capricious tycoon'. There is nevertheless a possible link between his failure to write satisfactory books about and for adults and his immense success as a writer for children which may explain the fact that neither Dodgson, Milne nor Grahame were anything like as successful as authors for adults as they were as writers for children. Children like to see things in black and white, as Dahl apparently did, and are not averse either to the instant gratification of chocolate or to sadism. If, as Jeremy Treglow suggests, Roald Dahl never entirely grew up, this puts him in the same company as Dodgson, Milne or Frank Richards, the creator of Billy Bunter. Richards never married, was passionately addicted – like his most famous creation – to jam tarts, and emerged only rarely from the room in which he wrote 1.5 million words a year. On one occasion, when he was living in Italy, there was an earthquake. Richards never heard it.'You see', he explained, 'I was at Greyfriars.' The fact that he himself left school at fifteen may also explain why none of the characters in the *Gem* and the *Magnet* ever leaves the Remove for the Sixth Form.

There are obviously exceptions. There was nothing odd about Arthur Ransome, and Michel Tournier was as good at writing about grown-ups as he was at writing for and about children. Although Richmal Crompton was an almost archetypal maiden aunt, she was – as Mary Cadogan's 1986 *Richmal Crompton: The Woman Behind*

William (Allen & Unwin, London) showed – eminently sane and level-headed. Enid Blyton, who in 1955 was the third most translated author in the world – Lenin was first, Simenon second – wrote her books in a kind of trance-like state, in which she seemed to go back to the days before her childhood ended with the sudden departure from her home of her father, when she was only thirteen. There is, however, nothing particularly odd about this. It is even recommended by poets such as Rimbaud.

6. Published in 1879 and much admired by the French. The tradition to which this book belongs was admirably analysed by Peter Coveney in his *Poor Monkey. The Child in Literature* (Rockliffe, London, 1957).

7. First published in French in 1954, and translated into English under the title *By Way of Sainte-Beuve* by Sylvia Townsend Warner (Hogarth Press, London), p.76. Proust's idea is not an entirely new one. As Kingsley Amis pointed out in his review of Martin Seymour-Smith's *Robert Graves: His Life and Work* (Hutchinson, London, 1982), Samuel Johnson observed the 'custom then prevailing' by keeping his observations on a poet's work quite 'separate from those of his life'. *The Amis Collection* (Penguin, 1991), p. 201.

8. *Les Mots* (Gallimard, Paris, 1964), p. 212, a translation by Irene Clephane is available in Penguin.

9. *Stanley and the Women* (Hutchinson, London, 1984), p. 127.

10. Quoted on p. 299 of Noel Annan's *Our Age* (Weidenfeld & Nicolson, London, 1990; Fontana, 1991), p. 299. Thomas Balogh went on to become an economic adviser to the Wilson government of 1964.

11. *Grapes of Wrath*, Chapter 19.

12. *Words*, p. 212.

13. See *Over Seventy: an autobiography with digressions* (Herbert Jenkins, London, 1957), p. 16. Quoted by R. B. D. French in his 1966 study of Wodehouse, published by Oliver & Boyd, Edinburgh, in the *Writers and Critics* series. This remains the best and most perceptive study of Wodehouse.

14. Quoted on p. 241 of Barry Phelps, *P. G. Wodehouse, Man and Myth* (Constable, London, 1992). This is the most informative of the books dealing with Wodehouse as a man. Like the other studies, it effectively disposes of the long-standing myth that he acted in a treasonable manner in making the 1941 Berlin Broadcasts. The text of these can be found at the end of *Performing Flea* (Herbert Jenkins, London; 1953; Penguin Books, 1961). A minor example of the existence of censorship in wartime Britain lies in the withdrawal of many of Wodehouse's books from the public libraries; and, in some cases, of their physical destruction. One of the side-effects of this act of vandalism has been to increase the price of pre-1939 Wodehouse first editions. The best guide to Wodehouse for bibliophiles is the 1991 *P. G. Wodehouse: A Comprehensive Bibliography and Checklist,* by Eileen McIlvain, Louise S. Sherby and James H. Heineman (New York: Heineman/Detroit. MI: Omnigraphics. Distributed in the UK by Folkestone: Dawson); well reviewed in the *TLS* for 26 April 1991.

It will be recalled that Anatole does not provide the meals at Blandings. He works for Bertie Wooster's Aunt Dahlia.

Chapter 3 Visions of Childhood II: The Child Wicked on its own Account

1. *Nineteen Eighty-Four* (Secker & Warburg, London, 1949; Penguin, 1954), p. 134.
2. All references are to the Bantam Book paperback (New York, 1965). The book is discussed in some detail in Laurence Langer's *The Holocaust and the Literary Imagination* (Yale University Press, 1975).
3. *Point Counter Point*, p. 312. *Point Counter Point* is something of a 'roman à clef'. Maurice Spandrell is based on Baudelaire, Philip Quarles on Huxley himself, Mark Rampion on D. H. Lawrence, Burlap on Middleton Murry.
4. Agota Kristof, *The Notebook*, translated by Alan Sheridan (Methuen, London, 1989), p. 31.
5. 'Politics and the English Language', 1946, *Collected Essays . . . Oruell*, vol. IV, p. 136.
6. *A High Wind in Jamaica* (London, 1929; Harper & Row, New York, 1987), p. 119 and p. 200.
7. The Questionnaire is reprinted in the Capricorne Books edition (New York, 1958).
8. For the quotations from *Lord of the Flies*, see Chapter IV for 'brilliant world of hunting' and Roger throwing the stones and just missing; Chapter V for 'mankind's essential illness' and Ralph's 'rules are the only things we've got'. Chapter VI for 'a human both heroic and sick', Chapter VIII for the beast telling Simon 'I'm the reason why it's no go'.
9. Gide (1869–1951) described the puritanical background in which he was brought up in his 1926 *Si le grain ne meurt* (*Unless it Die*; see John 12: 24, 'Except a corn of wheat fall into the ground and die, it abideth not; but if it die, it bringeth forth much fruit'); the implication of the title being that it is only by ceasing to be the person created by the religious beliefs inculcated in him during his childhood that Gide has been able to grow up both intellectually and spiritually, and become a writer. In 1951, in one of the many articles inspired by Gide's death, Sartre wrote that he was a man who had lived out, in and through his life and works, 'the final death agony of God'. This is how Martin du Gard saw Gide as well, and in August 1951 created something of a disturbance at the graveside by his protests against the insistence of Gide's still pious family on giving him a Christian burial.

   Sartre made a particular point of praising the way Gide had 'assumed his own sexuality', and saw this as the key to his mature agnosticism. Gide was a homosexual – or, more accurately, a pederast, being attracted to pubescent boys – and defended homosexuality as a perfectly natural form of sexual behaviour in *Corydon*, a set of dialogues privately printed in 1908 but made available to the general public in 1922. *Unless it Die* describes his early sexual development and inspired the short poem quoted by A. J. Ayer in the first volume of his autobiography:

The best known work by André Gide,
Is called 'If Perish not the Seed'.
Indeed, his own peculiar taste,
Ensures it does all go to waste.

Like the clerihew

People thought with horror,
Of Sodom and Gomorrah
Till they were given a boost
By Proust

the lines of Gide are a reminder of the difficulty which the English have in resisting the temptation to make jokes about matters often dealt with more seriously in France. They nevertheless hide the fact that while Proust described homosexuality without ever, as he put it in a conversation with Gide, 'using the pronoun "I"', Gide showed considerable courage in being the first writer to come out.

In 1892, in response to strong encouragement from his doctor, who assured him that he was attracted to boys only because he knew nothing of the delights of heterosexuality, Gide married his cousin Madeleine, with predictably disastrous results. When, in 1916, he broke his promise to give up a form of sexual behaviour which she found profoundly distasteful and went off to London with the young Marc Allégret, son of a Protestant pastor, Madeleine hit back in the way she knew would hurt her husband most. On every day that he had been away from her, even before their marriage, Gide had written her a letter, clearly looking forward to the publication of what critics might well have greeted as his greatest book, *André Gide: Lettres à sa femme*. Madeleine took each letter, read it through a second time, and burnt it. She then told Gide what she had done.

Marc Allégret seems to have suffered least from the encounter. In 1955, he helped to discover Brigitte Bardot. In his memoirs, published in 1993, he spoke with fond remembrance of his earlier encounter with Gide.

10. *I'm the King of the Castle* (1970; Longman's paperback, 1984), p. 181.
11. The matter is fully discussed in Philippe Aries *L'Enfant et la vie familiale sous l'ancien régime* (Plon, Paris, 1960), translated by Robert Baldick as *Centuries of Childhood* (Cape, London, 1962).

Chapter 4   Varieties of Realism I: Plays, Intertextuality and Myth

1. Published by Jonathan Cape (London, 1979). What James Mangan, the son of a successful newspaper editor, and grandson of an equally successful Canadian Pacific Railway comptroller, finds when he

goes back to Southern Ireland in search of his 'roots' is a land decaying with alcohol and drugs, living off theft and charity, held prisoner by its myths and its religion – a country, in short, attacked by all the evils afflicting any society whose most intelligent and enterprising members have, in the past 200 years, either been forced to emigrate or have chosen to do so.

Moore himself is no exception to this rule. After having provided, in *The Lonely Passion of Judith Hearne* (1955) and *The Feast of Lupercal* (1957), two highly vivid and convincing accounts of the Catholic Belfast middle class into which he was born in 1921, he went to live in Canada. To judge by the work of Roddy Doyle, the Catholic church plays virtually no role in the lives of the Dublin working class; except by the residual impact of its teaching on abortion and contraception.

2. See *Selected Essays*, p. 107: 'Hamlet (the man) is dominated by an emotion which is inexpressible because it is *in excess* of the facts as they appear'.

The concept of intertextuality is well explained by David Lodge in his *The Art of Fiction. Illustrated from Classic and Modern Texts* (Penguin, London, 1982). He takes a passage from Conrad's 1917 *The Shadow-Line* and shows how it presupposes a knowledge on the reader's part of Coleridge's *The Rime of the Ancient Mariner*.

3. Broadcast on Radio 3 in 1992 but not, unfortunately, available either in print or on cassette. Balthasar, who has been absent from the Danish court for three years, asks what has happened while he has been away. Phormio pithily acquaints him with the holocaust which took place 'last Saturday'. She then reveals that she is an illegitimate daughter of the old Hamlet, and thus sole heir to the Danish throne. At this, however, old Hamlet himself reappears, astounding Phormio by telling her that he was not slain by Claudius. 'Reeling with liquor', as was his wont, Claudius had poured the poison on to his ankle, not in his ear. Old Hamlet then foils the plan of Balthasar and Phormio to poison him by poisoning them first. In his death agony, Balthasar nevertheless manages to slay old Hamlet who dies, as Phormio puts it 'with no grand speech to make before he goes'.

4. *Tribune*, 3 December 1982. Quoted in the very useful 1986 Methuen Paperback volume on Stoppard in the *Facts on File* series. Stoppard did spend the first two years of his life in Czechoslovakia, which was not then the socialist state which it became during the 1945–90 Soviet occupation. He was born in 1937, and taken at the age of two to Singapore, where his father, Joseph Straussler, was manager of the Bata shoe-manufacturing company. Straussler was killed in the Japanese invasion, but Tom's mother escaped to India, where she met and married Major Stoppard.

5. See *Tom Stoppard: The Artist as Critic* (Macmillan, London, 1988), p. 42.

6. My translation of p. 43 of the 1972 'Points' paperback edition of Barthes's first book, *Le Degré zéro de l'écriture* (*Writing Degree Zero*),

first published in 1953. The view that there is something reactionary about clarity would have surprised thinkers as progressive as
Voltaire, Hume, Bertrand Russell and A. J. Ayer.

7. In *Language, Truth and Logic* (Gollancz, London, 1936).
8. Sammells, *Tom Stoppard*, p. 135.
9. *Collected Essays . . . Orwell*, vol. IV, p. 62.
10. See *The Liberal Imagination* (London and New York, 1951; Mercury
Books, 1961), p. 301.

Chapter 5   Varieties of Realism II: Censorship, the Novel and the City

1. All references are to the account of the trial by C.H. Rolph entitled
The Trial of Lady Chatterley, published by Penguin Books in 1961.
    Mr Griffith-Jones's remark was widely appreciated. It was perhaps
admissible, when Virginia Woolf made the remark in 1924, in her
essay *Mr Bennett and Mrs Brown*, for her to illustrate her contention
that 'human nature changed' . . . 'on or about December 1910', by
talking in the first instance about 'relations between masters and
servants'. In the 1920s there were still over half a million domestic
servants in London. By 1960, they were far rarer than Rolls Royces.
2. *Ulysses* (Shakespeare Press, Paris, 1922; Bodley Head edition, 1960),
p. 191.
3. See p. 20 of the Theatre Communications Group edition (New York,
1992). Subtitled 'A Gay Fantasia on National Themes', the play deals
quite fully with the impact of AIDS on American society. As Richard
Kramer put it, writing in *The New York Times* on 3 February 1994,
'Mart Crowley's *The Boys in the Band* flung open a door 25 years
ago. The gay closet hasn't been closed since.'
    The second part of *Angels in America, Perestroika*, is on the same
theme. It could be argued, with exceptions such as Fritz Peter's
1951 novel *Finisterre* and Radcliffe Hall's 1922 *The Well of Loneliness*,
that homosexuality itself comes out of the closet in a satisfactory
literary form only when it is implied rather than taken openly as a
theme. André Gide's 1919 novella *La Symphonie Pastorale*, for example,
keeps its place as the most widely read of his works because the
relationship between Gide and his male adolescent partners is
transposed into the relationship between the middle-aged Pastor
and the blind girl, Gertrude. In Proust, the relationship between
the narrator and Albertine is much more skilfully handled than
Charlus's affair with the violinist Morel. The same is true of Philip
Callow's relationship with Mildred in Somerset Maugham's *Of
Human Bondage*. It is unusual and refreshing to find a homosexual
in literature who is so free of guilt that he regards his sexual
preferences as totally natural. L'Oncle Alexandre in Michel Tournier's
1975 novel *Les Météores (Gemini)* is the best example. Bernard Sands,
in Angus Wilson's 1951 *Hemlock and After*, is one of those who
manages to transpose his feelings of guilt most convincingly into
a general context. There is also an entertaining window on the world
of homosexuality by Simon Raven in the essay which gives its title

to his 1963 book, *Boys will be Boys* (Anthony Blond, London), orig-inally published in *Encounter* in November 1960.

4. Details of this and other judgments can be found in Jonathon Green's *The Encyclopedia of Censorship*, Facts on File (1956).
5. *Collected Essays . . . Orwell*, vol. I, pp. 121 and 139.
6. In 1942, in his review of the first three of T. S. Eliot's *The Four Quartets*. Ibid., vol. II, p. 239.
7. See *The Art of T. S. Eliot* (Dutton, New York 1949), p. 85.
8. *Angels in America*, p. 56.
9. *Ulysses*, p. 267.
10. Joyce did have children, but neither his daughter, who went mad, nor his son, seems to have played a major part in his emotional life. Sartre had no children, and makes a remark comparable to that of Stephen Dedalus when he says on p. 13 of *Les Mots* that his father had 'versé les quelques gouttes de sperme nécessaires pour faire un homme' (shed the few drops of sperm needed to make a man). However, in *Les Mains Sales* (1947) Hugo is clearly looking for a spiritual and political father to replace the biological one whom he has rejected, and the relationship between Franz von Gerlach and his father is the most powerful emotional theme in the 1959 play *Les Séquestrés d'Altona*.
11. *Ulysses*, p. 427.
12. Ibid., pp. 284 and 286.
13. Ibid., pp. 239 and 428.
14. *Memories of the Ford Administration* (Knopf, New York, 1992), p. 176.
15. Ibid., p. 55.
16. *Love and Friendship* (Macmillan, New York, 1962), p. 275.
17. *Ulysses*, p. 877.
18. Ibid., pp. 83–4.
19. *Memories of the Ford Administration*, p. 130.
20. p. 206 of the 1985 Faber and Faber paperback edition.
21. See p. 409 of the 1982 Pléiade edition of *L'Age de raison*: 'il s'était laissé aller en moi comme un gosse qui fait dans les draps'.
22. See *The First Book of Gargantua*, Chapter XVIII, translated by Jacques Leclerc (New York, Modern Library, 1936).
23. *Ulysses*, p. 479.
24. Ibid., p. 643.
25. Quoted on p. 71 of Ronald Bush, *T. S. Eliot. A Study in Character and Style* (OUP, 1983), from Eliot's 1923 review in the *Dial*.

Chapter 6   Varieties of Realism III: Naturalism, Tragedy and the Unconscious

1. *In Cold Blood* (Hamish Hamilton, London, 1966), p. 6 and p. 10.
2. Ibid., p. 184.
3. *Schindler's Ark* (Hodder & Stoughton, London, 1982), p. 10 of Author's Note.
4. *The Bonfire of the Vanities* (Farrar, Strauss & Giroux, New York,

1987. Bantam Book paperback, 1988), p. 65. See also p. 61 for the link between the action of the novel, the atmosphere of the 1980s, and the events of the 1970s:

> Ever so quietly, the U.S. had started printing money by the billions to finance the war in Vietnam. Before anyone, even Johnson, knew what was happening, a worldwide inflation had began. Everyone woke up to it when the Arabs suddenly jacked up oil prices in the early 1970s. In no time, markets of all sorts became heaving crap-shoots: gold, silver, copper, currencies, bank certificates, corporate notes – even bonds.

A passage like this anchors *The Bonfire of the Vanities* just as firmly in the Reagan and Thatcher years of the 'golden boys' as the analysis of the Depression anchors Steinbeck's *The Grapes of Wrath* in the 1930s. It also makes it far less of a right-wing novel than has been alleged. Traditionally, the right has blamed the inflation of the 1970s and early 1980s exclusively on the rise in oil prices, alleging that this was a politically motivated decision aimed at reducing Western support for Israel.

5. Opening of Chapter 14 of *The Bonfire of the Vanities*.
6. Bibliographical and other details can be found in my *Albert Camus*, Macmillan Modern Novelists (London, 1990).
7. *The Grapes of Wrath* (Heinemann, New York, 1939), opening of Chapter 5.

Chapter 7 Moral Certainties and the Problem of Determinism

1. Quoted in Carlos Baker, *Ernest Hemingway. A Life Story* (Scribner's, New York, 1969), p. 252.
2. 'The Door of Opportunity' (1932). See vol. III of *The Collected Short Stories of Somerset Maugham* (Heinemann, London, 1951) p. 1079.
3. *The Short Happy Life of Francis Macomber* (1936; 1963 Penguin edition), p. 8.
4. 'The Door of Opportunity', p. 1107.
5. See 'England your England', *Collected Essays . . . Orwell*, vol. II, p. 75.
6. For Maynard Keynes, see O'Falain, *The Vanishing Hero* (Eyre & Spottiswoode, London, 1956), p. 22.
7. *Iliad*, Book III, lines 380–445.
8. See letter of 2 June 1950 in *Selected Letters, 1917–1961*, ed. Carlos Baker (Granada, London and New York, 1981), p. 697.
9. See Kenneth S. Lynn, *Hemingway* (Simon & Shuster, New York, 1987), p. 432.
10. See 'Hemingway's Women', in *Ernest Hemingway, the Man and his Work*, John McCaffery (World Publishing Company, New York, 1965), p. 349.

Chapter 8 Moral Dilemmas I: Religion, Ethics and Some Incidental Truths

1. *The Man Who Was Thursday* (London, 1908), Chapter 6, 'The Exposure'.
2. *Ulysses*, p. 444.
3. See *The Letters of Aldous Huxley*, ed. Grover Smith (Chatto & Windus, London, 1969), p. 576. See also p. 646 for the comparable view, expressed in 1952, that 'many of the world's artistic and cultural organisations are infiltrated by homosexuals, with the result that nobody who is vulgar enough to like women stands a chance'. *Those Barren Leaves* was originally published in 1925. See p. 92 of the 1951 Penguin edition.
4. Quoted by William A. Chace, in *The Political Identities of Ezra Pound and T. S. Eliot* (Stanford University Press, California, 1973), p. 79.
5. See the *Pléiade* edition of Claudel's poetry (Paris, 1967), p. 577.
6. See Sartre's preface to Fanon's *Les Damnés de la terre* (*The Wretched of the Earth*), 1961. Reprinted in *Situations* IV (Gallimard, Paris, 1964), p. 227.
7. *The Heart of the Matter* (Heinemann, London, 1948 Penguin edition, 1971), p. 272.
8. For a full discussion of this and other matters, see Alice K. Turner, *The History of Hell* (Harcourt Brace, New York, 1993). The doctrine of Apocatastasis, according to which we are all saved, is particularly attractive. For Scobie see *The Heart of the Matter*, p. 194.
9. *Heart of the Matter*, p. 58.
10. See *A Buyer's Market*, the second in Powell's 12-volume sequence *A Dance to the Music of Time* (Heinemann, London, 1952), p. 32.

    The only novels written by Englishmen about their experiences in the 1939–45 war to have gained widespread recognition in literary circles are Powell's *The Soldier's Art* and *The Military Philosophers* – 1966 and 1968; volumes 8 and 9 respectively in *A Dance to the Music of Time* – and Evelyn Waugh's *Sword of Honour* trilogy (*Men at Arms*, 1952; *Officers and Gentlemen*, 1955; *Unconditional Surrender*, 1961). In both cases, the main characters are officers, generally from the upper class. Neither Waugh nor Powell talks about the contribution which the British armed services made to the defeat of Hitler. If Waugh sees the Second World War as the great watershed in the social history of England in the twentieth century, it is to disapprove of it. Neither *The Bridge on the River Kwai* nor *The Cruel Sea* is taken seriously as literature; perhaps because Pierre Boule is a Frenchman, who also wrote the best-selling *Planet of the Apes*; and because Monsarrat gives no sign of doubting the justice of the cause for which his heroes are fighting.
11. *The Bonfire of the Vanities* (New York, 1988), Chapter 24.
12. *Stepping Westward* (Houghton Mifflin, New York, 1966), pp. 323 and 324.

Chapter 9 Moral Dilemmas II: Philosophy, Free Will and some Visions of the Future

1. Quoted by Bernard Crick on p. 92 of the 1984 Clarendon Press edition of *Nineteen Eighty-Four*.
2. Letter dated 13 July 1944, quoted on p. 315 of Bernard Crick, *George Orwell. A Life* (Secker & Warburg, London, 1980).
3. Updike, *Memories of the Ford Administration*, p. 152.
4. In an essay on *Heretics and Renegades* (Hamish Hamilton, London, 1954), reprinted in *George Orwell. A Collection of Critical Essays* (Prentice-Hall, New York, 1984), p. 119.
5. *Collected Essays, Journalism and Letters* (London, 1968), vol. IV, p. 451.
6. The publication by David Bradshaw of *The Hidden Huxley. Contempt and compassion for the masses* (Faber and Faber, London and Boston, 1994) suggests that the dream in *Brave New World* may well have been less ironic than earlier critics have generally thought. Huxley was so obsessed with the way ordinary politicians were making a mess of things that he looked quite favourably at the idea of a government by all-powerful and highly intelligent scientists.
7. *Brave New World* (1932). Quoted from p. 214 of the 1984 re-edition by Chatto & Windus, London, with a preface by Sybille Bedford and followed by *Brave New World Revisited* (1958).
8. From the General Confession: 'We have followed too much the devices and desires of our own hearts. We have left undone those things that we ought to have done and we have done those things that we ought not to have done.' The fact that so few people recognised the quotation suggests that there are disadvantages to the end of the compulsory church-going that Philip Callow found so boring in Maugham's *Of Human Bondage* (see Chapter 7, endnote 8).
9. *The Children of Men* (Faber and Faber, London, 1992), p. 11.
10. Ibid., p. 12.
11. Ibid., p. 87. It is improbable that the name is an example of intertextuality, but *Harriet Marwood, Governess* is a well-known novel of masochistic flagellation, originally published in semi-clandestinity in Paris, 1960, by Girodias's Olympia Press, and reprinted by the Grove Press in 1967.
12. *Children of Men*, p. 226.

Chapter 10 Moral Dillemas III: Ends, Means and Irony

1. *Major Barbara*, 1905, Act II. Penguin Books, 1960, p. 108.
2. See Michael Holroyd, *Bernard Shaw* (Random House, New York, 1991), vol. III, pp. 245 and 248.
3. See p. 106 of the 1962 Grove Press paperback edition.
4. *The Unbearable Lightness of Being* (Faber, London, 1984), p. 266.
5. *Le Dieu caché* (Gallimard, Paris, 1955). Published in England by Routledge & Kegan Paul, London, International Library of Philosophy and Psychology 1963, with incomprehensible success.

6. See *Situations* IV (Gallimard, Paris, 1954), 'Merleau-Ponty Vivant', p. 227.
7. *The Collected Essays, Journalism and Letters of George Orwell* (Secker & Warburg, London, 1968), vol. III, p. 30.

Chapter 11   Politics, Commitment and the Responsibilities of the Scientist

1. Quoted from pp. 929–32 of *The Basic Writings of Bertrand Russell* (Allen & Unwin, London, 1961).
2. Quoted by Bernard Crick on p. 92 of the 1984 Clarendon Press edition of *Nineteen Eighty-Four*.
3. See the *Proceedings of the Aristotelian Society*, 1956.
4. *Look Back In Anger*, Act III, Scene i (Faber and Faber, London, 1957), p. 84.
5. *Dürrenmatt* (Oswald Woolf, Berg, 1988), p. 124.
6. *Quartered Safe Out Here, A Recollection of War in Burma* (Harvill Collins, London, 1992; paperback, 1995), p. 221.

   George MacDonald Fraser is, of course, best known as the author of the Flashman books, an entertaining series of nine novels describing the adventures of the cad and bully expelled from Rugby in Thomas Hughes's 1857 *Tom Brown's Schooldays*. Although a congenital coward, as well as a compulsive lecher, Flashman always emerges triumphant, and ends his career as General Sir Harry Flashman, VC, DSO etc.

   In so far as the reader is assumed to know about *Tom Brown's Schooldays*, if not actually to have read it, the Flashman novels can be seen as an example of intertextuality, comparable on a frivolous level to Jean Rhys's reconstruction of the early life of Mr Rochester's first wife in *Wide Sargasso Sea* (André Deutsch, 1966; Penguin, 1968), to Keith Waterhouse's *Mrs Pooter's Diary* (Michael Joseph, 1983), or the continuation by Another Lady of the novel *Emma*, which Charlotte Brontë had sketched out before her death (Dent, 1980).

   Admirers of Kipling's *Gunga Din* will recognise the origin of MacDonald Fraser's title.
7. *The Physicists*, translated from the German by James Kirkup (Cape Plays, 1963), p. 54.
8. *Ibid.*, p. 54.
9. See *New Maps of Hell* (Gollancz, 1968; New English library edition, London, 1969), p. 61. For another view of science fiction, see Tom Shippey's Introduction to *The Oxford Book of Science Fiction Stories* (1993).
10. *The Physicists*, p. 58.
11. *Ibid.*, p.17.
12. *Put Out More Flags* (Book Club edition, 1943).

Chapter 12   Madness, History and Sex

1. Quoted by Malcolm Bradbury, *Evelyn Waugh*, Writers and Critics (Oliver & Boyd, Edinburgh and London, 1964), p. 66.

2. See Evelyn Waugh, *Essays, Articles and Reviews*, ed. Donat Gallagher (Methuen, London, 1983), p. 153.
3. See *The Third Man*, Modern English Film Scripts (Lorimer, London, 1969), p. 114.
4. Dürrenmatt, *The Physicists*, p. 8.
5. *Times Literary Supplement*, 20 November 1981. Reprinted in *The Amis Collection* (Penguin Books, 1991).
6. *Decline and Fall* (1928; Penguin Books, 1937), p. 33.
7. Dürrenmatt, *The Visit*, Act III, p. 67.
8. This remark encapsulates two comments in Russell's *History of Western Philosophy* (Allen & Unwin, London, 1948). On p. 771, Russell observes: 'At the moment [1943, the date he was writing], Hitler is the outcome of Rousseau, Roosevelt and Churchill of Locke'. On p. 667, he observes: 'Since Rousseau and Kant, there have been two schools of liberalism, which may be distinguished as the hard-headed and the soft-hearted. The hard-headed developed, through Bentham, Ricardo and Marx, by logical stages into Stalin; the soft-hearted, by other logical stages, through Fichte, Byron and Carlyle and Nietzsche, into Hitler.'

Chapter 13   Magic Realism, Post-modernism and Toni Morrison

1. *Cien años de soledad* (Buenos Aires, 1967), translated by Gregory Rabassa, *One Hundred Years of Solitude* (Jonathan Cape, London, 1970; Pan paperbacks, 1978), p. 91.
2. Ibid., p. 91.
3. Quoted in Andrew Graham-Yooll, *After the Despots* (Bloomsburg, 1988), p. 126.
4. *One Hundred Years of Solitude*, p. 177.
5. Langer, *The Holocaust* (Yale University Press, 1975), p. 18.
6. Christopher Isherwood, *Mr Norris Changes Trains* (London, 1935; Penguin, 1953), p. 62.
7. *The Trial* (*Der Prozess*, 1925), translated by Willa and Edwin Muir (Gollancz, London, 1935; Penguin Books, 1953), Chapter III, pp. 58–9.
8. Ibid., p. 59, Chapter III.
9. Lewis Carroll, *Alice Through the Looking-Glass*, Chapter V.
10. *One Hundred Years of Solitude*, p. 43.
11. Ibid., p. 75.
12. The Trial., p. 237, Chapter IX.
13. Salman Rushdie, *The Satanic Verses* (Viking Penguin, London and New York, 1988), p. 168.
14. Ibid., p. 270.
15. Ibid., p. 37.
16. Ibid., p. 75.
17. See p. 30 of the 1951 Penguin edition of *Work Suspended* and other stories.
18. *The Satanic Verses*, p. 180.
19. Ibid., p. 50.

20. Ibid., p. 424.
21. Ibid., p. 547.
22. Ibid., p. 295.
23. *A Passage to India* (1924), Chapter 15.
24. *The Satanic Verses*, p. 295.
25. Pipes, *The Rushdie Affair* (Carol Publishing, New York, 1990), p. 98.
26. *The Satanic Verses*, p. 455.
27. Ibid., p. 210.
28. Ibid., p. 214.
29. *The Handmaid's Tale* (McLelland & Stewart, Toronto, 1988), p. 279.
30. *The Satanic Verses*, p. 261.
31. Updike, *Memories of the Ford Administration*, p. 296.
32. *Small World* (Secker & Warburg, London, 1984), p. 25.
33. Quoted from *Contemporary Literary Criticism Yearbook* (1987). Published by Gale Research, Detroit, New York, Washington, Chicago and London, this is the most convenient work available for anyone in search of information about modern authors.
34. 13 May 1987, quoted on p. 130 of Daniel Pipes, *The Rushdie Affair*. My view absolutely.
35. Ibid., p. 44. Perhaps because of this, I found little sympathy for Rushdie at the time of the *fatwa* among conservatively minded colleagues on whose support for the principle of free speech I thought I would have been able to count.
36. Quoted from an interview republished in Nellie Y. McKay, *Critical Essays on Toni Morrison* (G. K. Hall, Boston, 1988), p. 51.
37. Ibid., p. 46.
38. Freude, schoner Gotterfunken,
    Tochter aus Elysium,
    Wir betreten Feuertrunken,
    Himmlische, den Heiligtum.
    Deine Zauber binden wieder,
    Was die Mode streng geteilt,
    Alle Menchen werden Bruder,
    Wo dein sanfter Flugel welt.
    (Joy, thou daughter of Elysium and of the Gods themselves, Oh maid divine, we tread your shrine. Although the excess of light may destroy our senses, Thy healing spell will restore again whatever the harsh use of the world has destroyed. Wherever thy gentle wings rest, we find all men to be our brothers.)
    On the evening of Saturday, 7 May 1994, after the sounding of the Last Post at the Menin Gate, Ypres, a group of German students sang the words to Beethoven's music. It was a most moving experience.
39. Toni Morrison, *Beloved* (Alfred Knopf, New York, 1987; Signet edition, 1991), p. 127.
40. Morrison, *Tar Baby* (Alfred Knopf, New York, 1981; Signet edition, 1983), p. 191.
41. Ibid., p. 227.
42. See her essay 'The Fabulous World of Toni Morrison's *Tar Baby*' in

Nellie McKay, *Critical Essays on Toni Morrison* (G. K. Hall, Boston, 1988).
43. Ibid., p. 144.
44. *Tar Baby*, p. 108.
45. Ibid., p. 175.
46. Ibid., p. 140.
47. Ibid., p. 45.
48. *One Hundred Years of Solitude*, p. 154.
49. See *The New Criterion*, 5(5), June 1988.
50. *The Satanic Verses*, p. 101.
51. Ibid., p. 457.
52. *Beloved*, pp. 131, 329 and 81.
53. Ibid., p. 191.
54. Maya Angelou, *Singin' and Swingin'* (Random House, New York, 1976), p. 23.
55. *Beloved*, pp. 146 and 247.
56. Quoted in *Contemporary Literary Criticism Yearbook* (1988).
57. *Beloved*, p. 221.
58. Ibid. p. 313.
59. *The Bluest Eye* (Chatto & Windus, London, 1979; Picador, 1990), p. 133.
60. Angelou, *Singin' and Swingin'*, p. 85.
61. *The Bluest Eye*, p. 126.

Index: Themes and Ideas Mentioned or Explored

Index: Names Mentioned in the Text

In some cases (e.g. Lewis Carroll, Freud and Marx) a reference to the name implies a reference to the work and ideas.